D1388002

GEORGE VI

GEORGE VI

A New Biography

PATRICK HOWARTH

HUTCHINSON

LONDON   MELBOURNE   AUCKLAND   JOHANNESBURG

This edition first published in 1987 by Hutchinson, an imprint of
Century Hutchinson Ltd, Brookmount House, 62–65 Chandos Place,
London WC2N 4NW

Century Hutchinson Australia Pty Ltd
PO Box 496, 16–22 Church Street, Hawthorn, Victoria 3122, Australia

Century Hutchinson New Zealand Limited
PO Box 40–086, Glenfield, Auckland 10, New Zealand

Century Hutchinson South Africa (Pty) Ltd
PO Box 337, Berglvei, 2012 South Africa

British Library Cataloguing in Publication Data
Howarth, Patrick
   George VI: a new biography
   1. George, *VI, King of Great Britain*
   2. Great Britain—King and rulers—
   Biography
   I. Title
   941.084′092′4   DA584

   ISBN 0–09–171000–6

Photoset by Deltatype, Ellesmere Port
Printed in Great Britain by
McKays of Chatham Ltd, Chatham, Kent

CONTENTS

ACKNOWLEDGMENTS

I wish to express my heartfelt thanks for help received in the course of my researches to:

Alfred Knightbridge and the staff of the Public Record Office, Kew;
  Nigel Evans and the staff of the Public Record Office, Chancery Lane;
Oliver Everett and the Windsor Castle Library;
Dr Benedikt S. Benedikz and the University of Birmingham Library;
Marion M. Stewart and Churchill College, Cambridge;
Miss C. M. Ritchie and University College, Oxford;
Dr D. M. Smith and the Borthwick Institute of Historical Research;
Mrs M. Chalk and the staff of Broadlands;
Dr E. G. W. Bill and the Lambeth Palace Library;
Dr D. M. Blake and the India Office Library;
The Bodleian Library;
Ministry of Defence Air Historical and Navy Historical Branches;
The Industrial Society;
Eric Carter and the Department of the Environment;
D. Wakefield-Harrey and the Women's Royal Voluntary Service;
William M. Redmond and the Australian Archives;
Brian Murphy and Paulette Dozois and the Public Archives of Canada;
Sherrah Francis and the New Zealand National Archives;
J. Dane Hartgrove and William Mahoney and the National Archives, Washington;
Raymond Teichman and the Franklin D. Roosevelt Library;
Benedict K. Zobrist and the Harry S. Truman Library;
Martin M. Teasley and the Dwight D. Eisenhower Library;
Chantal Bonazzi and Jean Favier and the Ministère de la Culture, Paris;
Australia House, London;
Anita Burdett and Elizabeth Ketchum and Canada House, London;
New Zealand House, London;
The Embassies of Ireland, Norway, South Africa and Spain.

I wish to add a special word of thanks to the staffs of the Richmond-upon-Thames and Kensington and Chelsea Public Libraries.

Many people have been kind enough to talk to me about their memories of the late King George VI, to write to me or give me, out of the kindness of their hearts, help in other ways. Those whom I would like to thank in particular are:

Sir Godfrey Agnew, Vice-Admiral Sir Peter Ashmore, Marshal of the Royal Air Force Sir Dermot Boyle, Lord Brabourne, the late Sir Norman Chester, Vice-Admiral Sir Peter Compston, Dr Ian Fergusson, Sir Edward Ford, Sir Martin Gilliatt, Marshal of the Royal Air Force Sir John Grandy, Carron Greig, the Earl of Halifax, the Dowager Viscountess Hambleden, Michael Hansell, the late Sir Philip Hay, Vane Ivanovic, Stephen Koch, J. A. McCracken, Dan Maskell, Bruce Mathalone, Sir Oliver Miller, Jean Orme, the Duke of Portland, Air Commodore H. A. Probert, Sir Anthony Quayle, Dr Robert Robson, Jim Smith, Prince Tomislav of Yugoslavia, Group-Captain Hugh Verity, Lord Wilson and Philip Ziegler.

Transcripts of Crown-copyright records in the Public Record Office appear by permission of the Controller of H. M. Stationary Office. In this connection I am grateful also to the Keeper of the Queen's Archives and Heinemann Ltd.

To my wife

FOREWORD

If at the beginning of the last quarter of the nineteenth century a political commentator had forecast that in Britain in a hundred years' time respect for the House of Commons would decline appreciably, respect for the House of Lords increase slightly, and respect and affection for the monarchy grow hugely, he would have been considered eccentric. Yet this is what has happened.

Why the House of Commons has come to enjoy less and less respect is debatable. There may have been a decline in the quality of membership, but it is by no means certain that there has been. Concentration in certain sections of the press on personalities and trivialities – some might call these realities – has been a contributory factor. But the main cause has probably been the diminution of the gap which once divided the electorate from its representatives. People can hear for themselves how members of the House of Commons behave at Question Time, and they have drawn their own conclusions.

The House of Lords, by contrast, has not suffered in esteem from exposure to television. There seems to be increasing respect for its role as a revising chamber, and the House is not today considered, as it was towards the end of the last century, a natural subject for satirical light opera.

But the institution which has undergone the greatest change in esteem is the monarchy. Rather more than a hundred years after Queen Victoria was being referred to in scurrilous pamphlets as 'Mrs John Brown' her great-great-granddaughter enjoys a popularity which far exceeds that of any contemporary political leader. How has this happened?

It can be argued that the British have been exceptionally successful in developing, clarifying and then utilising the concept of constitutional monarchy, and that this has served to enhance the reputations of the monarchs themselves. There is some truth in this, and much of the credit for what has happened should be given to people who saw little of the limelight: private secretaries and others who served the monarchs in their political roles.

It is also true that the longer it is conducted successfully the more the benefits of constitutional monarchy become apparent.

Republicanism appeals in the first instance as a means of removing tyrants. Where the monarch is precluded from becoming a tyrant its attractions may well fade.

But while the successful operation of a system may contribute to the respect felt for a monarch, it cannot be the cause of the affection which he or she enjoys. Other reasons must be found to explain this.

During the last hundred years successive monarchs have been brought closer and closer to their peoples through various media: illustrated magazines and newspapers, then cinema newsreels, radio and, finally, television. As a result people have come to feel they know their monarchs and their families personally and to react emotionally to them.

This has certainly inspired affection, but, as happened to the House of Commons, it could well have had the reverse effect. Cameras reveal disagreeable features as readily as they emphasise attractive ones.

For an explanation of affection personal qualities must be taken into account, and in any analysis of the status of the modern British monarchy primary consideration must be given to the personality of King George VI.

He, more than any of the monarchs who preceded him, caused his people – certainly in the United Kingdom – to love him. They began by pitying him and fearing for him. They came before long to respect him and then to admire him. Many ended by regarding him as the embodiment of much that they held dear and wanted to preserve, however keenly they may have wished to change other aspects of contemporary life.

The story of his reign, though it spanned years of destruction and distress, is more than a story of a personal triumph. It is, in my judgment, a record of a moral triumph. As such I find it both encouraging and inspiring.

CHAPTER ONE

Early Years: Early Influences
1895–1905

The man who was to reign as King George VI from December 1936 to February 1952 was born on 14 December 1895. He was given the names Albert Frederick Arthur George. When he was born his great-grand-mother, Queen Victoria, was still on the throne and was entering upon her final period of popular acclaim and reverence, of which the celebration of her diamond jubilee was the climax.

This reverence had not been shown to her predecessors, nor at all times to the Queen herself. Of England in 1819 Shelley had written:

> An old, mad, blind, despised, and dying king, –
> Princes, the dregs of their dull race, who flow
> Through public scorn, – mud from a muddy spring, –
> Rulers who neither see, nor feel, nor know,
> But leech-like to their fainting country cling,
> Till they drop, blind in blood, without a blow –

Twenty-seven years earlier still Tom Paine had greeted the flight of Louis XVI with an address to the people of France. In this he wrote: 'Royalty is as repugnant to common sense as to the common right . . . Of all superstitions, none has more debased men's minds.'

In 1871 republican clubs were formed in more than fifty towns in Britain.[1] An attempt on the Queen's life in March 1882 was reckoned by one of her biographers to have been the seventh of its kind, though the list did include a rather ineffectual effort by an Irishman named Arthur O'Connor, who pointed an unloaded pistol at the Queen, in the hope of obtaining the release of some Fenian prisoners.[2]

Much of the popular disapproval of Queen Victoria derived from her failure in the middle years of her reign to accept her responsibility to show herself to her people and to engage in the pageantry which they expected of her. That she overcame this unpopularity was partly due to her longevity – though, as Shelley's poem indicates, longevity had been a poor asset to the unfortunate George III. More important in increasing the esteem felt for the Queen was her excellent instinctive understanding of popular opinion. Lord Salisbury once said that when he knew what the Queen thought he knew pretty well what her subjects, particularly the middle classes, would think.[3] Most important of all was the growing popular consciousness of empire.

The genesis of this popular consciousness can perhaps be found in the Great Exhibition of 1851, where the impressive displays of colonial products understandably fired the national imagination. More and more during the half-century which followed her people became aware that the Queen was the sovereign ruler, not simply of a comparatively small European country, but of the largest empire ever established by any nation, and bore the specific title of Empress of India. Enthusiasm for empire was never stronger than in the final years of Queen Victoria's reign, even while a war of dubious merit, which brought British general international opprobrium, was being waged in South Africa. Of this enthusiasm Queen Victoria was the natural beneficiary.

In 1895 when the future King George VI was born, monarchy was still the generally accepted form of government in Europe. Admittedly Switzerland had long been a republic, but this was a part of the Swiss tradition of conducting the nation's affairs in a manner different from that of all its neighbours. France too was a republic, but in the past century there had been repeated alternations between republics and monarchy. Outside Europe, in the United States and in Latin America, republics were firmly established, but Europeans still tended to regard these countries, to some extent, as colonies which had rebelled.

As Prince Albert grew to manhood, pressures in favour of republicanism and for the overthrow of monarchs were to become powerful and widespread. Among the principal champions of republicanism were the leaders of the two countries which in the second half of the twentieth century were to become the most powerful in the world, the USA and the USSR. President Woodrow Wilson, while engaged in the business of peace-making after 1918, and Lenin, after the Bolshevik revolution of 1917, were both, in their different ways, believers in republicanism as a panacea for all social ills, and both were crusaders on behalf of their beliefs.

The aggressions of the Italian and German dictators in the 1930s, and later the advent of the Red Army into eastern and central Europe, were to drive a number of monarchs into exile. The process of removing kings and establishing republics continued after World War II, particularly in Islamic countries. There was indeed to be no significant reversal of the trend until King Juan Carlos came to the Spanish throne in 1975.

Furthermore, although the republican movement never became strong in Britain in the twentieth century, the unsatisfactory reign of King Edward VIII, although short, lasted long enough, and the circumstances of his abandonment of his throne were lamentable enough, for the monarchy to be shaken and to be seen to totter. One more disastrous king would almost certainly have been enough to bring the British monarchy to an end.

Yet, by the end of King George VI's reign of a little over fifteen years the monarchy in Britain enjoyed greater popular respect and affection than at any previous time since constitutional monarchy was established. This popularity moreover owed nothing to the kind of expanding national power which brought such esteem to Queen Victoria in her later years. George VI's reign was to see the beginning of the dismantling of empire and of a serious diminution of Britain's status as a great power.

In the judgment of history books, kings and queens of the past have tended to be assessed by victories or defeats in battle, by the flourishing or decline of their countries' arts, or by greater or lesser degrees of national prosperity. To modern constitutional monarchs, such considerations are hardly applicable. The most useful criterion by which a modern king in a country such as Britain can fairly be judged is perhaps the extent to which the esteem and affection felt for the monarchy is enhanced or diminished during his reign. If this standard is applied to George VI, he must be adjudged more than merely a successful king. He has strong claims to be considered a great one. Yet he came to the throne more reluctantly than any other monarch in the nation's history, and was faced with a widespread belief that he was unfitted, both physically and emotionally, for the task which had been thrust upon him. How wrong these judgments were, and why they were so wrong, is still little understood in the nation over which he reigned.

14 December, the date of Prince Albert's birth, was also the anniversary of the death of the Prince Consort. Because of the obligatory visit to the royal mausoleum at Frogmore, this day was known in the royal family, somewhat irreverently, as 'mausoleum day'. Prince Albert's parents, the Duke and Duchess of York, even felt some trepidation because of the coincidence of dates. This was fanned by the Duke's father, the Prince of Wales, who wrote that Queen Victoria was 'rather distressed'.[4]

Queen Victoria, who was a much kindlier woman than her rather forbidding features and her posthumous reputation have suggested, did not allow any such distress to affect her for long, and two days later the Prince of Wales wrote that it would gratify the Queen if the boy were to be named Albert. He became known in his family as Bertie, and it was commonly believed that if he ever did come to the throne it would be as King Albert I.

The christening was delayed by another, but contemporary, royal death, that of Prince Henry of Battenberg, who narrowly qualified as a member of the royal family, having married Queen Victoria's youngest daughter and having been granted the title of Royal Highness at the age of thirty-six. After volunteering to take part in the Ashanti expeditionary force he contracted fever and died at sea. His body was brought back to the country of his adoption preserved in rum.

Prince Albert had been born in a comparatively modest house built on the Sandringham estate in Norfolk and known as York Cottage. The great house at Sandringham was occupied from time to time by the Prince of Wales, the future King Edward VII. York Cottage had been designed by a colonel who was not an architect, had an inadequate number of bathrooms, and generally smelt of food. The Duke of York, the future King George V, however had taken an early liking to it and had had it furnished by Maple's. Being a man of extraordinarily conservative tastes, he continued to regard it as his favourite home. It was in fact an uncomfortable house, which Harold Nicolson, his official biographer, described variously as a 'glum little villa' and an 'undesirable residence'.[5]

The date eventually chosen for the christening of Prince Albert was 17 February 1897. The ceremony took place in St Mary's church in Sandringham. The godparents, predominantly of German extraction or title, were Queen Victoria, the Empress Frederick of Prussia, the Crown Prince (later King Christian X) of Denmark, the Grand Duke and the Grand Duchess of Mecklenburg-Strelitz, the Duke of Connaught and Prince Adolphus of Teck.

The difference in age between Prince Albert and his elder brother, Prince Edward, known in the family as David, was about eighteen months. In the ten years between 1895 and 1905 four more children were to be born to their mother. They were, in order of age, Princess Mary, later to be known as the Princess Royal; Prince Henry, who became Duke of Gloucester; Prince George, who became Duke of Kent; and Prince John. The youngest, Prince John, was an epileptic and backward child, who lived quietly at Sandringham with a male attendant until he died in 1919. It is perhaps a tribute to the good taste of the contemporary press that so little was known about him publicly.

These children were fortunate in that their parents were devoted to each other. Yet the circumstances of the future King George V's marriage were unusual.

Prince George, as he was at first known, was brought up in close proximity to his elder brother, Prince Albert Victor, who was known within the family as Eddy. Such education as they received took place largely on board HMS *Britannia*, in which they both served as cadets. During this period they were under the tutelage of a Windsor canon, the Rev. John Dalton, father of the future Cabinet Minister, Hugh Dalton.

It soon became apparent to Dalton, and to others, that Prince Albert Victor, who could reasonably be expected to succeed to the throne before long, was not an intelligent boy. One telling phrase used by Dalton was 'the abnormally dormant condition of his mental powers'. Prince George, by contrast, was found to be bright and lively. Of the two, the younger brother was clearly the leader.[6]

As he grew up Prince Albert Victor had a tendency to fall suddenly and inconveniently in love, even being unfortunate enough at one stage to have his passions aroused by a Roman Catholic, Princess Hélène of Orleans. Queen Victoria therefore very reasonably came to the conclusion that the best hope for Prince Albert Victor lay in the rapid provision of a sensible wife. Her choice fell on Princess May of Teck, whom she described as 'a very nice girl, distinguée-looking with a pretty figure'.[7]

The engagement of Prince Albert Victor, who was now Duke of Clarence, and Princess May duly took place, but on 14 January 1892, suddenly and unexpectedly, Prince Albert Victor died. With remarkable speed, and apparently without demur from either party, Princess May was transferred from one brother to the other. Within eighteen months of the Duke of Clarence's death she and his younger brother, who was now Duke of York, were married. Once married they became so close to each other in spirit that they disliked ever being separated, and when they had to be they would write to each other daily.[8] Yet as a father the Duke of York, later King George V, was stern, remote and rather forbidding.

Of the strength of his affection for his children there can be no doubt. When his only daughter, Princess Mary, married and left home George V recorded in his diary that he went up to her room to take leave of her and 'quite broke down'.[9] Even his eldest son, the future King Edward VIII, with whom he clashed more often and more strongly than he did with any of his other children, stated in his ghosted memoirs: 'Affection was certainly not lacking in my upbringing.'[10]

George V's shortcomings as a father stemmed chiefly from difficulties in communication and a reluctance to show his real feelings. These were in part a consequence of his own upbringing. When his Private Secretary, Lord Stamfordham, suggested to him in World War I that he might show a more genial image towards the general public, such as he often showed towards his own guests, he replied: 'We sailors never smile on duty.'[11]

His way of life was based on the discipline of the clock and the punctilious fulfilment of duty. Meals were expected to begin when the clock struck the hour appointed. By preference George V would dine alone with his family, wearing a white tie and the Garter star. When he left the dining-room his wife would remain standing and their sons, in order of age, would go up to her, bow and then withdraw.[12] As the future Duke of Windsor put it, 'my father literally pounded good manners into us.'[13]

Harold Nicolson, when working on his biography of George V, was distressed by what he saw as the tedium of his subject's life before he came to the throne. So much of his time, it seemed, had been expended on the slaughter of enormous numbers of birds.

George V had indeed few intellectual or artistic interests. He had been known to wave his walking-stick in indignation at a Cézanne painting. When asked which his favourite opera was he is reputed to have answered: 'Carmen, because it's the shortest.' His best-remembered saying consists of only two words, one of which was 'bugger'. He was also irascible and intolerant. Yet he had what Lord Esher called 'an instinct for statecraft',[14] and he had, above all, that sense of duty which the twentieth century has shown to be the most important quality in a constitutional monarch.

A royal librarian, Sir Owen Morshead, said to Harold Nicolson: 'The House of Hanover, like ducks, produce bad parents. They trample on their young.' Among others he no doubt had Nicolson's subject in mind, but the judgment in George V's case is only partially just.

Prince Albert, in a talk he had with Sir Walter Monckton after he came to the throne as George VI, gave an illuminating analysis of his father's role in the bringing up of his family. Monckton's biographer, Lord Birkenhead, quotes George VI as saying how difficult it had been to have discussions with his father, who had always treated his sons as if they were all alike, whereas they differed greatly in character. The King went on: 'It was very difficult for David. My father was so inclined to go for him. I always thought that it was a pity that he found fault with him over unimportant things – like what he wore. This only put David's back up. But it was a pity that he did the things which he knew would annoy my father. The result was that they did not discuss the important things quietly.' This, George VI had pointed out, was why Edward VIII had never told his father of his intention to marry.[15] That George V had, on the whole, a damaging influence on his eldest son is probable. His second son, by contrast, may well have gained more from his father's guidance and example than he suffered from his father's irascibility.

Princess May, who after Prince George's accession to the throne would adopt the name Mary, was in some respects much better educated than her husband. Her mother, Princess Mary Adelaide, popularly known as Fat Mary, was a granddaughter of George III and sister of the Duke of Cambridge, for many years Commander-in-Chief of the British Army. Princess May's father, the Duke of Teck, a handsome man with a taste for gardening and interior decoration, could have become King of Württemberg but for an earlier marriage in his family involving the beautiful Hungarian Countess Rhedey of Kis-Rede, who was deemed not to be of royal blood.

Princess May spent her early years in Kensington Palace, after which the family moved to White Lodge in Richmond Park. In spite of her German descent she considered herself wholly anglicised. During a visit, at the age of twenty-five, to Württemberg, which she described as 'a primitive place', she wrote to her old governess: 'I certainly do not like Germany . . . Thank God I belong to a great Nation.'[16]

Princess Mary Adelaide was notoriously extravagant, and in 1883, when Princess May was sixteen, they were obliged to leave England for a time. As the future Queen Mary herself put it, 'My family were always in short street, so they had to go abroad to economize.' As their resting-place they chose Florence, where the young Princess regularly visited museums and art galleries in the afternoons, and where she acquired tastes she would not be able to share with her future husband. (Her early experiences of relative poverty may also have helped to explain her subsequent practice of pointedly admiring her friends' possessions and thereby acquiring a number of them as gifts.)

Once she was married, however, since her sense of duty was no less strong than her husband's, Princess May subordinated everything to the maintenance of his comfort and well-being. In particular she knew that he did not like to be contradicted, especially at meal-times or by women,[17] and, so far as possible, she ensured that this did not happen. Prince George understandably found the marriage a perfect one.

Like her husband, she was an indifferent communicator. Asquith once said he was more exhausted by dining next to her than by a debate in the House of Commons.[18] But the charge, sometimes made, that she had a detached and distant attitude towards her children, is certainly refuted by her eldest son. Even in ghosted memoirs there is no mistaking the warmth with which he recalls the affection she showed to himself and his brothers and sister. The happiest hour of the children's day, he recollects, occurred when they were called at 6.30 in the evening from the schoolroom to her boudoir. There she would read or talk to them, impressing them with 'her soft voice and her cultivated mind'.[19]

As in most upper-class families of the time their parents played only a limited part in the children's upbringing. In the earliest years nannies served as continual intermediaries, and manservants too played roles of importance. In his official biography of George VI, published in 1958, Sir John Wheeler-Bennett reveals some of the more deplorable practices of those who had the young Prince Albert in their charge. One nanny he even describes as 'sadistic and incompetent'. She neglected Prince Albert even to the point of failing to feed him properly, chiefly because of her preoccupation with his elder brother. Fortunately she did not remain long in the royal service.[20]

Wheeler-Bennett's revelations have led a number of commentators to suggest that Prince Albert's early upbringing was bound to induce nervous disorders, some of which would inevitably remain with him in later life. This is questionable. That much more attention, and indeed love, should be bestowed on his elder brother than on him was understandable. Prince Edward not only enjoyed the prestige of probable succession to the throne, but he had the pretty-boy good looks which would remain with him well into middle age and which naturally appealed to older people. Prince Albert, on the other hand – although he developed in later life into a handsome man – as a child was ungainly and not very attractive physically. His ears stuck out, and he was also knock-kneed. His father, who was knock-kneed himself and acutely conscious of the fact, decided that Prince Albert would benefit from being obliged to sleep in splints. This was an extremely painful exercise, and probably quite useless. He was left-handed, but was instructed, as left-handed children at the time often were, to conform to most of the practices of the right-handed.

Yet neither as a boy nor as a young man did Prince Albert show any resentment of the adulation poured on Prince Edward. He was deeply fond of his elder brother, admired him and could even be said to have idolised him until circumstances forced him to change his judgment.

Certainly there was nothing warped or unfriendly in the character of the young Prince Albert as he began to emerge from the early care of parents, nannies and others. The Countess of Airlie, who as a Lady-in-Waiting became a close confidante of Queen Mary, gave a revealing picture of the three eldest children at the time when Prince Albert was six years old.

'Prince Edward,' she wrote, 'always called David, and Princess Mary were the least inhibited of the children – the former because as the eldest son he had the highest status in the family; the latter because she was her father's favourite . . . The child to whom I was most drawn was Prince Albert – Bertie – although he was not a boy who made friends easily . . . He made his first shy overture to me at Easter 1902 – after I had been only a few weeks in the Household – when he presented me with an Easter card. It was his own work, and very well done for a child of six – a design of spring flowers and chicks, cut out from a magazine, coloured in crayons and pasted on cardboard. He was so anxious for me to receive it in time for Easter that he decided to deliver it in person.'[21]

From his childhood onwards it is true that Prince Albert had to bear a number of handicaps, but the extent to which these were induced by upbringing is debatable. He did not have robust health, and a number of his weaknesses may have been hereditary in origin. His worst affliction, however, was a bad stammer. When he was in his early thirties he began to gain some control over this as a result of skilled treatment and his own persistence, but he could never be certain of being free from it. He was also liable to violent outbursts of temper, but these happily did not last long.

The first public event that can have made much impact on Prince Albert was the death of Queen Victoria. On a cold afternoon on 2 February 1901, when he was five years old, he stood in St. George's Chapel in Windsor to attend her burial service. The next month his father, now the heir to the throne, and his mother set off for Australia. They were away for more than seven months, and Prince Albert and the other children were left nominally in the charge of their grandparents, the new King Edward VII and Queen Alexandra. It was a relaxed, pleasant interlude, with Queen Alexandra's notorious lack of concern for punctuality serving to soften the normal rigidity of discipline. It also enabled the children to come to know their grandfather better.

Edward VII was a man of large appetites, which he invariably satisfied. He smoked too much and ate too much. He was consistently unfaithful to his wife, and gambling was among his favourite pastimes. (He was not a heavy drinker. Unlike many of his contemporaries in England he preferred champagne to port, and a man who is a huge eater is unlikely to become seriously drunk on champagne.)

Just as he reacted against the puritanism which was so prevalent among the British middle classes in the nineteenth century, and which Queen Victoria understood so well, so he reacted against the intellectual gifts and inclinations of his father, the Prince Consort. Courtiers observed that neither he nor Queen Alexandra ever seemed to open a book.

Nevertheless, while Prince of Wales he had prepared himself for his role as King much more thoroughly than was commonly supposed. Once he succeeded to the throne he showed that he had both an awareness of the dignity of the monarchy and the capacity to enhance it. He appreciated the importance of ceremony, dress and punctilio and used the expression, *le métier d'être roi*. In spite of his obesity he was impressive both in appearance and manner.

Although anti-intellectual, he was in fact a gifted linguist, and his outlook was cosmopolitan. He felt at home in Paris, in German spas and at Cannes to an extent which his son George must have found barely conceivable. Writing to him about his eldest son, Albert Victor (Eddy), Queen Victoria had made the comment: 'He and George are charming dear good boys, but they are very *exclusively* English which you and your brothers are not, and this is a great misfortune in these days.' He disagreed with this judgment, believing that being very English would make for greater popularity at home.

Yet he himself enjoyed considerable popularity among the masses in Britain – not least because of his interest in horse-racing. His affairs with women were conducted with sufficient discretion to prevent any public outcry. Although objections were voiced in some conservative circles to his evident enjoyment of the company of the newly enriched, and even Jews, this was criticism which he could bear with impunity. He could also be said to have had a better understanding of the proper role of a constitutional monarch than Queen Victoria showed, acting, as he did, consistently on the advice of his ministers.

When Edward VII came to the throne Prince Albert was aged five. He was fourteen when the King died. During those years, even within the somewhat restrictive family circle in which he lived, he was close enough to the Court to have formed some impression of how one monarch performed a role which he would later have thrust upon him.

CHAPTER TWO

Education and the Royal Navy
1905–1918

The arrangements which George V, when Prince of Wales, made for the education of his elder sons were based on two assumptions. One was that the kind of education which he had received had been good enough for him. The other was that it must therefore be good enough for his sons. Both assumptions were unfortunately wrong.

The man who played the principal part in the early education of Prince Edward and Prince Albert was Henry Hansell, a Norfolk schoolmaster. Hansell's son Peter, who became a solicitor in Cromer, would sometimes recall how his father came into the royal service. The Prince of Wales, he stated, was out shooting one day with some of his neighbours in the Sandringham area and mentioned that he was looking for a tutor for his boys. Somebody suggested Hansell; certain enquiries, seemingly rather perfunctory, were made, and Hansell was taken on.[1]

Hansell was not without qualifications. He had taught at a public school, Rossall, and a preparatory school, Ludgrove, and he had been a part-time tutor to Prince Arthur of Connaught. His physical appearance was impressive. The first biographer of the future King George VI, Taylor Darbyshire, who in 1929 brought out a book entitled *The Duke of York*, described Hansell after he had ceased to instruct the young boys. 'His tall slim form and keen intellectual face,' Darbyshire wrote, 'may still be seen at Buckingham Palace in his capacity of Gentleman Usher to the King.'[2] But the qualities in Hansell which appealed most to the Prince of Wales were that he was a keen yachtsman and a Norfolk man. It did not seem to occur to the Prince that in selecting those who would help to form the minds of his children he could have had the advice of the best educational authorities in the country.

Hansell believed, reasonably enough, that the proper place for the royal children to be taught was a school. As the Prince of Wales disagreed, he tried to create the atmosphere of a British public school and to introduce as many of its trappings as possible, even appointing Prince Edward as head boy. The experiment was largely unsuccessful. Children learn from competition, inspiration and the mutual imparting of the kind of semi-secret information whereby much of folk-lore is preserved. All this was lacking in Hansell's regime. In particular Hansell himself lacked the ability to inspire.

In later life the Duke of Windsor, recalling how he, as the eldest boy, fared, wrote of Hansell: 'If he harboured strong views about anything, he was careful to conceal them. I am today unable to recall anything brilliant or original that he ever said.' He added: 'Looking back over those peculiarly ineffectual years under him, I am appalled to discover how little I really learned.'[3]

For Prince Albert the instruction was even less effectual. He was very conscious of his stammer, which he had developed at an early age. This largely precluded him from taking part in the oral practice of foreign languages, and sometimes, when asked a question to which he knew the answer, he would not give it because it contained a word he knew he would have difficulty in getting out. He was described, probably unjustly, as 'inattentive'.

Hansell, in short, was a man who was given, through his employer's misjudgment, a difficult task which was clearly beyond his capacities. Of this he was probably aware, just as he was of the restraints on his personal freedom which his appointment imposed. One of the most moving passages in the Duke of Windsor's memoirs is his description of how Hansell would sometimes walk up onto some high ground and stand there 'looking into space and smoking his pipe'. In trying to explain to the children why he was there he said: 'I don't suppose you will understand, but for me it is freedom.' The high ground became known in the royal family as 'freedom'.

Hansell had a number of specialist teachers to help him. An elderly professor named Eugen Oswald taught German. He complained that Prince Albert pulled his beard, but he seems to have been more successful with Prince Edward, who acquired a liking for the German language. A Frenchman named Gabriel Hua, who had taught the young Prince George on board HMS *Britannia*, was called back into service to teach his children. There was also for a time a French mistress called Mlle Dussau, who had been governess to three sons of Lord Tennyson. Princess May seems to have obtained Mlle Dussau's services with the same skill whereby she acquired *objets d'art*, Lady Tennyson letting her go with considerable reluctance.[4]

Another instructor from the past who was recalled was the Rev John Dalton, for a long while the principal tutor to Princes Albert Victor and George. Now a formidable figure in his sixties, he had the task of giving religious instruction. In this he may well have had some success, for throughout his life George VI was to retain a strong and uncomplicated religious faith.

The most distinguished of the various teachers was Cecil Sharp, the collector of folk-songs, who taught the royal children singing. Unfortunately they were not musically gifted.

One form of instruction given was directly related to the roles which the royal children would have to perform in later life. Its purpose was to train the royal memory so that faces could be more easily recalled. It was a variant of the game which Kipling's Kim had to play during his initiation into the secret service. One of the boys would go into a room where there were some fifty people and be introduced to them all. He would then go into another room, where a sketch showed the guests in roughly the same positions, and be asked to identify as many as possible. Proficiency was soon acquired.

There were also outings of a kind which could not so easily be enjoyed by royal children of later generations. These were visits under Hansell's guidance to cathedrals and museums. Popular photography was still crude, and in a number of newspapers and magazines illustrations were still provided by artists rather than cameramen. As a result Prince Albert and his family could mingle with other sightseers without necessarily being instantly recognized and harassed.[5]

Although the training of their young minds and the imparting of instruction were both inadequate, the royal children were, on the whole, a happy group and created a pleasant impression. This was attested to by a number of eye-witnesses. Lord Esher, describing a visit to Balmoral, stated: 'The house is a home for children – six of them at luncheon – the youngest running round the table all the while.'[6] The Austrian Ambassador, Count Albert Mensdorff, described the children as 'very nice and well brought up'.[7]

Although the family pattern of life had been considerably altered in 1903 when, with the belated move of King Edward and Queen Alexandra to Buckingham Palace, his heir was able to occupy Marlborough House in London, the rhythm of early education was scarcely broken until the spring of 1907, when Prince Edward was sent as a cadet to the recently established Royal Naval College at Osborne. Hansell appointed Prince Albert, now aged eleven, head boy, Prince Henry, the future Duke of Gloucester, taking his place as a kind of second-in-command. Prince Albert, Hansell noted approvingly, took his new responsibilities seriously.

Before Prince Albert followed his elder brother to Osborne Hansell wrote in a final report: 'I have always found him a very straight and honourable boy, very kind hearted and generous; he is sure to be popular with other boys.'[8]

Recalling in later life his days as a naval cadet, Prince Albert's father, King

George V, said that he had had no advantages from being a prince. He was rather small; he was expected to challenge bigger boys, and he regularly received a hiding.[9] He overcame all this, just as he did a tendency to be seasick. Superior officers noted his indifference to hardship or danger,[10] and he ended with an abiding affection for the Royal Navy, in which he would gladly have made a career had not his elder brother died so young.

With this experience behind him he issued instructions that his sons were to be treated at Osborne like all the other cadets, with no favours granted.[11] This he must have felt particularly important in the case of Prince Albert, for whom he envisaged the career in the Royal Navy of which he himself had been deprived. While Prince Albert was a cadet at Osborne he wrote to him: 'You know it is Mama's and my great wish that you should go into the Navy.'[12]

Prince Albert entered Osborne as a cadet in January 1909, shortly after his thirteenth birthday. The grounds of Osborne House in the Isle of Wight had been largely designed by the Prince Consort. The house became Queen Victoria's favourite residence in England, but Edward VII, having no desire to live there, presented it to the nation as a convalescent home for officers. Space for the naval college was found in the stables and in newly erected bungalows.

The regime was in many respects similar to that of other expensive boarding schools. In winter the day began with reveille at 6.30, followed by a plunge into cold water. It indicated no lack of respect that a royal or aristocratic bottom could be flogged by a petty officer wielding a bamboo cane, with a naval doctor in attendance to see fair play.

In one respect, however, the instruction given at Osborne differed from that in most other establishments. This was the reiterated assertion that where there were two ways of doing something, one was the right, or Royal Navy, way; the other was the wrong way.[13] This may not have encouraged breadth or depth of speculation, but to a natural conformist who wanted to be accepted by the Royal Navy it was a convenience. By the time he came to Osborne Prince Albert was already showing clear signs of being a conformist by temperament. Prince Edward, by contrast, though never a whole-hearted rebel, had a detectably rebellious streak.

When Prince Albert arrived at Osborne his older brother was able to warn him of likely pitfalls as they went for walks together beyond the college's playing-fields. The chief difficulty they shared was their lack of previous schooling. The elder brother later stated: 'The fact that I had never been to school before caused me to be regarded as a freak.'[14]

For Prince Albert the immediate consequence was to be placed near the bottom of his intake, or 'term', and there he remained. When he eventually rose from 67th to 61st place place it was a noticeable advance. He does not seem to have been much disturbed by his low ranking. He entered readily into college activities and made friends fairly easily, and he learnt to handle a boat with some skill. He also made the acquaintance of a man who was to be important to him as mentor and formative influence.

This was Surgeon-Lieutenant Louis Greig, the Assistant Medical Officer, who had played rugby football for Scotland and who coached the boys in the game with vigour and enthusiasm. Greig was later to serve the Prince in a variety of capacities, to transfer with him from the Royal Navy to the Royal Air Force, and to partner him in the Wimbledon tennis championships. Like a number of the other boys Prince Albert had for him a kind of hero-worship. Greig said later that the principal service he rendered Prince Albert was to 'put steel into him'.[15]

Education at the Royal Naval College, Dartmouth, in south Devon, which Prince Albert entered in January 1911, was largely an extension of that provided at Osborne. The Prince's academic record remained dismally bad, and at one point he was placed 67th out of 68. But he had learnt, or instinctively knew, how to conduct himself in a manner that would gain the respect and liking of his fellow-pupils. A contemporary said of him later: 'One knew instinctively that he would never let you down. He never once asked for a favour all the time he was at Dartmouth, nor did he once use his position to gain a favour for anyone else.'[16]

Increasingly during his Dartmouth days Prince Albert found affairs of state and the change in his father's role intruding upon, or at least varying, the life of a naval cadet. At the age of fourteen, looking out one day from Marlborough House, he suddenly noticed that the royal standard was at half-mast. Shortly afterwards he and Prince Edward were summoned to their father, whose face, in his eldest son's words, was 'grey with fatigue'. He told them that their grandfather was dead. Prince Albert mentioned the royal standard, and his father, overcome by grief though he was, remained sufficiently master of himself and of ceremony to point out that a mistake had been made. 'The King is dead. Long live the King,' he told them. The mistake was soon put right.[17]

For King George V's coronation in 1911 the two Princes were granted special leave. On their return to Dartmouth Prince Edward, now heir to the throne, observed among his contemporaries what he described as 'a subtle respect' for his new position. Prince Albert enjoyed no such benefit, but he did have the privilege of accompanying his father on a review of the fleet from 7 to 11 May 1912. On this occasion he met for the first time his future Prime Minister, Winston Churchill, who was then First Lord of the Admiralty. He also had what was at the time the rather unusual experience, even for a naval man, of putting to sea in a submarine which then submerged.

The final stage in Prince Albert's training as a cadet was a cruise in foreign waters aboard HMS *Cumberland*, a 9800-ton cruiser. At first he was extremely seasick, but, like his father, he was able in time to master this unpleasant weakness. As the cruise continued he enjoyed it more. For the first time he was engaged in activity of some consequence while not in the presence of, and therefore under the shadow of, his elder brother. As there were ports of call in the Canary Islands, Bermuda, Barbados, Jamaica, Trinidad, Puerto Rico and Newfoundland, there was plenty of sight-seeing. The cruise also gave Prince Albert an early insight into some of the problems liable to arise when a member of the royal family appears in public. One of his duties was to open a new wing of the Kingston yacht club. In doing so he found himself surrounded by Jamaican girls who competed in trying to touch the royal person as many times as possible. After that he took his duties sufficiently lightly to appoint a fellow-cadet, who resembled him physically, to stand in for him on certain occasions.[18]

The final outcome of Prince Albert's naval training was his appointment as a midshipman in the Royal Navy on 15 September 1913. Shortly afterwards, as the twelfth of thirteen midshipmen, he joined HMS *Collingwood*, the flagship of the vice-admiral commanding the 1st Battle Squadron, the Hon. Sir Stanley Colville.[19] *Collingwood* was a 19 250-ton battleship. On board Prince Albert was known, for the easier enforcement of discipline, as Mr Johnson.

A little more than a month after he joined her *Collingwood* sailed from Devonport to take part in manoeuvres in the Mediterranean. For Prince Albert these served mainly as an exercise in adaptability. For the great bulk of the time he had to conduct himself as the most junior of officers in a large ship's company. But when *Collingwood* called at Alexandria he and Admiral Colville were invited to stay with Lord Kitchener in Cairo, where he met the Khedive. When the battleship anchored in the Bay of Salamis he received King Constantine and Queen Sophie of Greece (Uncle Tino and Aunt Sophie, as he knew them) on board.

After the 1st Battle Squadron returned to home waters Prince Albert resumed normal naval duties with no interruptions except to accompany his father in a naval review off Spithead in July 1914. On 4 August he was keeping the middle watch on board *Collingwood* when war between Britain and Germany was declared.

The war that followed was to be for Prince Albert largely a period of illness, disappointment and frustration. But it also gave him the opportunity to be the first King or future King of England to take part in a naval battle since William IV, who was present at the battle of Cape St Vincent.[20]

Within three weeks of the outbreak of war Prince Albert was attacked by severe stomach pains. Appendicitis was diagnosed, and an operation was performed in Aberdeen, where he had been taken by hospital ship. Whether the diagnosis was correct may be questioned, for though the pains were relieved for a time they recurred later. Sir Frederick Treves, the eminent surgeon who had served both Queen Victoria and Edward VII, was of the opinion that the Prince ought not to go to sea on active service again. Prince Albert was unwilling to accept this verdict, and a compromise was reached, which enabled him to work on a temporary basis in the Admiralty. After a few months he was deemed fit to rejoin *Collingwood*, but the attacks returned, and once again he was transferred to a hospital ship, where he spent more than two months. A period of convalescence followed, but Prince Albert had exacted a promise from his father that if the fleet were to put to sea he would be allowed to rejoin *Collingwood*. This was a promise to which his father attached importance, and a letter was sent to the captain of the hospital ship which read: 'The King would prefer to run the risk of Prince Albert's health suffering than that he should endure the bitter and lasting disappointment of not being in his ship in the battle line.'[21] Prince Albert was therefore on board, albeit in the sick bay, when the 1st Battle Squadron put to sea on the evening of 30 May 1916.

By dawn the next day Admiral Jellicoe, in command of the Grand Fleet and flying his flag in *Iron Duke*, had concentrated a force which included twenty-four battleships. Ahead of him Admiral Beatty was in command of the 5th Battle Squadron.

The battle which followed off the west coast of Jutland has been considered remarkable by naval historians mainly for two reasons. One was the indecisive nature of its outcome. The other was the total failure of British naval intelligence. Beatty's remark, 'There's something wrong with our bloody ships today, Chatfield', has passed into folk-lore. Jellicoe might well have spoken in much more decisive terms about his lack of information. Time and again he asked where the German battle-fleet was, and no one was able to tell him.

The Germans inflicted considerably more damage on the British than the British inflicted on them, and on these grounds claimed a victory. But since the main object of British naval strategy in the North Sea was to prevent the German fleet from putting out in force, and since it never did so again after the battle of Jutland, any victory claimed was of little benefit to Germany.

Of his part in the action Prince Albert wrote for the benefit of his father: 'I was in A turret and watched most of the action through one of the trainer's telescopes. At the commencement I was sitting on top of A turret and had a very good view of the proceedings. I was up there during a lull, when a German ship started firing at us, and one salvo "straddled" us.' Wisely he took evasive action. He went on: 'The hands behaved splendidly and all of them in the best of spirits as their hearts' desire had at last been granted, which was to be in action with the Germans ... My impressions were very different to what I had expected. I saw visions of the mast going over the side and funnels hurtling through the air etc. In reality none of these things happened and we are still quite sound as before.'

Later he wrote to his elder brother: 'When I was on top of the turret I never felt any fear of shells or anything else. It seems curious but all sense of danger and everything else goes except the longing of dealing death in every possible way to the enemy.'[22]

For the part he played in the battle Prince Albert was commended in a despatch which Jellicoe made public. Two months after the battle he was promoted to the rank of lieutenant. His father expressed his pride and satisfaction in conferring on him on his twenty-first birthday the Order of the Garter.

The battle of Jutland was the principal engagement in which the Royal Navy took part in World War I. In World War II George VI was continually conscious, as he sometimes made clear when he conferred medals for gallantry, that he was not himself engaged in the actual fighting. But the knowledge that he had personally taken part in the battle of Jutland remained as a source of some satisfaction for him.

In the following year the Prince's attacks of gastric pain were more frequent and violent. He became deeply depressed and eventually accepted that he was physically unfit for service at sea. He therefore suggested to his father that he might be transferred to the Royal Naval Air Station at Cranwell. His father agreed, and his appointment was gazetted on 13 November 1917. Louis Greig undertook to accompany him.

Before he could take up his new appointment Prince Albert's doctors at last took the course which, it seems in retrospect, they might reasonably have taken two years or more earlier. This was to perform an operation based on their sudden discovery that what he had been suffering from all along was a duodenal ulcer.

The training station at Cranwell in Lincolnshire was named HMS *Daedalus* in conformity with the Royal Navy's practice of giving ships' names to its shore stations. The site was one of a number of flat stretches of ground which the Admiralty acquired in World War I in order to supplement the work of the Coastguard by the use of reconnaissance aircraft. It became a training station early in 1916, when an Admiralty memorandum stated: 'All officers and men under instruction in aeroplanes, kite balloons and airships will be sent to Cranwell for a finishing course and for graduation.'[23]

At Cranwell Prince Albert was put in charge of cadets under instruction, Greig taking command of the school of physical training. When the Royal Air Force was formally brought into being the Prince was given the rank of flight-lieutenant in the new service. Later in 1918 he was assigned to another cadet training post at St Leonards-on-Sea in Sussex. His final appointment was to General Trenchard's staff. In this capacity he at last succeeded in reaching France on active service on 23 October 1918.

When the war came to an end less than three weeks later he was nearly twenty-four years old, an unassuming young man, liked by his contemporaries, not very well educated, with a strong sense of duty, who had shown tenacity and courage of an unspectacular kind in struggling with physical difficulties.

CHAPTER THREE

Cambridge Undergraduate
1918–1919

In the year which followed the ending of World War I there were a number of events which served to broaden Prince Albert's experience and to develop his understanding. For the first time he acted as the King's representative at an occasion of political consequence; he entered on the last stage of his formal education, and he learnt to fly. He also made contact with the welfare organisation which was to provide him with one of his principal interests during the next twenty years, and which was to help shape his opinions on social problems.

King Albert of the Belgians had decided to make an official and spectacular entry into Brussels on 22 November 1918 to mark the final liberation of his country. He asked for a member of the British royal family to accompany him, and George V decided that this should be Prince Albert. The Prince therefore rode into Brussels alongside members of the Belgian royal family, to be greeted at the Place des Nations by the two most famous figures of Belgian passive resistance to the Germans, Burgomaster Max and Cardinal Mercier.[1]

It was a moving ceremony, but there was some disquiet behind it, and the Allied solidarity, which it was intended to convey, was far from complete. This was shown in a series of despatches from Sir Francis Villiers, the British Minister in Brussels.

On 3 December Villiers reported a conversation he had had with Major Barber, the British liaison officer with General Degoutte, who commanded the French Sixth Army in Belgium. Five French divisions, Villiers reported, had already passed through Brussels. Triumphal marches had been made through Liège, Tirlemont and Louvain, and Degoutte had stated in Barber's presence that this was part of a deliberate policy of impressing the Belgian people with what the French had done to bring about their liberation. The policy, Degoutte had said, would be continued. Villiers proposed as a counter-measure a march through

Brussels by British troops with a band. 'Although the effort we have made is fully appreciated by the upper classes in the country,' he wrote, 'the lower classes have been so cut off from the outer world, and under the influence of German propaganda, that they do not appear to realise it.'[2]

The War Office's reply was chilly. 'It is considered undesirable on military grounds,' the Director of Military Intelligence wrote on 23 December, 'to send British troops to march through Brussels at the present time.' Some war films, he added, would be sent instead.[3] Prince Albert on horseback in the company of the Belgian royal family was therefore the principal visible representative the British Government felt able to offer the people of Brussels as a counterweight to the manifestations of French martial power.

Whatever the masses may have thought, there could be little doubt about the cordiality of the feelings of the King of the Belgians towards Britain. On 8 December he received the British Military Attaché, Brigadier-General Francis Lyon, in audience on his appointment. The King, Lyon reported, was 'most enthusiastic about the work done by our army in the field . . . He regarded our attack near Cambrai as the most important contributory factor in the German defeat.'

Lyon went on: 'The King considers that it is on our friendship that his country must chiefly rely in the future . . . The King also spoke with great enthusiasm of M. Clemenceau, who visited him on the Yser, and for whom he has an admiration that he does not give the impression of having for the French in general.'[4]

Efforts to strengthen Anglo-Belgian links were also made in other directions. Before the end of the year M. Delacroix, the Belgian Prime Minister, visited London to discuss with Lloyd George what were described as 'matters of great importance regarding the present and near future'. Lloyd George himself was made a Doctor of Law by the University of Ghent.[5]

As was to happen on other occasions in the near future while he was still inexperienced, Prince Albert does not seem to have been made aware of the intricacies of the policies of which he was to some extent an instrument. In a letter which he wrote to his father from Brussels he told him only of the 'impressive sight' which the procession made and the 'wonderful welcome' which King Albert received.

After the ceremony in Brussels Prince Albert accompanied the King and the Prince of Wales on a visit lasting some two weeks to battlefields in France and to Paris. He was posted for a time as an Air Force officer to a headquarters in Spa, and in February 1919 he returned to England. He worked for a short time in the Air Ministry, where, as he afterwards made clear, he acquired a proper respect for the industry and ability of the civil servants whom he encountered.[6] But as a serving officer in the Royal Air Force he felt it his duty to qualify as a pilot. His father accepted this and agreed that he should learn to fly.

The aircraft in which Prince Albert learnt was an Avro 504. His instructor was Lieutenant Alec Coryton, who later became an Air Chief Marshal, and they operated from a base which afterwards became part of Croydon airport. Louis Greig, now aged thirty-nine, decided he must learn to fly at the same time.

Prince Albert did not much enjoy flying. After his first flight he wrote to his mother: 'I don't think I should like flying as a pastime.'[7] Nevertheless he persisted and after 23 hours 10 minutes flying time passed as a pilot in Category A. He received his wings on 31 July 1919.[8] Greig also qualified.

Prince Albert did not make a career in the Royal Air Force. In later life he stated that the principal reason why he did not do so was the ban which his father subsequently imposed on his flying because of the risks involved.[9] But to be the first member of the royal family to qualify as a pilot gave him understandable satisfaction. This may have been all the greater because, as with much else that he set himself to do, he had to overcome a considerable personal reluctance.

The King was of the opinion that Prince Albert and his younger brother, Prince Henry, might benefit from a few terms at Cambridge, and in October 1919 they were enrolled as undergraduate members of Trinity College. The decision to send them up to Cambridge was in itself reasonable enough, but, as he had done before, the King imposed educational conditions of his own idiosyncratic choice.

The princes' period of residence was to be only a year, even though in that time a normal undergraduate can do little more than peck at an honours degree course. The King also decided that his sons should not live in college. Instead Louis Greig, now a Wing-Commander and with the formal post of Equerry, was installed with his wife in a house a mile from the college, and here the princes were to live. The King took the view that it would be unfair to ask his sons, who had seen something of the outside world, to accept the restrictions of living in a college. In fact, as a consequence of the war there were plenty of adult undergraduates, some of whom had been markedly matured by the experience of the trenches, with whom the princes could have mixed easily had they been resident in Trinity. As it was, they remained outside the mainstream of university life. They were seen occasionally among the athletes in the Hawks Club, and they seem to have spent not a little of their time touring the countryside on motor-cycles. To Prince Albert in particular, who was considered an exceptionally shy undergraduate, the presence of Prince Henry, for whom he had affection but who was far from intelligent, could hardly have been stimulating.

In contrast with his earlier educational experiences, Prince Albert now found himself being instructed by men with first-class minds, in particular the distinguished historian, J. R. M. Butler. Among the work which was brought to his attention was that of Walter Bagehot.

A nineteenth-century political journalist, who stood for Parliament once without success, Bagehot had the extraordinary distinction of being the author of a book which, in the absence of a written British constitution, came to be widely accepted as an adequate substitute for one. His dictum that in a constitutional monarchy the sovereign has the right to be consulted, to encourage and to warn, has not only been quoted innumerable times, but has become vested with an authority not greatly different from that of an Act of Parliament. Bagehot considered monarchy as the natural form of government, yet readily conceded that adherence to the hereditary principle was unlikely very often to put on the throne a man of exceptional ability. One section of his work, *The English Constitution*, consists largely of sensible suggestions on how constitutional monarchy, as defined by him, can best serve the nation.

To some extent Bagehot echoed the historical assumptions and prejudice of his period. Writing in the Victorian age, he stated: 'It is only in the period of the present reign that in England the duties of a constitutional monarch have ever been well performed. The first two Georges were ignorant of English affairs ... George III interfered unceasingly, but he did harm unceasingly; George IV and William IV gave no steady continuing guidance and were unfit to give it.'

Some passages in Bagehot's work, however, might be seen as blueprints for aspects of the future reign of George VI, others as forecasts of some of the temptations which would be put before his elder brother.

'We have come,' Bagehot wrote, 'to regard the Crown as the head of our morality. The virtues of Queen Victoria and the virtues of George III have sunk deep into the popular heart.' In another passage he wrote: 'There is no royal road to political affairs: their detail is vast, disagreeable, complicated, and miscellaneous. A king, to be the equal of his ministers in discussion, must work as they work.'

He wrote too: 'A family on the throne is an interesting idea also. It brings down the pride of sovereignty to the level of petty life ... The women – one half the human race at least – care fifty times more for a marriage than a ministry. All but a few cynics like to see a pretty novel touching for a moment the dry scenes of the grave world.'

On the subject of temptations Bagehot wrote: 'The place of a constitutional king has greater temptations than almost any other and fewer suitable occupations than almost any other ... Whatever is most attractive, whatever is most seductive has always been offered to the Prince of Wales of the day, and always will be. It is not rational to expect the best virtue where temptation is applied in the most trying form at the frailest time of human life.'[10]

That Prince Albert studied Bagehot with particular care while he was up at Cambridge has been established beyond doubt.[11]

The Boys' Welfare Association, with which Prince Albert first came into contact in 1919, was largely the creation of one man. This was the Rev. Robert Hyde, who, as a temporary wartime civil servant in the Ministry of Munitions, had made a study of the working conditions of boys in factories.

Hyde's father had died when he was nine. His principal memory of his father was of accompanying him to distant parts of London, where they went to dispose of family possessions in order to keep their home going. He himself left school at fourteen. In his first job the only pay he received was sixpence a week tea money on Thursdays, when he was obliged to work late.

After working for seven years as a porter for a firm of importers of colonial wares he decided to take holy orders. For this he needed a knowledge of Greek, Latin, Euclid and biblical history, none of which he had ever studied. A doctor friend, who had come into a legacy, lent him £100, and with this he was able to enter the theological faculty of King's College, London.

His first parish was Hoxton in London's East End, where there were numerous garment factories. As a memorial to the Christian socialist, Frederick Denison Maurice, a group of his admirers had established the Maurice Hostel Settlement there. Hyde was put in charge of this in 1906, and he remained there for ten years. A frequent visitor to the hostel was Clement Attlee, who was then engaged in similar welfare work in the Haileybury Cadets' Club in Stepney.

Hyde's appointment to the Ministry of Munitions was part of a governmental plan to improve working conditions in factories. In this, philanthropy and the need to increase wartime production both played a part. In the course of his duties Hyde received some sensible advice from the poet Humbert Wolfe, also a civil servant, who told him that in order to persuade the owners of the factories which he visited to introduce welfare schemes he must first persuade them that it would be profitable to do so. Hyde caused something of a stir by writing three articles for the *Daily Telegraph* on 'The Boy in Industry', and he can perhaps be given credit for creating a new profession, that of welfare officers in factories.

In the course of his duties Hyde made the acquaintance of a number of sympathetic employers, among them Sir William Beardmore and Steven Alley of Alley and McLellan. They encouraged him in his plan to form a boys' welfare association, and Beardmore agreed to be the first chairman of the association's council. Premises were found in Tothill Street in Westminster, Alley and McLellan paying the office costs. Hyde left his civil service job, gave up his living in Hoxton, from which he had been granted leave of absence, and decided to devote his energies entirely to the new association. The Boys' Welfare Association was established on 3 April 1918. There was not enough money to pay Hyde a living wage, and his wife went out to work to support him.[12]

In later life Hyde's appearance was thought to resemble that of Chesterton's Father Brown. Maude Reed, a member of the staff of the Industrial Society, which grew out of the Boys' Welfare Association, wrote of him: 'A man of superb judgment, strategy and foresight, and intensely alive, he appeared to have few personal needs and ambitions.'[13] It was evidence of his resourcefulness that within a few months of the formation of the Boys' Welfare Association he was able to discuss its affairs with a member of the royal family. This was brought about by the Rev. G. K. A. Bell, later Bishop of Chichester, who was at that time Chaplain to the Archbishop of Canterbury, Randall Thomas Davison. The Archbishop discussed the project with George V's Private Secretary. This was Lord Stamfordham, whose advice George V usually, and wisely, took. The King once said of him: 'He was the most loyal friend I ever had. He taught me to be a king.'[14]

In the advice which he eventually gave about the Boys' Welfare Association Stamfordham was probably influenced by reports of social unrest. There had already been some disturbing signs of this, and another was to occur the next year, when at a meeting in the Albert Hall to celebrate the third anniversary of the October revolution in Russia, the King's name was hissed.[15] Stamfordham agreed to meet Hyde. The Assistant Private Secretary, Clive Wigram, was also present.

That the idea of inviting Prince Albert to become President of the Association was discussed seriously at the first meeting was evidence of Stamfordham's far-sightedness. Public bodies can normally expect the stamp of royal patronage only when they have proved their value and good repute over a number of years. The Boys' Welfare Association was new, small and potentially controversial. Its stated aims, 'to encourage the study among employers and managers of labour of questions affecting the welfare of persons engaged in industry' and 'to advise and assist employers in starting and improving welfare schemes', were harmless enough. But the trades union movement was sceptical, and the number of employers who actively supported the association was minuscule.[16]

One of the questions which Stamfordham put to Hyde was: 'Are you going to set the King's son against the King's Government?' This was a reasonable question. Hyde was soon to learn that there were officials in the new Ministry of Labour who looked forward to his downfall. One of them even said: 'If Hyde now makes a mistake we'll take away his Prince Albert.'[17]

Hyde evidently satisfied Stamfordham of his intentions, and soon afterwards he was received by Prince Albert. The Prince showed immediate interest, but was quoted by Hyde as saying: 'If I accept, there must be no fuss, no publicity and no red carpet.'[18] These were conditions which Hyde could not possibly fulfil, but he must have given a reasonably satisfactory answer, for on 21 March Prince Albert became President of the Boys' Welfare Association. He attended his first meeting of the association's council on 1 May, accompanied by Louis Greig. In a short speech in which he overcame his stammer as best he could, he said he felt the welfare movement had come to stay and prosper, and he contributed thirty guineas to the fund.[19]

His acceptance of the presidency seems to have had an immediate effect on the association's finances. A guarantee fund of £6500 was provided by individual guarantees ranging from £250 to £500. The council also decided that, in recognition of the fact that the work had begun to extend far beyond the welfare of boys, the association should be renamed the Industrial Welfare Society.[20]

While a Cambridge undergraduate Prince Albert had a number of official functions to attend and other official tasks to perform. On 28 October 1919 he received the freedom of the City of London. Two days later he greeted the Shah of Persia at Dover. Less than two weeks after that he was again at Dover, this time to greet the President of the French Republic, Raymond Poincaré. These were obligations he could fulfil without serious difficulty. More demanding were a number of tasks assigned to him as a result of the new responsibilities of his elder brother, who was now Prince of Wales. The government in general, and Lloyd George in particular, had come to the conclusion that the greatest service the Prince of Wales could now render his country was in strengthening imperial links. This meant extensive tours of Empire, inevitably beginning and ending with long sea voyages. In the Prince of Wales's absence more engagements at home had to be met by his younger brother. Many of these involved the making of speeches.

Prince Albert's stammer had not improved, and speech-making had not become any easier. Most people who are affected by bad stammers can arrange their lives in such a way that they are rarely, if ever, called upon to make public speeches. This course was not open to Prince Albert.

It was noticed that he stammered less when he was not reading from a script,[21] but the opportunities for princes of the royal blood to give impromptu public speeches are limited. They cannot be expected to have detailed expert knowledge of all the causes and concerns in which they are involved, and if there is also a political significance to the functions they attend they must act on governmental advice. For Prince Albert the ordeal of public speaking from a script had to be endured year after year. Yet no evidence has come to light that he refused any duties reasonably asked of him on the grounds that he would be obliged to make a speech.

CHAPTER FOUR

Balkan Interlude
1920–1922

On 5 January 1920 Prince Albert wrote to his cousin, Lord Louis Mountbatten, to explain why he could not attend a social function in ten days' time. 'I have got to go down to Wales,' his letter stated, 'to see a coal mine!!!!' The four exclamation marks are his.[1]

That the King's son should visit a coal mine was indeed a surprising event, and the visit to Wales was followed by a further one to Tyneside, where the Prince was shown over a number of factories. At the annual general meeting of the Industrial Welfare Society on 29 October 1920 he made a report on these visits, in which he said: 'The saving and brightening of the worker's life should be, and must eventually be, an industrial issue, and when the community realizes that that country is richest which nourishes the greatest number of happy people a big step will have been taken towards the contentment and prosperity of the nation.' In the same speech he called attention to a passage in the latest report of the Chief Inspector of Factories, which recorded a 'marked increase in the introduction of welfare conditions'.[2]

When he made this speech Prince Albert was already known as the Duke of York, his father having conferred this title on him during his final term at Cambridge, on 5 June 1920. With it came the additional titles of Earl of Inverness and Baron Killarney. In answer to his son's letter of acknowledgment and thanks King George V wrote: 'I know that you have behaved very well in a difficult situation for a young man and that you have done what I asked you to do.' He went on to express the hope that his son would always look upon him as his best friend.[3]

The Duke of York's earliest engagements on behalf of the Industrial Welfare Society were no doubt undertaken out of a sense of duty, but before long they were to give rise to one of his most abiding interests.

In March 1921 a football match was played between a team of boys from the Briton Ferry Steel Works in South Wales and one representing

Westminster School. This pioneering event aroused some public interest, and when, shortly afterwards, the Duke of York, accompanied by Robert Hyde of the Boys' Welfare Association, visited the sports ground of the biscuit company, McVitie and Price, its chairman, Sir Alexander Grant, suggested to him that more could be done to bring boys in industry and boys in public schools together.[4] As a result the Duke invited Hyde and a naval officer, Commander B. T. Coote, to Buckingham Palace to discuss Grant's idea. The upshot was the decision to organize a camp that would serve the purpose Grant had in mind.

Grant accepted financial responsibility for the camp. A disused airfield near New Romney in Kent was chosen as a site. The support of other industrialists was obtained, as was that of the chairman of the Headmasters' Conference, Dr David of Rugby. All this was done with remarkable speed, and on 3 July 1921 the first of the camps was formally opened.

These camps became an annual event, their site being later changed to Southwold in Suffolk. Except for one year, when he was incapacitated, the Duke was to attend every camp before he was called to the throne. His first Private Secretary after he became King, Sir Alexander Hardinge, wrote: 'I believe that, of all his activities, the annual boys' camp gave him the greatest pleasure.'[5] In the public mind the name of the Duke of York was probably more readily associated with his annual camp than with anything else he did before he became King.

The effectiveness of the camps in breaking down social barriers is easily exaggerated. The introduction of national service, or conscription, was to be vastly more beneficial in this respect. But, apart from the pleasure they undoubtedly gave, the camps must have taught an appreciable number of boys something of the living conditions and habits of thought in areas of society of which they otherwise would have had no knowledge. Among those who learnt much was the Duke of York himself.

In 1920 and 1921, although he had many official engagements, the Duke of York was able to indulge his social and sporting tastes more freely than at any time in his adult life. At Buckingham Palace, family evenings ended at 10 or 10.30, and before they went to bed the King liked to interrogate his children on how they had spent the day. Increasingly the sons found reasons not to be present on such evenings.[6]

The Duke of York danced well. Lady Helen Hardinge described him as 'particularly nimble and expert in the most complicated steps'. She also wrote that at skating 'the Duke of York was – typically – much better than he thought he was'.[7] He was a good enough golfer to bring his handicap down to nine without much effort, and he achieved some distinction at tennis.

Louis Greig, who in 1920 became the Duke of York's Comptroller, was his principal tennis instructor and more importantly taught him how to conduct himself on the court. The Duke's outbursts of temper were sometimes excessive, but through Greig's firmness and his own efforts he succeeded in bringing them increasingly under control.

In that year the Duke reached the singles semi-final of the RAF tennis championships after two hard matches, in both of which he lost the first set. Greig beat him easily in the semi-final, but, playing together, they won the doubles.

Dan Maskell, who was to attain a position of unique authority in British tennis, was a ball-boy at Queen's Club in London when the Duke of York played there. He recalled the Duke as a left-hander with a good top-spin forehand but a weak backhand. His best shot was a forehand taken about shoulder-height. Maskell was to find greater natural talent in George VI's granddaughter, Princess Anne, who could in his judgment have become a Wimbledon player had circumstances been different.[8]

Among those whom the Duke of York met socially in 1920 were members of the Bowes-Lyon family, including the youngest daughter, Lady Elizabeth. In September of the following year he visited the family's ancestral Scottish home, Glamis Castle, where the principal occupation was to be shooting.

George V's favourite recreational activities were philately and shooting, and his younger son markedly inherited his taste for the latter. Modern sensibilities tend to be offended by the killing of birds simply for sport. Indeed, when George VI died in 1952 and a BBC newsreader, after announcing his death, said that on the last day of his life he had been able to indulge in his favourite sport, shooting, a feeling of public disquiet was fairly widespread. Nor can it be denied that at times the royal carnage was on a massive scale. On one afternoon at the home near Beaconsfield of the owner of the *Daily Telegraph*, Lord Burnham, some 4000 pheasants were killed, George V himself bagging more than 1000 of them. Afterwards the King admitted to his eldest son that they had gone a little far that day.[9]

In his own approach to shooting, George V's second son accepted the conventions of his class and age. The sport was an important part of upper-class social life, especially in the autumn, and he himself was taught to shoot when very young. Two days before Christmas 1907, when aged twelve, he recorded in a game-book the shooting of one pheasant and forty-seven rabbits by his father, his elder brother and himself. The record ended: 'My first day's shooting. I used a single barrel muzzle loader with which Grandpapa, Uncle Eddy and Papa all started shooting. I shot three rabbits.'[10]

Throughout his life he kept records in game-books with scrupulous care of birds and other animals shot. He had both natural ability in shooting and acquired skill. An exceptionally kindly man, he was also, in the words of one who knew him well, 'a compulsive shot'.[11]

In April 1922 King George V received a letter from Queen Marie of Roumania about the forthcoming marriage of her daughter, also called Marie, to King Alexander of Yugoslavia. Queen Marie was the grand-daughter of both Queen Victoria and the Emperor Alexander of Russia. A woman of exceptional beauty, she had exercised great political power in Roumania in World War I. Her personal ascendancy over the royal families of south-east Europe was such that she has been described as a kind of Queen Victoria of the Balkans. In the words of her biographer, 'her love life was the gossip of three continents.'[12] Certainly not all her children were her husband's. In her letter Queen Marie pointed out that at the marriages of the Kings of Serbia it had been customary to have three sponsors, or 'Kooms'. The chief of these was traditionally the Emperor of Russia. As there was no longer a Russian Emperor she asked King George to be the principal sponsor, and to send one of his sons to represent him.

Stamfordham referred Queen Marie's letter to Lord Curzon, the Foreign Secretary, and wrote: 'The King asks whether you see any political objection to his agreeing to this proposal. As he is the first cousin of the mother of the bride, he is the Sovereign who is most closely interested by family ties in this matter, and he feels it will be difficult to refuse the Queen of Roumania's request unless on political grounds.' He reminded Lord Curzon that Serbia, now a principal part of Yugoslavia, and Roumania had both been Britain's allies and added: 'No doubt the Queen of Roumania wishes to give as much prestige and *éclat* as possible to the marriage.'[13] The decision taken was that King George V should accept the invitation and that the Duke of York, 'attended by one gentleman', should represent him. No special mission would be sent, but a monitor of the Royal Navy would be despatched up the Danube to Belgrade.

The British Foreign Office clearly attached importance to the Duke's visit. Even though a Secret Intelligence Service report had recently been received, suggesting that if the Duke did go to Belgrade he would be in some personal danger, this did not deter the Foreign Office from recommending the visit. Nor is there any evidence that the contents of the SIS report were conveyed to the King or to his son.

In April the SIS representative in Austria had warned that 'certain Croatian revolutionaries, aided and abetted by the Bulgarian Macedonian revolutionaries, were forming a plan to assassinate King Alexander'. Further enquiries were made, and two months later the SIS representative sent a report based on information from another source. This was even more specific. 'It is hoped to put the plan into operation,' the new report stated, 'during the forthcoming wedding festivities in Belgrade.' The name of the proposed assassin was given as Marion Kilifarsky, described as a former Bulgarian Macedonian Comitadji and 'now an independent desperado'. The effective controller of the plot was thought to be a

Hungarian agent named Stipetitch, who was of Croatian extraction and held the rank of major. He had been engaged for some time in disseminating anti-Serbian propaganda and had founded a West Hungarian Croat Party.[14]

The SIS report containing all this information was dated 1 June 1922. Its contents were reported to the British Minister in Belgrade, Sir Alban Young, on 5 June. It was on that day that the Duke of York, travelling by Simplon–Orient Express and accompanied by his Private Secretary, Sir Ronald Waterhouse, arrived at the Yugoslav frontier. A special train conveyed him to Zagreb, where on his way from the railway station to the palace he was enthusiastically welcomed by a large crowd.

The wedding ceremony and festivities took place without incident. How imminent the threat was to King Alexander and to those in his vicinity at the time of the wedding is open to speculation. Certainly the SIS reports were not without substance. Croat revolutionaries did intend to take King Alexander's life, although it was not until 1934 that they succeeded.

The Duke was exposed to another, though minor, hazard while in Belgrade. The Serbian royal stables had recently been replenished with some fine Irish horses. All were said to have been well trained except one. This, for some reason, was allocated to the Duke when he took part in the parade. The horse became extremely restive, but the Duke kept it under control in a manner which was much admired.

After the festivities the British Minister in Bucharest, Sir Herbert Dering, returned to Bucharest together with the Roumanian Foreign Minister. From Bucharest he wrote to the Foreign Office: 'The Minister for Foreign Affairs . . . stated the excellent impression made at Belgrade by the Duke of York. Monsieur Duca added an expression of his own admiration for the Duke's horsemanship.'[15]

Among those whom the Duke of York met at the festivities was Prince Paul of Yugoslavia, brother of King Alexander, who after the King's assassination was to become Regent. During and after World War II George VI was to become much concerned with the fate of Prince Paul and other members of his family.

Within a few months of his return to England the Duke of York had to travel once again to south-east Europe. This was a consequence of the decision to hold a belated coronation ceremony at Alba Julia in Roumania. Queen Marie was the guiding spirit in this enterprise, and for inspiration she turned to the records of imperial Russian coronations.[16]

George V was again asked to send a son to represent him, and on this occasion he showed strong reluctance. In particular he wanted to know who was going to pay for his son's journey. This sent the Foreign Office in search of precedents. The most recent was that of the coronation of the King of Norway in 1906, which was attended by the Prince and Princess of Wales with a suite of nine persons. They had lived on board the royal yacht, and the Foreign Office had defrayed the expenses, which had amounted to £1450. The official of the Central Department, whose advice had been called for, added: 'Times have changed since 1906, and I should say that if the Duke of York represents the King, he could, not being the heir to the throne and being unmarried, attach Sir Herbert Dering to his suite and take out two others, a Secretary and an Equerry.'[17]

The Foreign Office agreed to foot the bill, and with the somewhat grudging acquiescence of his father the Duke of York set off on 9 October 1922 on another long train journey. He was accompanied this time by Admiral Sir Henry Campbell, whom George V had known for a long time and had personally selected for the mission, as well as by Colonel Waterhouse.

The coronation ceremony seems to have been as colourful as Queen Marie had hoped. Sir Herbert Dering reported: 'About twenty richly-clad prelates stood on the steps leading to the altar screen of old oak and formed a most picturesque group. The choir in the gallery, all in Roumanian national costume, at once commenced the service which was fully choral and, as is customary in the Orthodox Church, unaccompanied and very beautiful. His Majesty wore Field Marshal's uniform and carried the baton as well. The Queen was a striking figure in cloth of gold with a Roumanian headdress of the same material.' Dering went on to refer to the 'admirable impression' which the Duke of York had made and to quote an officer who had been attached to him, General Mircescu, as expressing the wish that the attachment could be permanent.[18]

On his return the Duke of York, whose style as a letter writer was decidedly more succinct than that of Sir Herbert Dering, wrote to Mountbatten of his visit: 'I had quite a good time there, and all the festivities went off all right. I was only there five days and took four days to get there and four days to get back. Too long a journey to my mind and one does get so fed up with a train.'[19]

Letters between Lord Louis Mountbatten and the Duke of York were at this period fairly frequent. Mountbatten had become engaged in February 1922 to Edwina Ashley while she was staying in India with the Viceroy, Lord Reading. The Prince of Wales, who was to be best man, was also in India, and the Duke of York undertook to organise details of the wedding, which was to be held in London. 'It is a great responsibility,' he wrote to Mountbatten on 18 May 1922, 'to arrange somebody's wedding, especially when both bridegroom and best man are at the other end of the world.'[20]

For the most part the Prince of Wales conducted himself admirably on his tours of the empire, but there were occasional lapses. One such occurred in New Zealand, when he failed to turn up at a returned soldiers' function. Offence was also caused when he failed to get out of his bed on the royal train to acknowledge a crowd's greeting in Australia.[21]

In consequence, perhaps, the Prince of Wales's visit to India clearly caused his younger brother some anxiety. On one occasion he wrote to Mountbatten: 'I am so glad to hear David is in good form now. I did hear to the contrary the other day, but no doubt that was only a passing phase.' In India the Prince of Wales's task was certainly more difficult than it had been in Australia or New Zealand, because of the political demonstrations which confronted him. To Edwina Ashley the Duke of York wrote: 'I am very thankful that David is out of India at last, as from what one hears at this end . . . things did not seem to be too easy or comfortable.'[22]

CHAPTER FIVE

Marriage and East Africa
1922–1925

During 1922 the Duke of York was engaged in wooing Lady Elizabeth Bowes-Lyon. Perhaps only the somewhat old-fashioned word 'wooing' can properly describe what occurred. In the words of Lady Airlie, a close confidante of Queen Mary, the Duke of York was 'deeply in love but so humble'.[1] As he himself put it in a letter to Mountbatten, 'it took some time and no mistake.'[2]

That the King's son should have to persist for so long before he could persuade a young girl to be his bride may seem surprising. To a small extent the conventions of the time may have been responsible. P. G. Wodehouse understood these well when he portrayed his heroes, even those who had a boxing blue behind them and the prospect of a dukedom ahead, as trembling with fright when they proposed marriage to nice, uncomplicated girls. But there were also more cogent reasons for the Duke of York's difficulties.

The Bowes-Lyon family were Scottish aristocrats. Lady Elizabeth's father was the Earl of Strathmore. Her mother, Nina Cavendish-Bentinck, was descended from the Dukes of Portland. Of them Horace Walpole had written: 'No wise King of England would think it for his credit that he considered himself, or was considered by others, as personally at variance with a Duke of Portland.' Members of the family were not therefore dazzled by the presence of royalty. They were also sharply aware of what being a member of the royal family entailed.

The Duke of York's parents were indeed keener than the parents of the bride that the marriage should take place. Queen Mary even invited Lady Strathmore to come to see her in order to enlist her help. At the meeting Lady Strathmore tactfully suggested that the question of marriage was one which the young people should decide for themselves. In telling of this conversation to an old friend, the Earl of Strathmore made a prescient comment. He had, he said, grave doubts about the Prince of Wales. He described him as 'nervy' and said he might never come to the throne, adding that, even if he did, it might not last. 'Then,' he is reported to have said, 'where should we be?'[3]

In time Lady Elizabeth Bowes-Lyon's feelings for the Duke of York overcame her doubts and her family's, and she accepted his proposal of marriage. With characteristic brevity and an awareness perhaps of the insecurity of the open telegraph service, he conveyed the news of his engagement to his parents on 13 January 1923 in a telegram which read: 'All right Bertie.'

Rather more sonorously King George V informed the Privy Council: 'I do hereby declare my Consent to a Contract of Matrimony between My Most Dearly Beloved Son His Royal Highness Prince Albert Frederick Arthur George, Duke of York, K.G., G.C.V.O., and Lady Elizabeth Angela Marguerite Bowes-Lyon, youngest daughter of the Right Honourable Claude George, Earl of Strathmore and Kinghorne, which Consent I have caused to be signified under the Great Seal and to be entered on the Books of the Privy Council.'[4]

The marriage was solemnized in Westminster Abbey on 26 April 1923. Against the advice of the Dean, the Chapter of the Abbey had turned down the BBC's request to broadcast the service,[5] but this did not diminish popular enthusiasm for the event. By her looks alone Lady Elizabeth had easily been able to capture public affection, and there was understandably much interest in what she wore. This was reported to be 'a medieval-style chiffon moiré wedding dress embroidered with silver thread and pearls and incorporating sleeves of Nottingham lace.'[6] The Duke of York wore RAF full-dress uniform. It was the first time since 1383 that a prince of the royal blood had been married in Westminster Abbey.[7] Among the guests at the wedding were thirty boys from factories, selected through the Industrial Welfare Society.[8]

For the first part of their honeymoon the Duke and Duchess of York chose Polesden Lacey, a house near Dorking, which they had been offered by its owner, Mrs Ronald Greville. For Mrs Greville, an ambitious hostess who had successfully fought her way through to the upper reaches of society, this was perhaps her greatest triumph. The illegitimate daughter of a Scottish brewer named William McEwan, she had married the grandson of the Duke of Montrose. While retaining close control of the conduct of the brewery, she found time to entertain with a skill and a splendour which made her highly regarded as a hostess. Harold Macmillan wrote of her: 'Perhaps Mrs Ronnie Greville exercised more political power in the Conservative Party than Lady Astor achieved by her membership of the House of Commons.'[9] If this judgment was correct it was in some respects unfortunate. Among those who cultivated Mrs Greville's company was Joachim von Ribbentrop when he was German Ambassador in London, and she was well received at a

Nuremburg rally. In spite of this she was able, perhaps by the sheer force of her personality, to retain the friendship of the Duke and Duchess of York. They were to dine with her shortly before the abdication in 1936, and in her will she left the Queen Mother, as she had then become, £1½ million.[10]

The second part of the honeymoon was spent at Glamis. Here the bride had the misfortune to contract whooping-cough.

King George V and Queen Mary welcomed the new Duchess of York with a warmth they were not always able to show to their sons. It was evidence of the unusual place she had in the King's affections that when on one occasion she appeared two minutes late for a meal, he had the gallantry to say the meal had been started two minutes early. She herself stated that, unlike his own children, she was never afraid of the King.[11] When George V died she described him as 'angelic'.[12]

The first home of the Duke and Duchess of York was White Lodge in Richmond Park, where Queen Mary had spent some of her childhood and where her eldest son had been born. In a letter of unusual length, after congratulating the Duke on his choice of a wife and expressing the hope that his new home would be as happy as the one he was leaving, the King, his father, wrote: 'You have always been so sensible and easy to work with and you have always been ready to listen to any advice and to agree with my opinions about people and things, that I feel that we have always got on very well together.'[13] In parenthesis he added: 'so different to dear David.' With these last words he expressed perhaps as clearly as he was able the blend of affection and irreconcilability which formed his feelings towards his eldest son. The Duke of York for his part, with typical thoughtfulness, expressed the hope that his parents would not miss him too much.[14]

White Lodge was a house of splendid appearance, which had been built in the 1720s for George II and had been known at one time as 'Stone Lodge'. Oaks and chestnuts proliferated in the section of the park which it adjoined. But in 1923 it was not a pleasant house to live in. It was still lit by gas, the water supply was inadequate, and there were not enough bathrooms. In the necessary tasks of renovation and redecoration, the leading parts were played by Queen Mary and the Government Department responsible for royal residences, which was then known, rather uninspiringly, as the Office of Works. 'My mother,' the Duke of York explained in a letter, 'wants everything arranged at once . . . HM Office of Works is of course the exact opposite . . . We want a happy medium.'[15]

In spite of all that was done the house remained extremely difficult to heat, and eventually the Duke and Duchess decided to give it up and to find a home in the centre of London. For a time they were lent

Chesterfield House by Princess Mary. Some four years later they were able to find a London residence of their own at 145 Piccadilly.

The Duke of York's only overseas engagement in 1923 was once again in the Balkans. As godfather he had to attend the christening of King Alexander of Yugoslavia's young son Peter. On this visit he was accompanied by the Duchess. The christening was followed the next day by the marriage of Prince Paul and Princess Olga of Greece. Some years later the Duke of York's ties with the Yugoslav royal family were to be strengthened further by the marriage of his brother, the Duke of Kent, to Princess Olga's sister, Princess Marina.

At home the General Election of 1923 brought into power the first Labour Government in the nation's history. The Duke of York had the opportunity to observe that his father found the outcome fairly easily navigable. In 1924 the Duke and Duchess of York paid a visit to Northern Ireland involving numerous public functions. Shortly before this the Duke had welcomed to London a royal figure whom he was to encounter again before and during World War II. This was Ras Tafari, later to become the Emperor Haile Selassie of Ethiopia.

In the winter of 1924–25 the Duke and Duchess of York made their first lengthy visit overseas, to East Africa. Ostensibly the purpose of their visit was simply to have a holiday, but there was a political background which suggested that the presence of a member of the royal family might be desirable. Of this the general public in Britain knew remarkably little.

In December 1922 a letter had been sent to all Labour Members of Parliament in Britain from a body representing the Indian population in East Africa. It pointed out that elections were due to take place in Kenya in April 1923 and made four demands on behalf of Kenyan Indians. These were:

(a) The right to vote as British subjects equal to other British subjects.
(b) The right to live our own lives in our own way wherever we like, providing we are not usurping the rights of anyone else.
(c) The right to purchase land in the Highlands for purely agricultural and pastoral work.
(d) The throwing open of the Civil Service for the promotion of Asians to higher posts in the country and for their appointment to such posts in India.

On 15 January the next year the Governor of Kenya, Sir Robert Coryndon, sent a telegram to the Secretary of State for the Colonies in which he reported that rumours had reached him of British plans to introduce a new franchise bill which would apply to Kenya and would give 'large concessions to Indians'. These rumours, he stated, were causing concern among local white settlers. 'Public feeling,' he reported, 'is at present being kept in hand, but it is very strong and stiffened by such press headlines as "Be prepared", "No compromise on Indian question", and "Asiatic claims to be resisted at all costs".'[16]

The Secretary of State for the Colonies was the liberal-minded Duke of Devonshire. Of him Harold Macmillan was to write: 'During his tenure of the Colonial Office in 1923 he left his mark on British colonial policy by the famous declaration of "paramountcy" in East Africa. This formally declared that on any question which might arise where the interests of the settlers and the native inhabitants were in conflict those of the latter must be regarded as "paramount".'[17] Between the Duke and the Kenyan Governor, who came from South Africa, there was little sympathy.

On 1 February Coryndon reported that '36 leaders of all shades of European opinion including three of the leading missionaries' had held a secret conference for three days. They decided they could not accept any proposals for extending the franchise and considered it 'quite useless to submit them to public opinion'. On the same day he forwarded to London a report from a Ugandan newspaper of a petition which began: 'We, the educated Natives of this country, view with alarm the fact that an Indian deputation is going to London to lay their claims before the responsible authorities.'[18]

Two days later Coryndon went even further. The white settlers, he reported, were preparing extreme measures in order to maintain their position. They would begin by refusing to pay taxes and establishing 'the most stringent commercial and personal boycott against Indians'. Further actions might include seizure of the Treasury, armoury and the railway, telegraph and customs offices 'with the same general object of paralyzing the Government'. They were even thinking of the wholesale expulsion of Indians from Nairobi to Mombasa Island.

The Duke of Devonshire remained sceptical, and in a further telegram Coryndon laid out what he believed to be the settlers' philosophy. 'The Colony,' he reported, 'is absolutely solid that in this part of Africa, with five and a half million natives, the ultimate responsibilities of government must remain in European hands and must not be diluted by being shared with an eastern race, alien in spirit and recognized as being lacking in the genius of government of backward subject races.'

The Duke replied that he did not propose at that stage to answer specific points Coryndon had made beyond observing that 'it is His Majesty's Government which is charged with imperial interests whether in Africa or elsewhere; that the interests of natives in Africa are the peculiar responsibility of the Secretary of State for the Colonies, and that nothing that I can think of is more likely to damage the imperial cause in Africa than the example of direct action in a British African colony by Europeans.'[19]

This served to calm down the tone of the correspondence, but the white settlers continued to prepare for action, if it should be needed, with the setting up of 'vigilance' bodies and plans for a descent by motor-car on Nairobi in order to overthrow the Government.

Meanwhile the Colonial Office in London tried to find a compromise, the Duke of Devonshire insisting that the form it took must be acceptable to the Government of India. By the late autumn agreement was reached, and on 16 October 1923 the Kenya Executive Council approved a draft bill. This provided for the election of ten European members, which was the same number as before, as well as five members to 'represent the interests of the Indian community' and one for the Arab community. The Secretary of State for the Colonies remained responsible, in so far as he could be, for the interests of the indigenous population. In this way violence was avoided, and it was to a land of restored calm, with little real change in the make-up of its government, that the Duke and Duchess of York sailed from Marseilles on 5 December 1924. They were accompanied by a new Comptroller, Captain Basil Brooke, RN, for Louis Greig had left the Duke's service on the most amicable terms early in 1924. The other members of the party were a new Equerry, Colin Buist, who was also a naval officer and who had been a contemporary of the Duke's at Osborne and Dartmouth; a Lady-in-Waiting, Lady Annaly; a maid and a valet.[14]

Sir Robert Coryndon clearly wanted to make the visit of the Duke and Duchess of York to Kenya something of a triumphal progress. As such it could be interpreted as a seal of royal approval on the measures which had been taken for the future government of the colony. On 4 September 1924 he submitted a draft programme. This included an extensive tour of the colony, a dinner at Government House, visits to the Nairobi Club and the Muthanga Country Club and a formal opening of the Nairobi City Park. The royal couple would, it was suggested, also be the guests of a number of the leading settlers, including Lord Delamere and Lord Francis Scott.

As a consequence of the 1923 General Election, the Duke of Devonshire was no longer in office, and the Secretary of State for the Colonies was now J. H. Thomas, an ex-railwayman and a forthright, pragmatic politician with whom George V quickly established an excellent rapport. Thomas informed Coryndon that his programme was not acceptable.

'Their Royal Highnesses' visit to Kenya,' he wrote, 'is in the nature of a holiday and for shooting, and it is not the intention to make a comprehensive tour of the Colony as proposed in your despatch . . . Their Royal Highnesses do not wish to suggest any visit to private residents in the Colony as giving undue formality to their tour. They are quite willing to give inhabitants of the Colony opportunities of meeting them, but it is considered that this should be arranged quite informally.'[20]

Coryndon conceded defeat and responded with a programme of animal slaughter, the richness of which could be matched by few other countries. In proposing a site for a hunting camp he wrote: 'Elephant, buffalo, lion and rhino are found in the vicinity, and His Royal Highness will no doubt indicate his wishes in this direction . . . The bag may reasonably include most of the following: giraffe, Grevy's and common zebra, waterbuck, palla, oryx, eland, Grant's and Thomson's gazelle, other small buck, and cheetah and hyaena. Leopards are improbable.' He went on to offer suggestions for presents to be given to representatives of seven different African tribes, stating: 'Presents are confined to Arabs and Natives as being natives of the country. Europeans and Indians are not included.' He added: 'Reporters will be excluded if it is desired, and information will be supplied to the press.'

The P & O liner bringing the Duke and Duchess reached Mombasa after a brief stop at Aden. In Nairobi the Duke had a number of talks with the Governor and quickly formed a favourable impression of him. 'Sir Robert Coryndon,' he wrote to his father, 'seems to be a very nice man and very alive to his responsibilities out here.'[21] The Duke enjoyed the shooting, but the method used to give information to the press did not work as well as the Governor had hoped. One report, which received wide circulation in Britain, stated quite incorrectly that the Duke had been charged by a rhinoceros, the implication being that his life had been in serious danger.

This report disturbed the King, and in turn the King's alarm disturbed the Governor. 'I am deeply concerned,' Coryndon telegraphed to London on 5 January 1925, 'that the press cables should have caused annoyance to His Majesty.' He went on to explain that he was empowered to intercept or detain messages only in the event of a public emergency or for public safety. He added: 'I may say that the Government has already delayed certain non-European telegrams to places outside England so that possible undesirable deductions would be nullified.'[22]

After he had been in Kenya a few weeks the Duke of York wrote to his mother: 'We are both so impressed with this wonderful country and it has certainly come up to and passed our expectations.' He expressed confidence in its future, and in his opinions on how that future should be arranged the influence of Coryndon is apparent. Kenya, he wrote, needed 'the best people we can produce from home'. He added: 'I don't mean the settlers, who are a very nice lot on the whole . . . but the official side of the life of Kenya. I have had several talks with the Governor, Sir Robert Coryndon, and he is sorry to have to say that things are not quite as they should be owing to lack of first hand and personal knowledge of the officials at home.' In this respect Coryndon achieved what he wanted from the visit. The Duke for his part was enquiring and learning.

An attempt by the settlers to enlist the Duke on their side did not however succeed. To his surprise he was informed by Coryndon that the colony wanted to present him with a farm. He reported the offer to his father, who replied that he agreed with the Colonial Office's opinion that the offer must not be accepted because of the precedent it would create. The King went on: 'What would you do if the farm didn't pay? The only way would be to buy a farm yourself (and you have no ready money) like David did in Canada and I thought that was a mistake.'[23]

The holiday away from the capital, in Rongai, which the Duke and Duchess were enjoying at that time, was cut short by the sudden and totally unexpected death on 10 February of Sir Robert Coryndon after an emergency operation. The King, who from a distance was watching his son's activities closely, sent him a telegram to express his pleasure that he had made the 250-mile journey from Rongai to Nairobi to attend the late Governor's funeral.

The remainder of the Duke and Duchess's African holiday was spent in Uganda and the Sudan. In Uganda they met the Kabaka of Buganda, who, the British Government had decided, should be made KCMG, and the Duke invested him with the order. In Sudan they were shown the site of the battle of Omdurman. They finally reached England, again by P & O liner, on 25 April 1925.

CHAPTER SIX

Empire Commitments
1925–1927

During the two years which followed his return from East Africa the Duke of York's official duties were largely directed towards the consolidation of empire. The first of these was performed only two weeks after his arrival in London.

On 23 April 1924 King George V had opened the most ambitious exhibition devoted to the theme of the empire which Britain was ever to stage. It was held in Wembley, and over an area of 220 acres was spread what the King, in his opening speech, described as 'a vivid model of the architecture, art and industry of all the nations which come under the British flag'. A hundred thousand spectators watched the opening ceremony, and for the first time ever a speech by the King was broadcast on what was then known as 'the wireless'. It was unfortunate that the style of many of the exhibits was such that for years afterwards the term 'Wembley Exhibition' became almost synonymous among designers and architects with bad taste.

The exhibition had been formally closed by the Prince of Wales on 1 November 1924, but in response to popular demand the Government decided to reopen it, with many new exhibits, the next year. The reopening ceremony on 10 May 1925 was the Duke of York's first official duty on his return from East Africa. He also became the new Exhibition President. His opening speech was one to which he looked forward with particular dread, and there were indeed long pauses, painful moments of paralysed articulation, during which he was unable to utter a sound.

The exact nature of the relationship between the self-governing dominions and Great Britain was a subject which had long been exercising the minds of politicians and civil servants, and in 1926 Lord Balfour, as Chairman of an Inter-Imperial Relations Committee, finally arrived at a definition which met with general approval. The Dominions, he stated, 'are autonomous communities within the British Empire, equal in status, in no way subordinate one to another in any aspect of their domestic or external affairs, though united by a common allegiance to the Crown, and freely associated as members of the British Commonwealth of Nations.' Four years later it was to be agreed by the various governments concerned that Balfour's formula should be given statutory effect. The outcome was the Statute of Westminster of 1931.[1]

This formal recognition of the supreme importance of the Crown in providing the principal link between the nations of the Empire implied clear obligations on the part of the king, and therefore of members of his family. When Balfour's definition was formulated plans were already being made for a visit by the Duke and Duchess of York early in the coming year, 1927, to two of the dominions, New Zealand and Australia.

On 21 April 1926 the Duchess of York gave birth to her first child, a girl who was given the names Elizabeth Alexandra Mary. The birth was caesarean and took place at 17 Bruton Street, the London home of the Earl and Countess of Strathmore, for the Duke and Duchess had not yet found a house they wanted. In accordance with the established practice designed to ensure the legitimacy of kings and queens by preventing, for example, child-swapping in the event of a still-birth, the Home Secretary, Sir William Joynson-Hicks, was present in the house. On the strength of a certificate signed by Sir Henry Simon, the doctor in charge, Joynson-Hicks wrote to inform Lord Balfour, the Lord President of the Council, that 'Her Royal Highness the Duchess of York was delivered of a strong healthy female child at 2.40 am this morning'. Balfour, being in Cannes at the time, was unable to receive the notification in person.[2]

A fortnight after the birth of the future queen Britain faced one of her gravest industrial crises of the twentieth century, a general strike. Royal intervention in an event of this nature was clearly undesirable; instead the Duke of York sensibly learnt what he could of day-by-day developments by listening to debates in the House of Commons.

Though the strike was widespread and potentially catastrophic, it did not last long. Once it was over life, for the more favoured sections of society at least, reverted to normal almost overnight. Among the familiar events staged in its aftermath were the Wimbledon tennis championships, which in 1926 were given exceptional royal patronage. The King and Queen attended the opening ceremony on 21 June, and in partnership with Wing-Commander Louis Greig the Duke of York played in the doubles championship. In the first round they were drawn against a pair named A. W. Gore and H. Roper Barrett.

Largely because lawn tennis was a British invention there were then more players of good quality in Britain than in almost any other country. Gore and Roper Barrett were in the upper reaches of these, certainly as a doubles pair. They beat the Duke of York and Greig 6–1, 6–3, 6–2. For the Duke this was not altogether discreditable.

The championships were still predominantly contests between genuine amateurs. Among the first-round winners in the singles, for instance, were a Scottish clergyman and an English peer of the realm.[3] There were no great British tennis players at the time, however, and in the absence of the American William T. Tilden the men's events were dominated by the French. Jean Borotra won the singles and Jacques Brugnon and Henri Cochet the doubles.

The principal official reason for the Duke of York to visit Australia was an invitation for him to open the new Parliament House in Canberra. This and other events would clearly call for a great deal of speech-making, and the Australian Prime Minister, Stanley Bruce, who issued the invitation and who had heard the Duke speak, had understandable doubts about his capacity to meet the demands which would be made on him.[4]

Some three months before he was due to sail the Duke made the acquaintance of an Australian speech therapist living in London named Lionel Logue, and turned to him for help. King George VI's official biographer, Sir John Wheeler-Bennett, himself suffered from a speech impediment, and in his description of how Logue treated the Duke a new quality enters his writing. He quotes too Logue's own description of how there came into his consulting room 'a slim, quiet man, with tired eyes and all the outward symptoms of the man upon whom habitual speech defect had begun to set the sign.' The Duke visited Logue nearly every day for ten weeks, and although he was never to be wholly free from difficulty when speaking in public, he gained from Logue's treatment a measure of control over his stammer, and therefore confidence such as he had never known before.[5]

On their voyage to the Pacific the Duke and Duchess of York sailed on 6 January, 1927, in the battle-cruiser HMS *Renown*. In her wake at home she left the makings of a political storm.

This broke in the House of Commons on 17 February, when there was a debate in Committee on a supplementary estimate of £7000 to meet costs incurred on the journey of the Duke and Duchess. One Labour MP, the future Lord Ammon, said that 'the Labour Party were not criticizing Their Royal Highnesses' but added that some people thought the expenditure involved was on 'what seemed to be a pleasure'. The MP for Mile End went further and said the royal couple were 'practically wrapped in cotton wool'. When David Kirkwood, the uncompromising Member for Dumbarton, said that 'it would not matter one iota to the welfare of the country if they never returned', he was duly rebuked by the Deputy Chairman, Captain Fitzroy. From the Conservative side it was pointed out that the royal couple were making a considerable sacrifice by having to leave their infant daughter behind.

The King was enraged by this debate. Stanley Baldwin, as Prime Minister, made his normal report on the proceedings, and on this Lord Stamfordham wrote in reply: 'You take a less serious and, I suppose, "House of Commons" view than does the King ... Though Parliament may discount these utterances as the irresponsible babble of the extremists of the Labour Party for the consumption of their constituents, His Majesty takes a grave view of these flippant, discourteous, if not insulting allusions to his Family.'

Stamfordham went on: 'The King has decided in future to refuse permission for any Member of the Royal Family to pay such official visits, unless the expenses incurred are defrayed by the respective Dominions: and His Majesty desires that this decision may be duly recorded.'[6]

On her west route *Renown* called first in the Canary Islands, then at Jamaica. After a stop-off in Panama she then sailed into the Pacific, where her first call was in the Marquesas. Fiji came next, and then on 22 February the Duke and Duchess arrived in Auckland. The voyage had lasted nearly seven weeks.

At the Domain in Auckland the number of people who turned out to see the Duke and Duchess was estimated at 80,000, probably the largest until then to have assembled for any event in New Zealand's history. In the course of the tour there were official welcomes in forty towns, and formal greetings were brought from a variety of peoples, both from within New Zealand and from other dependencies.

A Samoan delegation stated: 'While our country is small and far removed from the heart of the Empire to which it has been joined for only thirteen years, we wish to assure His Majesty that our hearts are true and sincere in our devotion to our King and flag.' An address from the City of Auckland announced: 'We have never sought to found in these fair islands a new race; rather is it our proud claim that we are a new England, a southern Britain.'

On arrival in the South Island the Duchess suffered an attack of tonsillitis, and after that the Duke had to carry out on his own the task of laying wreaths, visiting hospitals, reviewing parades and attending banquets. One event in the South Island took place on St Patrick's Day, when an address was received stating that 'men and women of Irish birth and descent are deeply sensible of the freedom and happiness they enjoy as subjects of His Majesty'.

The Duke made a particularly good impression at a meeting of the Returned Soldiers Association, thereby atoning for his brother's lapse seven years earlier. He left to the singing, tuneful or otherwise, of 'Madam-a-zell from Armen-teers'[7] and said he would always remember the evening as one of the happiest of his life.

The Governor-General, Sir Charles Fergusson, in a report to Leopold Amery, the Secretary of State for the Dominions, described the benefit derived from the visit as 'unmistakable' and the value of the presence of the Duke and Duchess as 'immeasurable'.[8] A more colourful tribute came from the Labour Mayor of Christchurch, who sent a message to 'brother Laborites' in Australia. In this he stated: 'My association with the Duke convinces me that he has a very impressive personality that grows upon one all the time. Undoubtedly he is immensely interested in social and economic conditions, and desires to see exactly how the workers of the Dominions are housed, and also how they are looked after during their hours of employment . . . A particularly noticeable feature of the Duke's character is that it makes a special appeal to men, and to working-men perhaps more than others.'[9]

The visit to Australia began in Sydney. This gave rise to a controversy over who would greet the royal couple first, the representatives of the Federal Government or those of the State of New South Wales. In the end a pontoon was built out from the shore, which was declared to be Federal territory. Here the Federal representatives lined up for presentations before handing the Duke and Duchess over to those of the State, waiting on the shore.[10] At the State reception in Sydney women were not included in the official groups for presentation. This precedent having been established, it was followed in other states.[11]

Popular enthusiasm was no less in Australia than it had been in New Zealand. In Sydney an Australian army general was seen climbing to the top of a lamp-post solely in order to catch a glimpse of the royal couple.[12] The Duke also endeared himself to the crowds in Newcastle when he insisted on leaving the hood of his car open in pouring rain to enable the crowds to see him and the Duchess, and in Queensland when, after watching a display of stock-riding, he rode a stock-horse himself and took part in drafting bullocks.[13]

One of the main events was the Anzac Day parade and service in Melbourne on 25 April. Another was the opening ceremony for the new Parliament House in Canberra. Here the Duke shared the limelight with Dame Nellie Melba, who at the age of sixty-six raised her still beautiful voice to sing 'God Save the King'.[14]

On the journey home there were calls at Mauritius, Malta and Gibraltar. Lord Louis Mountbatten was in Malta at the time, and he seems to have relieved the royal couple of some of the burden they might otherwise have borne. After returning to London the Duke wrote to Mountbatten: 'I haven't had a moment in which to thank you for all you did to make our stay in Malta so easy and enjoyable. It would have been a fierce affair had you not been there. I simply loved the polo and the ponies were marvellous.'

In the same letter the Duke wrote: 'Everything seems so strange now that we are at home. I can't settle down to anything, I find. It comes from pure tiredness, I suppose.'[15] He was only thirty-one when he wrote this, but evidence of strain was already apparent.

CHAPTER SEVEN

Return to Home Duties
1927–1935

The Duke of York's letter to Mountbatten thanking him for what he did in Malta was written from 145 Piccadilly. This house, newly moved into, was to be the London home of the Duke and Duchess for nearly ten years. The house, which had once belonged to the Rothschild family, no longer exists. On its site has been built part of the Intercontinental Hotel.

The Duke made a practice of inviting to 145 Piccadilly people whom he met in the course of his duties: leading figures in Commonwealth countries, those attending international conferences, ambassadors and others. He had an office in his home, where he worked daily with his staff until noon. He would then regularly walk with the Duchess in Green Park or along Piccadilly or Bond Street.[1]

A number of people who observed the Duke and Duchess of York commented on how devoted to each other they evidently were. In December 1927 Duff Cooper, writing to his own wife Diana about a visit to a theatre, which the Duke and Duchess had also attended, was emphatic about this. 'They reminded me of us,' he wrote, 'sitting together in the box having private jokes.'[2]

Their marriage was indeed extraordinarily successful, as harmonious as that of the Duke's own parents. To the Duchess's charm there were many tributes. Queen Marie of Roumania described her as 'one of the dearest, sweetest, most gentle . . . and most agreeable women I have ever met.'[3] Her husband, King Ferdinand, decided that her eyes reminded him of the rock-plant saxifrage and thereafter knew her as 'la duchesse saxifrage'.[4]

From Australia and New Zealand there was evidence of the impression the Duchess had made in the collection of three tons of toys for an infant daughter whom none of the donors had ever seen. In Australia and New Zealand too it become apparent to many observers how important the help and encouragement he received from his wife was to the Duke. The support his wife clearly gave him has sometimes brought the accusation that, both before and after he came to the throne, King George VI was over-dependent on her and even dominated by her. This is certainly a misconception. As one who worked closely with them both put it: 'She was a marvellous helpmeet to him, but he was perfectly his own man. She provided him with just the sort of ambience that he liked.'[5]

The Duchess also took easily to the new duties which her position required of her. A few years after the Duchess's marriage a friend asked Lady Strathmore whether her daughter was not bored by laying foundation stones and similar tasks. Lady Strathmore replied that she genuinely enjoyed the work because of her interest in the people she met.[6]

Among the societies for which the Duke of York worked actively in 1928 were, in addition to the Industrial Welfare Society, Dr Barnardo's Homes, the National Playing Fields Association, the Fresh Air Fund and the Gordon Boys' Home.[7] New tasks were to be added to these in the following year, as a consequence of the grave illness of King George V. This occurred in November 1928 and was diagnosed as a severe general infection of the blood and toxaemia following pleural pneumonia.[8] So serious was the condition that six Councillors were appointed to act jointly in the King's place. They were Queen Mary, the Prince of Wales, the Duke of York, the Archbishop of Canterbury, the Lord Chancellor and the Prime Minister.

The King recovered slowly during the winter, but he had to delegate some tasks to his sons. One which fell to the Duke of York, as Lord High Commissioner to the General Assembly of the Church of Scotland, was to preside over an assembly in which the Church of Scotland and the United Free Church of Scotland, which had broken apart, were reunited.

Duties of this kind were clearly important and demanding, yet in retrospect it seems strange that, after the evident success of the tour of New Zealand and Australia, the services of the Duke and Duchess of York were so little used to promote British interests overseas. It may partly be explained by the diminishing interest of governments after the late 1920s in empire, and particularly imperial trade. But the main reason was probably the justifiable belief that it was the Prince of Wales whom people in countries overseas really wanted to see. This is certainly suggested by the Government's handling of an episode in Anglo-Argentinian relations.

On 12 April 1929 Sir Malcolm Robertson, the British Ambassador in Buenos Aires, wrote a despatch to the Foreign Office in which he called attention to the efforts being made by the United States to promote their trade interests in Argentina. 'There can be but little doubt,' he wrote, 'that the main efforts of Mr Hoover's administration, in the foreign sphere, will be directed towards this sub-continent with a view to the furtherance of American business generally . . . The offensive may be said to have begun seriously with Mr Hoover's visit and his subsequent taking over of the Presidency. A somewhat startling indication has been the purchase for an

Embassy of what is perhaps the biggest and finest house in all Buenos Aires.'

As a counter-measure the British were to stage an industrial exhibition in Buenos Aires the next year, and Robertson asked: 'Could you possibly prepare the ground for the Duke and Duchess of York to come out and open the Exhibition somewhere about the middle of October next year?' He went on to suggest that the Duke should also visit Brazil, Chile and Uruguay.

Robertson's request was considered in the Foreign Office by Roger Makins, a future Ambassador to the USA, who concluded: 'Sir M. Robertson's proposal merits favourable consideration.' This did not please Makins's superior, Robert Craigie, who was later to become Ambassador to Japan. Pointing out that the Prince of Wales had been in Argentina in 1925, Craigie commented: 'We must not turn Argentine heads by an excess of attention and the visit of a Royal Prince to South America should be regarded as something altogether exceptional and flattering – not as something which can be repeated every four or five years.' On the subject of possible visits to Brazil and other countries Craigie wrote: 'I do not think the time has yet come for another royal progress.'[9]

This seems to have effectively brought to an end any suggestion that the Duke and Duchess of York should visit Latin America. Yet only a year later the Prince of Wales revisited Argentina. He was accompanied by his youngest brother, Prince George. He opened a British exhibition; he visited Brazil, Chile and Bolivia; and on his return he addressed the Manchester Chamber of Commerce on British trading opportunities in Argentina and the extent to which British advertisers lagged behind their American opposite numbers.

The official overseas visits which the Duke of York did make in the late 1920s and early 1930s were mainly in response to invitations from foreign royalty. In 1929 he and the Duchess attended the wedding of Crown Prince Olav of Norway and Princess Martha of Sweden. They spent only four days in Oslo, but this enabled the Duke to see something of King Haakon, whom he was to know much better during World War II and for whom he developed both affection and admiration. With Crown Prince Umberto of Italy, whose wedding in January 1930 the Duke also attended, his wartime relations were to be rather less cordial.

The Duke also visited Paris when a colonial exhibition was being held. A member of the Embassy staff who attended him recalled how eager he was to telephone his older brother to tell him everything of importance that had happened.[10] The distinguished French soldier, Marshal Lyautey, seems to have met the Duke on the same occasion, and, according to Princess Bibesco, a gossip-writer of some skill, he commented: '*Il a plus d'étoffe que son frère.'* ('There's more to him than to his brother'.) He added: *'Et la duchesse est délicieuse.'*[11]

On 21 August 1930 the Duke and Duchess of York's second daughter was born. She was given the names Margaret Rose. Like her elder sister she was born in a home belonging to her grandparents, in her case Glamis Castle near Dundee. The Labour Home Secretary, J. R. Clynes, seems to have been misinformed of the probable date of the birth and arrived at Glamis on 5 August. The Earl of Strathmore was not enamoured of the prospect of having to entertain a socialist politician for what seemed likely to be a long time, and a hospitable friend, the Dowager Lady Airlie, came to his help. Under her roof the Home Secretary, in order to satisfy the requirements of royal births, had to spend more than two weeks.[12]

Late in 1930 it seemed possible that the Duke would again be assigned a role of importance in the affairs of the Commonwealth. Lord Willingdon, the future Viceroy of India, was about to retire as Governor-General of Canada, and the Duke of York was among those whom the Canadian Prime Minister, R. B. Bennett, considered as possible successors. However, J. H. Thomas, who was now Secretary of State for the Dominions, was firmly of the opinion that because of Canada's proximity to the United States she should not have a royal Governor-General. George V was obliged to accept his advice.

In the year following Princess Margaret's birth her parents were granted a new home by the King. This was Royal Lodge in Windsor Great Park, a former residence of George IV. Here the Duke interested himself closely in the planning of the gardens, showing a taste and talent which he shared with his maternal grandfather and which was to pass to his eldest grandson.

Increasingly in the early 1930s the Duke and Duchess of York were preoccupied with their family life. Other concerns naturally made their claims, among them the Industrial Welfare Society. At one point its financial difficulties were such that the Duke was advised to resign. This he refused to do, and in January 1933 he sent an eight-page letter written in his own hand informing the Society with evident delight of a gift of £30,000 from a man named Fred Young. Nothing, he wrote, had given him more pleasure than Young's express wish that 'a minimum sum of £600 be set aside for the benefit of Mr and Mrs Hyde'.[13]

There were, too, factories to be visited, hospitals, museums and halls of residence in university colleges to be opened. But to a public servant as experienced as the Duke now was these made no great demands other than the very act of public speaking, with which he still had difficulty. Moreover there were his two younger brothers with whom such duties could now be shared.

Extra duties were imposed on all the members of the royal family in

1935, when George V celebrated his silver jubilee, the twenty-fifth anniversary of his accession to the throne. The King and Queen made long processions through London and, later, other cities, and for a week they appeared every night on the flood-lit balcony of Buckingham Palace. The warmth of their reception wherever they went was beyond doubt and certainly surprised George V himself. In trying to analyse the reasons for this, Harold Nicolson offered as one explanation the King's practice, begun somewhat reluctantly in 1932, of making Christmas broadcasts to the nation.[14] This had been in response to the combined persuasions of the Prime Minister, Ramsay Macdonald, the Director-General of the BBC, John Reith, and his own Private Secretary, Clive Wigram.[15]

The Duke and Duchess of York represented the King at the jubilee celebrations in Edinburgh. Then in November the Duke visited Brussels, when he presented a gift from George V to the King of the Belgians. This was a silver model of the belfry in Mons. Some concern was felt about the Duke's presence because shortly before his arrival there had been anti-British demonstrations in Brussels. These, according to the British Minister, Esmond Ovey, had been a consequence of 'a fascist meeting of Italian waiters'.[16] The disturbances were not repeated when the Duke arrived.

In the last years of his father's reign the Duke of York's life can be seen as one of public usefulness, in which reliability and tact were called for and humour was welcome, but in which neither imagination nor originality was required. He was shown no confidential State papers and was not normally consulted on matters of great moment. This was a role with which he was content, for he was not ambitious and did not seek power.

His family gave him great happiness, and his social and sporting life was fairly full. Words used to describe the private life of the Duke and Duchess of York in this period by those who shared some of it include 'relaxed' and 'fun'. Among those whose acquaintance he and the Duchess made in the winter of 1932–33 were Mr and Mrs Ernest Simpson. The Simpsons do not seem to have created any deep impression. Indeed there was no reason why they should. Mrs Simpson informed her aunt, Mrs Bessie Merriman: 'We have been skating out on the water with the Duke and Duchess of York. Isn't it a scream.'[17]

To the general British public the Duke of York appeared an amiable man, who was sometimes seen in cinema newsreels in shorts and open-necked shirt as he joined a group of campers in singing, with all the ritual gestures, 'Underneath the spreading chestnut-tree'. Of the qualities which lay behind this facade the public knew little. Some people expressed concern because his older brother, the Prince of Wales, showed no signs of marrying, but as there was little difference between the ages of the two men, speculation was largely confined to the problems which might face the young Princess Elizabeth if she were ever to become Queen.

There were a few people who contemplated the future with rather more anxiety. One of them was King George V. He had learnt to respect his second son and thought him superior in general character, certainly in courage, to the other members of his family. To his Prime Minister, Stanley Baldwin, he confided his doubts about his eldest son in words which have frequently been quoted: 'After I am dead the boy will ruin himself within twelve months.'

CHAPTER EIGHT

The Reign of Edward VIII
1936

On 20 January 1936 King George V, too weak to do more than make a sign with his hand, appointed a new Council of State to act for him. It consisted of Queen Mary and his four sons. During the night that followed the King died. For the first time the nation had learnt of the impending end of a reign through the medium of broadcasting, millions hearing the statement that the King's life was 'drawing peacefully to its close'.

Not until more than fifty years later did it become public knowledge that the King's life was terminated by his principal medical adviser, Lord Dawson of Penn, who injected morphia and cocaine into the King's jugular vein. Lord Dawson did this, according to his own written account, when he reached the conclusion that 'the last stage might endure for many hours . . . little comporting with the dignity and serenity which he so richly merited.'

Lord Dawson was also influenced by his desire that the King's death should be announced by the BBC in time for the first press comment to be made by *The Times* rather than by 'the less appropriate evening journals'.[1] Even in the timing of their death, he was implying, constitutional monarchs may be expected to abide by the wishes of their principal advisers.

On 24 January King George's body was brought to Westminster Hall, where it lay in state for five days. On the last night the King's four sons kept watch in uniform, one at each of the four corners of the catafalque. The idea that they should do so was that of the new King. It was an impressive start to a new reign.

Although the Prince of Wales had enjoyed a popularity without precedent, when he came to the throne there was no widespread feeling that the new reign would bring new splendour. This may have been partly because of a growing awareness of the threat of war. In the preceding year

Italian armies had swept into Ethiopia, and Germany had reintroduced compulsory military service. In two months' time German armies would reoccupy the Rhineland, and four months after that civil war would break out in Spain. But there were people too who noticed that when he was publicly proclaimed King on the day following his father's death Mrs Wallis Simpson was standing beside him.

Some who were close to the new King also noticed disturbing signs. Lady Helen Hardinge observed that in private his grief at the death of his father was 'frantic and unreasonable'.[2] To anyone with an intimate knowledge of his relationship with his father this must have suggested that the grief had causes other than mere bereavement.

The first task of importance which the new King entrusted to the Duke of York was to investigate the management, and particularly the cost, of the Sandringham estate. The Duke enlisted the help of Lord Radnor, who was responsible for much of the administration of the Duchy of Cornwall, made a detailed study himself, and produced a report. The King considered this too moderate and believed that greater economies could be made. Later the King decided to introduce economies in the running of Balmoral. This time he did not consult the Duke, which as the Duke commented in a letter to his mother, made him 'rather sad'.[3] Other economies which the new King made included a 10 per cent cut in the wages of household servants.[4] At a time when he was seen to be showering gifts on Mrs Simpson this did not endear him to those who served him.

His more senior advisers also had grounds for complaint. The chief of these was Sir Alexander Hardinge, his Private Secretary. Hardinge came from a family with a remarkable tradition of public service. His father had been Permanent Under-Secretary in the Foreign Office and Ambassador in Paris. Both his grandfathers had been soldiers who had reached the rank of field-marshal.

Edward VIII did not take to Hardinge, and Hardinge, though he served him conscientiously, disliked the King's methods of conducting business. In the words of Hardinge's wife, the new King 'was full of ideas, with which he bombarded my husband day and night, calling him out of his bath and away from his dinner guests and even out of bed.' But while expecting his staff to be always available, the King worked only when he chose, and as time passed he showed less and less inclination to read State papers.[5] In his own memoirs the King confessed: 'I have never had much zest for paper work.'[6]

Government ministers too began before long to be puzzled by the King's attitude towards a number of his obligations. Early in his reign, for example, it was necessary to make plans for the King's coronation and also for the equivalent ceremony which was expected to take place in India and was known as a durbar. On 2 March 1936 the Marquess of Zetland, who was Secretary of State for India, wrote to the Viceroy, Lord Linlithgow, about a conversation he had had with the King on the subject of a durbar: 'I found that he was at present not much inclined to favour the suggestion as he still remembers his tour of India in 1921–2 with a certain amount of distaste . . . He was clearly anxious that, at the present time, no countenance should be given to any rumours of such a ceremony which might gain currency either here or in India.'

The delays in reaching a decision disturbed those Indian princes who were in the Viceroy's confidence, and on 30 May the Maharajah of Patiala wrote to him: 'The very idea that no decision will be taken for a considerable time, suggesting that His Majesty may, by political considerations, be prevented from coming out to India, is likely to cause consternation.'

By October the Viceroy's patience was lessening, and in a private letter to Hardinge he wrote: 'I have felt bound to urge an early decision owing to the great amount of parliamentary work that will have to be done in this country if the King is to take a Durbar here at the end of next year.' Hardinge spoke to the King on the 27th, and the next day he reported to Linlithgow that, although the King had at first seemed reluctant to come to a decision, he had 'finally agreed to consider a sentence in his speech from the Throne'.[7]

The planning of Edward VIII's coronation was entrusted to a Coronation Committee of the Privy Council. Of this the Duke of York was chairman. There were thirty-seven members in all, of whom any five could form an effective quorum. Soon after its formation the committee chose 12 May 1937 as Coronation Day.[8]

The King does not seem to have done anything to hinder the deliberations of the committee, but it was noted that he appeared to treat the Duke not so much as a committee chairman but as his personal stand-in, one who must himself learn exactly what a coronation involved for the principal figure. Among those who made this observation was the Archbishop of Canterbury, Dr Cosmo Gordon Lang.

Many of those who had official dealings with the King were aware that Mrs Simpson occupied much of his time and thoughts. The King had known Mrs Simpson for about five years before he came to the throne and for most of that time had seen her mainly in the company of her second husband, Ernest Simpson. Mrs Simpson was an American, but her husband, although born in New York and Harvard-educated, was a British subject. They were married in 1928 and had lived in London since then.

In August 1934 Mrs Simpson came without her husband to join the future King Edward VIII's holiday party in Biarritz, and, as he later told Sir Walter Monckton, one of his principal confidants, it was in that year that he decided to marry her.[9] This intention he kept secret for a long time from his family and his official advisers.

That the King did not seek official advice on his matrimonial intentions was understandable, for he could have had no doubt that the advice he would receive would not be the advice he wanted to hear. He spent more and more of his time in his private residence, Fort Belvedere, near Sunningdale. Here he was relatively isolated, and his companions tended to be sycophants or friends of Mrs Simpson. State duties were increasingly neglected, and Charles Murphy, the ghost-writer of the Duke of Windsor's memoirs, and his collaborator with whom he wrote *The Windsor Story*, later stated that one of the frequenters of Fort Belvedere, Mike Scanlon, whom the King allowed to take boxes, which contained secret papers, to Sir Alexander Hardinge, was in fact a United States intelligence officer.[10]

Members of the royal family did meet Mrs Simpson from time to time. In the spring of 1936 the King drove over to Royal Lodge in Windsor with Mrs Simpson to show the Duke and Duchess of York a new American station wagon which he had bought. Some years later the Duchess of Windsor, as Mrs Simpson had by then become, was to comment: 'I left with a distinct impression that while the Duke of York was sold on the American station wagon, the Duchess was not sold on David's other American interest.'[11] No doubt Mrs Simpson confided her impressions to the King, and this may have been among the reasons why the Duke found the King, as he put it, 'very difficult to see'. The new King knew he would get little help from the somewhat wooden Gloucester, and the only member of his family whom he saw at all frequently in the summer of 1936 was the youngest prince, now Duke of Kent, whose relative youth and inexperience, quite apart from his considerable charm, made him the royal companion with whom the King could be most at ease.

One event did bring the two elder brothers momentarily together. On 16 July they presented new colours to battalions of the Brigade of Guards. Afterwards they were riding towards Buckingham Palace when a man named George McMahon, who was armed with a loaded revolver, advanced towards them. McMahon was seized by a special constable, but his revolver flew across the road and struck one of the rear legs on the King's horse. Neither of the brothers exhibited any concern. They were both accomplished horsemen, and, like their father, both were habitually calm in the presence of physical danger.

For his summer holiday in 1936 the King chartered the yacht *Nahlin* for what became the notorious cruise in the Adriatic, when he was frequently seen in the company of Mrs Simpson and their movements were widely reported in newspapers and magazines of various countries. In the British press, by contrast, a conspiracy of silence prevailed. This was instituted by Lord Beaverbrook and Esmond Harmsworth. Their motives were clearly open to question, for both were driven, in part at least, by an intense personal dislike of the Prime Minister, Stanley Baldwin. Neither of them had forgiven, or was likely to forgive, Baldwin for publicly likening press barons to 'the harlot through the ages' because of their exercise of power without responsibility. Beaverbrook, in particular, was to play a wholly unscrupulous role in the months which followed. Yet somehow they persuaded their fellow newspaper proprietors to maintain silence on the subject of the King's association with Mrs Simpson.

A situation was thus created which might have recalled that in Bavaria in the late 1840s, when King Ludwig's Ministers felt obliged to point out to him that, although the Bavarian press remained silent, foreign newspapers were writing daily about the power which Lola Montez exercised over him, and that it had become a common talking-point almost everywhere in the kingdom.

Privately the King clearly felt he could no longer keep silent, and he began to take his family into his confidence. When he told the Duke of York of his firm intention to marry Mrs Simpson the Duke found it difficult to express his feelings immediately. Shortly afterwards he wrote to his brother to say that he longed for him to be happy and that he was convinced that whatever the King decided would be in the best interests of the country and empire.[12]

Queen Mary, on the other hand, implored him not to take the step he intended, both for his own sake and that of the country. She found him unable to understand any point of view except his own.

The Prime Minister, Stanley Baldwin, was suffering from strain and fatigue. He had indeed been near to a nervous breakdown in the summer and was looking forward to retirement after the coronation in May 1937. This did not prevent him from having a clear understanding of the issues involved and of how to handle them.

The relationship between the Crown and the Church of England being what it was, there was no possibility, in Baldwin's judgment, of the King marrying a woman with two living ex-husbands and remaining on the throne. Nor, Baldwin knew, would the proposed marriage be acceptable to the great bulk of the people in Britain and the Dominions. On his return from his summer holiday he read all the official papers on the subject of Mrs Simpson that were put in front of him. Then he told the Foreign Secretary, Anthony Eden, that he hoped he would not be troubled much in the near future with foreign affairs.

With part of his mind the King, too, was aware of the reasons why he could not marry Mrs Simpson and remain on the throne. Mrs Simpson, quite clearly, was not. Though she had a lively mind and a clear understanding of what she wanted, she seems to have been unable at times to distinguish between the role of a British constitutional monarch and that of an American President. Many years after the event she was to say to her husband: 'If you had brought in a first-class public relations man from New York there'd have been no abdication.'[13] She probably died with this belief.

The King was under the influence of Mrs Simpson to an extent which people who dealt with him found difficult to credit. Dr Alan C. Don, Chaplain to the Archbishop of Canterbury, who, as his diaries show, was extremely well informed, wrote at one point: 'I should suspect that H.M. is sexually abnormal which may account for the hold Mrs S. has over him.'[14] Later he was to describe a conversation with Sir Walter Monckton, in which Monckton described the Duke of Windsor, as he had then become, as being, in the presence of his wife, 'like a rabbit in the presence of a ferret'.[15]

The King's feelings towards Mrs Simpson also caused him on one celebrated occasion to give deep offence to loyal but outspoken subjects. This occurred in June 1937 in Aberdeen, where he had been invited by the Lord Provost to open some new hospital buildings. Almost at the last minute he delegated the task to his brother, the Duke of York, while he himself, without any attempt at concealment, met Mrs Simpson at Aberdeen railway station. The excuse offered was that the Court was still in mourning, a restriction which was transparently just as applicable to his brother as it was to him. The Duchess of Windsor was later to describe the King's conduct on that day as 'a thoughtful act towards me that was to drive another spike in the growing structure of public misunderstanding'.[16]

The silence of the British press was broken when the *Yorkshire Post* had a leading article based on a sermon preached by the Bishop of Bradford, Dr Alfred Blunt, in which he had said that the King would abundantly need God's grace. He had added: 'We hope that he is aware of this need. Some of us wish that he gave more positive signs of such awareness.' Once the unofficial veil of secrecy was raised, public debate was vociferous, and it soon became clear that Baldwin had a great weight of opinion behind him in his attitude of firmness yet sympathy towards the King.

The opposition elements were oddly assorted, and their motives were various. George Bernard Shaw, the Irishman to whom the British had accorded the status of a kind of national jester, delighted in the spectacle of the Church of England, as he saw it, encouraging – if not actually obliging – the King to live in adultery with Mrs Simpson. Other champions of the King were Lord Beaverbrook, Winston Churchill and Sir Oswald Mosley.

Beaverbrook's motive was clear. It was, as he stated unequivocally to Randolph Churchill, 'to bugger Baldwin'. He withdrew his support once he learnt that the King was prepared to abdicate. His own words to Churchill were: 'Our cock won't fight.'

Churchill, no doubt because of his later services to the nation, has been credited with supporting the King out of a romantic dedication to monarchy. This may to some extent have been true, but, like Beaverbrook, he too had scores to settle with Baldwin. There is some evidence that he was prepared to make political capital to the extent of offering to form an alternative government if the issue of Mrs Simpson divided the nation, and that the King was mistakenly encouraged by believing this.[17]

The motives of Mosley, the leader of the British Union of Fascists, may be thought to have been made clear in a Foreign Office paper dated 18 December 1936. This was written by Orme Sargent, a future Permanent Under-Secretary, and described a conversation he had had with a German diplomat named Dr Jäckh.

Jäckh told Sargent that he had seen a despatch sent to Berlin after the abdication, 'in which Herr von Ribbentrop had explained that the real reasons for the recent crisis were not those constitutional and moral considerations which had been publicly announced. On the contrary, Mr Baldwin's real motive was a purely political one, namely to defeat those Germanophile forces which had been working through Mrs Simpson and the late King with the object of reversing the present British policy and bringing about an Anglo-German entente ... Herr von Ribbentrop held this view strongly, more particularly as he had based the whole of his strategy on the role that Mrs Simpson was expected to play in Anglo-German affairs. Her disappearance had completely disconcerted him and he now views the future with considerable anxiety, since he feared – to quote Dr Jäckh's words – "that the new King would be content to follow the Foreign Office policy".'

The despatch went on: 'Dr Jäckh had also gathered ... that the Führer himself was very distressed at the turn that affairs had taken in this country, since he had looked upon the late King as a man after his own heart who understood the Führerprinzip and was ready to introduce it into this country.'[18]

As a direct consequence of the popularity he had enjoyed when Prince of Wales there was much public support for the King in the difficulty he was seen to be facing, but it was emotional in nature and had little political basis. Neither Clement Attlee, the leader of the Labour Party, nor Sir Archibald Sinclair, the Liberal leader, could envisage their parties as champions of the cause of Mrs Simpson and the King, and both were too responsible to use the issue simply in order to embarrass Baldwin and his Government.

Baldwin also ascertained that the leading political figures in the self-governing dominions were, as he had expected, opposed to a marriage with Mrs Simpson. Joseph Lyons, the Australian prime minister, said in the Australian parliament: 'The proposed marriage, if it led to Mrs Simpson becoming Queen, would evoke widespread condemnation ... The alternative proposal of something in the nature of a specially sanctioned morganatic marriage would run counter to the best popular conception of the Royal Family.'[19]

Mrs Simpson, mindful of the success of President Roosevelt's so-called 'fireside chats', suggested to the King that he should broadcast directly to the nation, and the King put the idea forward himself. No British Government, however, could countenance a constitutional monarch appealing to the people over its head on a political issue, and the King finally did not press the matter, and events moved rapidly towards the climax.

It was on 1 December 1936 that the Bishop of Bradford had preached his sermon on the King's need of God's grace. More than two weeks before that, on 13 November, Sir Alexander Hardinge had written his now famous letter of warning to the King. In this he advocated that Mrs Simpson, who had already begun divorce proceedings against her husband, should leave the country. She did so, leaving for Cannes shortly afterwards.

The Duke of York seems to have received his first serious warning of the likelihood of abdication from Hardinge. He was clearly appalled and unwilling to believe what he had heard,[20] but did not waver in his loyalty or his determination to support the King. He made repeated attempts to see him in the first days of December, but was continually put off. In his diary he wrote: 'As he is my eldest brother I had to be there to try and help him in his hour of need.' When he did succeed in seeing the King he wrote: 'I then had a long talk with D but I could see that nothing would alter his decision.' After speaking to the King he went to see Queen Mary. To her he expressed his feelings of near desperation in a highly emotional scene.[21]

Among the admirers of the Duke's conduct during the final weeks of crisis were Lord and Lady Louis Mountbatten, who, in the words of Mountbatten's biographer, Philip Ziegler, came to appreciate his 'integrity and radiant decency'.[22] To the general public, however, he doubtless seemed an inadequate figure to replace the man who remained the focus of so much attention. Even such a sophisticated observer as Dr Don wrote in his diary less than a week before the abdication: 'The Duke of York, if he ascended the throne, would be in a most awkward position and would have to face a period of much unpopularity as having "supplanted" the idol of the multitude.'[23] There were even suggestions that the succession might pass, not to the Duke of York, but the Duke of Kent. One reason advanced for this was that it might serve to spare a woman from having to bear the excessive burden of the crown.

In the last few days of his reign the King saw much of two men. One was Walter Monckton, who in 1932 had been appointed Attorney-General to the Prince of Wales and legal adviser to the Duchy of Cornwall, and who was now called upon in effect to replace Hardinge as the King's Private Secretary. The other was George Allen, a solicitor. No matter how much public attention might be concentrated on the political implications of abdication, there were private and financial affairs to be considered.

The political settlement was, in any event, now in the hands of Baldwin. Mrs Simpson wrote from Cannes that 'no one but Baldwin and the dominions want you to go',[24] but the King had abandoned the struggle, and he cooperated with Baldwin when the Prime Minister was preparing his final report on the abdication to Parliament. One phrase which the King suggested, and which Baldwin used, was that he and the Duke of York had 'always been on the best of terms as brothers'. At the King's request too Baldwin added: 'The King is confident that the Duke deserves and will receive the support of the whole Empire.'[25]

In his speech to Parliament Baldwin expressed with clarity and distinction his views on the monarchy. Commenting on his discussions with the King he said: 'I reminded him of what I had told him and his brother in years past. The British monarchy is an unique institution. The Crown in this country through the centuries has been deprived of many of its prerogatives, but today, while that is true, it stands for far more than it ever has done in its history.' He went on to say that while the feeling which the people had towards the Crown 'largely depends on the respect that has grown up in the last three generations for the monarchy, it might not take so long, in face of the kind of criticisms to which it was being exposed, to lose that power far more rapidly than it was built up, and once lost I doubt if anything could restore it.'

In what was in effect a farewell, all-male dinner in Fort Belvedere the Duke of York, the Duke of Kent and Baldwin were among the eight guests present. The King, with the prospect of relief from the cares of office, was in sparkling form. In admiration the Duke of York whispered to Monckton: 'And this is the man we're going to lose.' Baldwin reported to the cabinet the next day that 'the King appeared happy and gay, as if he were looking forward to his honeymoon.'

In his final broadcast to announce his abdication on 11 December, and indeed in all the final stages of departure, the King, free of political responsibility and with Mrs Simpson safe in Cannes, comported himself with striking dignity. Both Churchill and Monckton had a hand in the preparation of his broadcast speech. Of the choice he had made he said: 'The decision has been made less difficult for me by the sure knowledge that my brother, with his long training in the public affairs of this country and with his fine qualities, will be able to take my place forthwith . . . And he has one matchless blessing, enjoyed by many of you and not bestowed on me – a happy home with his wife and children.'

His brother's first official action after the King had announced his abdication was to create him Duke of Windsor. In his diary he described 11 December as 'that dreadful day'.

CHAPTER NINE

Accession and Coronation
1937

On 3 January 1937 Neville Chamberlain, who was shortly to succeed Baldwin as Prime Minister, wrote to his old friend Alfred Greenwood: 'Yes, we had a most anxious time over E's escapades, but in the end all turned out for the best. I soon made up my mind that we should never be free from anxiety while he was King though we might get over the immediate crisis. With the present King and Queen we can all feel safe.'[1] Earlier Sir John Reith, the Director-General of the BBC, had noted in his diary: 'We felt as if a cloud of depression of which we had been almost physically conscious had lifted. Poor Edward. But thank God he and his ways have passed and there is a new King and Queen.'[2]

In the first few days of his reign the new King saw much of the Archbishop of Canterbury. On the day following the King's accession the Queen wrote to the Archbishop: 'The curious thing is that we are not afraid. I feel that God has enabled us to face the situation calmly, and although I at least feel most inadequate, we have been sustained during these last terrible days by many, many good friends.'[3]

The King was able before long to set the ecclesiastical leaders an example of charity. Shortly after the abdication the Archbishop of Canterbury had preached a sermon in which he reproached the departed King for seeking happiness 'in a manner inconsistent with the principles of marriage'. This provoked Gerald Bullett's famous verses ('Oh, Cosmo Cantuar, how full of cant you are') and also, as Dr Don recorded, 'a perfect deluge of letters . . . the majority abusive and even vituperative'. But when William Temple, the Archbishop of York, went even further and spoke of 'the wrong way of falling in love with someone else's wife', a telephone call came to Lambeth Palace to say the King wanted to know 'whether nothing could be done to exhort the leaders of religion to reticence'.[4]

To Baldwin the King expressed his appreciation by letter on

31 December. 'I do want to tell you,' he wrote, 'how much I admired the dignified way in which you carried out a very diffiult and very delicate task in that most unfortunate affair, and to congratulate you on the way that all parties rallied to you in the House of Commons during those fateful days.'[5]

In his personal staff the King made one important, though temporary, change. Sir Alexander Hardinge had thought that the new King might wish to dispense with his services. In fact the King asked him to stay on, but immediately granted him three months' leave of absence in recognition of the strain which he had undergone. Lord Wigram was called back from retirement to stand in for him. For services rendered, chiefly to Edward VIII, the King took an early opportunity of knighting Walter Monckton.

These were all generous and thoughtful actions. The public at large did not of course know of all of them, but one early decision which the King made seemed to meet with general approval. This was to take as his title 'George VI'. That he did so was probably as much in recognition of the general desire for a return to stability as in order to honour the memory of his father.

Shortly before coming to the throne the Duke of York, as he then was, had told Mountbatten of his doubts and anxieties and said that he had had no training other than that of a naval officer. Mountbatten replied that his father had heard almost the same words from the future King George V when the Duke of Clarence had died. In fact of course both future kings were wrong: they had both had long training in the essential duties of royalty and had learnt much both from precept and example. It was this training, combined with his own innate qualities, which gave George VI such a sure touch in the early weeks of his reign.

Foreign affairs were soon to occupy much of the King's attention. This was a direct consequence of the coronation. Public interest might be primarily in the pageantry, but distinguished figures from most of the countries of the world came to Britain for the occasion, and with many of them the King was to become acquainted for the first time.

The planners of the ceremonies themselves could rely largely on the detailed arrangements which had already been made for Edward VIII's coronation. These could now be applied to that of the new king, and dates in particular could remain unaltered. For the benefit of spectators, it was decided that the coronation procession should be twice as long as on previous occasions, and a kind of preliminary procession in the form of a state drive was staged in February. This was to the East End of London and involved a call at the People's Palace in Mile End Road.

The principal anxiety of the planners was a strike, still in operation early in May which had taken the London buses off the road, but a settlement was reached before coronation day. For the King himself his greatest concern was probably the broadcast which he had to make to the nation. For this he was attended by both Sir John Reith and Lionel Logue, his speech therapist.

The speech, which was broadcast on the evening of 12 May, was both moving and effective. 'I cannot find words,' the King said, 'with which to thank you for your love and loyalty to the Queen and myself. I will only say this. If in the coming years I can show my gratitude in service to you, that is the way above all others that I should choose.' The King's other main speech was at a luncheon in Westminster Hall attended by Prime Ministers and other leading figures in the Empire. On this occasion he had to address, as he was told, the representatives of some 400 million of his subjects. Neither speech was easy for him, but he managed both with dignity.

Among the happy decisions taken was one to send an individual letter on behalf of the King to every pensioner from World War I who had served in any of His Majesty's forces and was still receiving institutional treatment at public expense on coronation day. Special amnesties, it was decided, were an anachronism, and they would not be applied except in South Africa and Rhodesia.

The preparations for the actual ceremony were meticulous, and even members of the press were told exactly what they would have to wear if they were allowed to attend the service in Westminster Abbey. Whereas gentlemen were required to wear full dress uniform or full velvet court dress and ladies full dress as for a court with feathers and veils, members of the House of Commons, representatives of friendly societies and of trade unions and members of the press were allowed 'alternative court dress'. This included black silk hose, white evening dress tie, white gloves and plain black breeches.

Arrangements for the foreign delegations caused problems, however, the country whose demands were the most difficult to satisfy being Germany. At the coronation of King Edward VII in 1911 the German Crown Prince and Crown Princess had been first in order of precedence of the foreign delegates. But Germany had then been a monarchy, and in the order of precedence decided for 1937 first place was to be given to princes representing great powers who were brothers to their sovereigns. Then came the brothers and sister of King George VI and their wives and husband, followed by heirs to kingdoms, and the great-uncle and great-aunts of the King. The non-royal representatives of great powers came only fifth in order. This was acceptable to the United States, France, the Soviet Union and other powers which were not monarchies. It was not acceptable to Ribbentrop. At a meeting at the Foreign Office he protested angrily, being particularly incensed because the standard procedure of placing ambassadors in accordance with the length of their appointment was to be adopted, and he himself had arrived in London only recently.[6]

There were also doubts until almost the last minute about the composition of the German delegation. On 12 March the British Ambassador in Berlin, Sir Eric Phipps, reported on a meeting he had had with Baron von Neurath, the German Foreign Minister. Neurath informed him he still could not say who would be leading the delegation. He himself was urging that it should be Field-Marshal von Blomberg, but Hitler would not make up his mind until he knew who would be representing Italy. Neurath went so far as to tell Phipps in confidence that 'he had impressed upon the Chancellor that this was a question that did not concern Germany, but he could not move Herr Hitler.'[7]

In the end Blomberg did come. No member of the Italian royal family attended the coronation because the now deposed Emperor of Ethiopia had been invited. Germany, Italy and, for some reason, Finland were the last three countries to announce their delegations. The German delegation had to accept its position as twelfth among the non-royal representatives of great powers, ahead only of Portugal and the Holy See. The first of the foreign delegates in the procession were Prince and Princess Chichibu of Japan.

There were difficulties too with other powers. The Iraqi Minister in London had to explain that his government had changed its mind five times about the composition of its delegation.[8] The Yemeni representative and son of the king decided at the last minute not to attend a state banquet because he did not like the place he had been allocated. It was explained to the Palace by the Foreign Office that he had never left his country before and that the king, his father, treated all his sons like children.[9]

Generalissimo Chiang Kai-Shek at one time expressed a desire to come himself and bring his wife, but when he concluded, wrongly as it happened, that China was to be treated as a third-rate power, he decided to send his Finance Minister, Dr Kung, instead.[10] The Vatican representative stated that he could not attend the service in the abbey but asked for seats to see the procession. As a consequence of problems of these kinds it was not until 1 May, only eleven days before the coronation, that the King was able to agree the order of precedence.

Within the Commonwealth the principal problem was ecclesiastical and liturgical. As the sovereign of nations with a wide variety of faiths, Ireland being among them, the King could no longer satisfactorily promise, as his predecessors had, to uphold the Protestant faith. Instead he undertook to maintain 'the true profession of the Gospel'.

In the selection of those invited to attend the Abbey service it was decided that no foreigners would be included other than members of the official delegations. A single exception to this rule was made in favour of the United States, Mrs Gerard, the wife of the American Ambassador, and Mr and Mrs James Roosevelt being among the guests. The personal intervention of the King was clearly seen in the inclusion of four boys selected through the Industrial Welfare Society.

The Abbey service and the procession were carried out with the colour, precision, solemnity and sense of theatre which habitually characterise such events in Britain. 300,000 visitors from overseas were estimated to have come to London for the occasion, and some half a million people spent hours in darkness and rain in order to watch the final rehearsal of the coronation procession, which took place at dawn on the Sunday before the actual event. The proceedings in the Abbey were broadcast on the radio, but access was denied to the newly established BBC television service.

Not everyone was satisfied with what was done. The day after the coronation Winston Churchill called the attention of the Coronation Committee to certain weaknesses which, he wrote, ought to be 'placidly, but adequately considered with a view to the future'. One was 'the impossible attempt to bring 4000 cars to meet over 4000 individuals.' Another was the evidence that Privy Councillors and Cabinet Ministers were 'afforded no sort of distinction over the general mass of peers and Members of Parliament.' Churchill pointed out that he had no personal interest, as he could not expect 'according to the ordinary life statistics' to see another coronation. In fact of course he did.

Churchill's criticisms were presented to the Lord President of the Council, J. Ramsay MacDonald, who shortly afterwards retired from office. MacDonald passed them on to his successor, Lord Halifax. In doing so he referred to Churchill as 'our friend of the very poor judgment'.[11]

For the King the coronation service in Westminster Abbey was only one of a range of events requiring his participation. In the last three weeks of May there were two state banquets; a dinner given by the Prime Minister and one given by the Foreign Secretary; a reception for foreign delegates and a luncheon for Commonwealth representatives; a visit to the Guildhall to receive an address and a reception by the London County Council; an Empire Day service in St Paul's Cathedral and an investiture; the opening of new buildings for the Tate Gallery, and two Court balls. Visits to Scotland and Wales followed shortly afterwards.

For the talks he had with representatives of a variety of countries the King required briefs on the main subjects which might be raised. These he had to memorise. The brief he received on the far eastern countries, to cite only one example, mentioned that the Chinese might seek foreign assistance against Japanese aggression and explore the possibility of raising loans and credits in London; that in Japan a struggle for power continued between civil and military elements; that the Nepalese Government might hope to receive, instead of its annual subsidy from

Britain, some territory in India or a capital grant; and that a new Anglo-Siamese treaty was being negotiated.[12]

The guests staying at Buckingham Palace whom the King had to entertain included the Count of Flanders, Princess Juliana and Prince Bernhard of the Netherlands, the Crown Princes and Crown Princesses of Norway and Sweden, the Regent Prince Paul of Yugoslavia and Princess Olga, the Crown Prince of Greece, Crown Prince Michael of Roumania and the Bulgarian Prince of Preslav. Among the most famous of the other guests were the veteran American soldier, General John Joseph Pershing; Colonel Józef Beck, the Polish Foreign Minister; and the future Turkish President, General Ismet Inönü.

Although sovereign rulers were not invited to the coronation service, there was one monarch in Britain at the time for whom the King felt some personal responsibility. This was the 20-year-old King Farouk of Egypt. In February 1937 Sir Miles Lampson, the British Ambassador in Cairo, sent two lengthy despatches about Farouk's visit. In one he expressed the hope that efforts would be made to 'keep in friendly contact with him and to maintain his confidence in us and in our good intentions towards him.' Lampson added: 'He certainly is quite a nice boy: what the man will be, who knows?' The other despatch described a meeting Lampson had had with one of the regents, Aziz Izzet Pasha, who had said: 'His Majesty was increasingly unpunctual and not always even suitably dressed on formal occasions: he completely neglected his English studies; the Regents were never consulted as they should be.' Aziz went on to express his anxiety about what might happen when the king came of age the next year. On 4 March 1937 Lord Wigram wrote to Sir Robert Vansittart, then Permanent Under-Secretary at the Foreign Office: 'The King read with much concern Lampson's telegram ... regarding Aziz Izzet Pasha's account of the young King of Egypt. His Majesty was wondering whether there was any way in which he could bring a steadying influence to bear upon King Farouk, who evidently has no idea of the responsibilities of a Constitutional Monarch.'[13]

The Duke of Gloucester was despatched to meet King Farouk at Victoria station, and soon after his arrival George VI invited him to lunch at Buckingham Palace. He was also invited to a court ball and to the King's review of the fleet. He did not endear himself to Anthony Eden by arriving three-quarters of an hour late for a meeting, but shortly before leaving he announced his intention of returning to Britain for a few weeks every summer.[14]

Another visitor whom George VI entertained in the summer of 1937 was King Carol of Roumania, who had come to Britain on a private visit. He lunched at Buckingham Palace on 22 July, having shortly beforehand informed Eden that he had seen no signs of aggression in Germany, and that Hitler had informed friends of his that he had no intention of making war on anyone. It was announced that King Carol had been invited to pay a State visit to Britain the following year.

Stanley Baldwin carried out his intention of retiring shortly after the coronation and was succeeded as Prime Minister by Neville Chamberlain. To Baldwin the King wrote: 'You take with you into retirement the abundant goodwill of our people – and, heavy as their loss will surely be, I regard it as in one sense my gain – for in my inexperience I shall look to you for guidance and advice in the difficulties with which I know that I shall from time to time be faced.'[15]

On 18 May the King wrote to Winston Churchill to thank him for a letter of good wishes which Churchill had sent him. In this the King stated: 'I know how devoted you have been, and still are, to my dear brother, and I feel touched beyond words by your sympathy and understanding in the very difficult problems that have arisen since he left us in December.'

Describing himself in retrospect as 'one whose political influence at that time had fallen to zero', Churchill wrote that 'this gesture of magnanimity . . . will ever be a cherished experience in my life.'[16]

CHAPTER TEN

The Windsors Abroad
1937

Throughout the year 1937 King George VI was seldom free from problems and anxieties arising from the status and activities of his elder brother. For a time after his abdication the Duke of Windsor telephoned the King fairly frequently, expecting him to be available when he did so and even offering advice on affairs of state. This he clearly felt entitled to do, and he may well have thought his advice would be helpful. The King, after a time, found these telephone conversations a worrying distraction, and he succeeded in bringing the practice to an end. But difficulties remained, a number of them connected with the Duke's wedding plans.

There can be little doubt that the King originally intended that there should be family representation at his brother's wedding. Mountbatten, acting as intermediary, informed the Duke of Windsor on 5 May 1937 that he had fixed a date for the wedding which 'suited Bertie, George etc.'[1] Clearly, however, official advice must have been given against royal attendance at a wedding not blessed by the Church.

Owing to the complexity of the English divorce laws Mrs Simpson was obliged, because it was she who had brought the action against her husband, to live apart from the Duke until her divorce was made absolute. She stayed with her friends Herman Rogers and his wife in Cannes, while the Duke stayed in Austria, and during this period of separation they exchanged frequent letters. The Duke's letters for the most part consisted of endearments. Those from Mrs Simpson tended to be more practical in nature, and when she learnt that the royal family were not to be present at the wedding she found it, understandably from her point of view, unacceptable. Worse was to follow. The King informed the Duke by letter that by renouncing the throne he was no longer in line of succession and had thereby lost the right to the title of Royal Highness. He wished him nevertheless to keep this title, but it would not be conferred on his wife.

On receiving this letter the Duke is said to have exclaimed: 'I know Bertie. I know he couldn't have written this letter on his own.'[2] The Duke was no doubt right. Once again the King was acting on advice. The title of Royal Highness, once conferred, could not be taken away, and among the King's advisers there were some who questioned whether the Duke of Windsor's marriage would be a lasting one. Had the King fought hard enough he could no doubt have obtained for the Duke's wife the royal title. In all fairness there was no particular reason why he should have fought at all, but if he had known how the question of title would rankle over the years, he might perhaps have had it conferred out of charity when the question first arose.

The Duke of Windsor and Mrs Simpson were married at the Château de Candé near Tours, which was lent to them by Charles Bedaux, a Frenchman who had become an American citizen. Bedaux, whom Mrs Simpson had first met through Herman Rogers, was a rich industrialist and an admirer of fascism who was to work actively for Germany in World War II.

It was clear that after the marriage the Windsors would wish to travel in Europe, and before the marriage actually took place the heads of the British missions in both Paris and Vienna asked for instructions on how they should be treated. This question was referred personally to the King, who on 1 May asked the Foreign Office to put forward suggestions. After considerable deliberation a formula was devised. This was conveyed by Sir Alexander Hardinge, who had returned to duty as Private Secretary, in a letter to Sir Robert Vansittart, the Permanent Under-Secretary, on 2 September.

'The most important point, in His Majesty's opinion,' Hardinge wrote, 'is that His Royal Highness the Duke of Windsor and the Duchess should not be treated by His Majesty's representatives as having any official status in the countries which they visit. For this reason it seems to the King that, except under special instructions, His Majesty's representatives should not have any hand in arranging official interviews for them, or countenance their participation in any official ceremonies.'

Private entertaining was to be left to the representatives on the spot. Security measures should automatically be put into operation, and at railway stations a member of the Embassy staff, but not the ambassador or minister, should meet the Duke.[3]

Shortly before the King's decision on how the Duke and Duchess should be treated was conveyed to British representatives abroad Geoffrey Knox, the British Minister in Budapest, reported that they were about to visit Hungary. He asked for instructions on what to do if the Duke wanted to present the Duchess to the Regent Horthy. He added: 'While Admiral de Horthy entertains considerable sympathy and friendship for the Duke, whom he knows well, he expressed himself in strong terms about the Duchess.' Before Knox received an answer Horthy solved his problem for him by going off on manoeuvres the day after the Duke and Duchess reached Budapest.[4]

Late in September 1937 it was learnt that the Duke was planning to visit both Germany and the United States. The ostensible reason in each case was 'to see what is being done to improve working and living conditions in several of the larger cities'.[5]

The visit to Germany duly took place in October under the auspices of Dr Ley, the chief of the Labour Front. A large crowd greeted the Duke and Duchess on their arrival in Berlin, and numerous press and cinema photographers were present. They had tea with Hitler and talked to Goebbels. Both Ribbentrop and Rudolf Hess entertained them to dinner, and the Duke inspected the National Socialist party headquarters in Nuremberg. The Duke was careful not to make any speeches which could embarrass the British Government, but a report received by the British Foreign Office stated:

'The visit of the Duke of Windsor seems to have made a bad impression. His entire journey and expenses were paid by the German Labour Front. He was always with Dr Ley who is invariably drunk and is of second rate importance among the Nazis . . . Even the bill for the manicure of his secretary was paid by Dr Ley and no tips were given at the Kaiserhof where he stayed . . . The whole visit is described as lacking in dignity for one who has held such a great position.'[6]

While staying in the Kaiserhof Hotel in Berlin the Duke of Windsor wrote a personal letter to Sir Ronald Lindsay, the British Ambassador in Washington, to inform him that he would be arriving there on 11 November. 'If therefore,' he wrote, 'you could arrange for us to be received by the President and Mrs Roosevelt some time on the Friday, I would appreciate it very much.' He typed the letter himself and apologised in a postscript for his bad typing.

Two days after this letter was written the British Chargé d'Affaires in Berlin, George Ogilvie Forbes, dined with his American opposite number, Prentiss Gilbert, and learnt who was the inspirational source behind the Duke's apparent interest in international housing and labour problems. Gilbert, Ogilvie Forbes reported, 'raised the subject of the Duke of Windsor and of His Royal Highness's intended visit to the United States. He said that Mr Bedaux, the French-American millionaire host of the Duke's, had been approaching him with a view to obtaining from the United States Government official recognition of the forthcoming visit and also, I think, treatment of the Duchess as a Royalty . . . He said that the American press correspondents, who had hitherto painted in vivid colours the trivialities in the life of a married couple . . . had now decided that HRH had entered the arena of politics and that they would now develop that aspect.'

Ogilvie Forbes's report continued: 'He also said that as a result of the approaches which Bedaux had made to him, it was clear that this individual was "running" HRH and probably paying his expenses for the tour outside Germany . . . Bedaux also told him that it was the intention that HRH after the visit to the United States should visit Italy and Sweden in which latter country he would be placed in contact with a Swedish millionaire whose name he did not know and who was interested in World Peace through Labour reconciliation. Bedaux said it was also intended that HRH should take up this line and even went so far as to express the opinion that HRH might in due course be the "Saviour" of the Monarchy!' Ogilvie Forbes typed this report himself, informing the Foreign Office that he was not even putting a copy in the Chancery archives.[7]

Sir Ronald Lindsay happened to be on leave in England when he first heard of the proposed visit of the Duke and Duchess to the United States. On the very day on which the Duke had written to him from the Kaiserhof Hotel he wrote to Vansittart: 'The impending visit of the Duke and Duchess of Windsor to Washington fills me with unmitigated horror, though in the light of what I have heard while in England I cannot say I am surprised.'

Five days later, on 18 October, Lindsay came to Balmoral at the invitation of the King. Anthony Eden was also present, and after some discussion Lindsay was authorised to invite the Duke and Duchess to stay at the Embassy in Washington, to give a small dinner party for them, and to ask the President to receive them, but not to accompany them if he did so. This was a generous variation of the earlier guidance, and it seems reasonable to suspect the hand of the King in it.[8]

On his return to the United States Lindsay was surrounded by press reporters, who gave him what he described as 'one of the worst experiences I have ever had'. The United States government he found accommodating. The Secretary of State, Cordell Hull, was on holiday, and Sumner Welles, whom Lindsay described as 'the Vansittart of America', was in charge of the State Department. Welles told Lindsay that 'the President was most anxious to avoid doing anything that could give any embarrassment to the King or to his government,' but that he felt he must give the Duke a dignified reception. If he did not, 'it would be ascribed to British pressure and the President would be in a false position and the Duke would be a martyr.'

In the end the President was not obliged to make any decision. Bedaux's reputation, both as a sympathiser with fascism and as an industrialist with strong views on methods of increasing production, had spread to America. The Duke's visit to Germany had made a bad impression, and American organised workers, led by the Baltimore Federation of Labor, protested so strongly that Bedaux decided to withdraw from the enterprise. The Duke wondered half-heartedly for a time whether he should carry on without Bedaux, but it was not difficult to persuade him to give up all idea of an American visit.

In reporting to Eden on the whole affair Lindsay wrote: 'I remember how at Balmoral I accused you all (including, I think, Their Majesties) of exaggerating . . . I entirely underestimated the amount of "hostility" that would manifest itself here, perhaps because I knew nothing at all then about Bedaux.'[9]

It was not only through the enterprises conceived by Bedaux that the Duke's conduct aroused anxiety. On 28 December 1937 Sir Eric Phipps, who was now Ambassador in Paris, passed on a report to Eden in a letter which ended: 'I am not informing anyone of the above except yourself.' The report had come to him from Sir William Tyrrell, the former Ambassador, who had been staying in the Embassy for a week.

'Some time ago,' Phipps wrote, 'a special correspondent of the *Daily Herald* came over here to interview the Duke of Windsor. Tyrrell was shown the account of this interview, in which it was stated that His Royal Highness said that if the Labour Party wished, and were in a position to offer it, he would be prepared to be President of the English Republic.'

Tyrrell, who had described himself as 'shocked and horrified', had persuaded the newspapers's management not to publish the report.[10]

In the first six months of his reign George VI received official invitations to visit a number of countries. One of these came from Belgium, the country to which as Duke of York he had paid his first official visit as a representative of his father. It was decided that the King's other commitments would not allow him to go to Belgium in 1937 or 1938. Instead it was agreed to invite King Leopold of the Belgians to pay a state visit to Britain in November 1937, even though he could not stay in Buckingham Palace because the decorators would be at work. The British Minister in Brussels, Sir Noel Charles, learnt that the idea of a state visit to Britain attracted King Leopold greatly. He was even willing to turn down an invitation to visit France to open an international exhibition in order to make sure that he came officially to Britain first. Eden too passed on a report that 'King Leopold was the staunchest possible friend of Britain. He had been educated at Eton, was proud of it, and had the greatest admiration for this country.'[11] George VI also welcomed the visit, Lord Wigram telling Eden of the King's personal liking for King Leopold.

At a state banquet held on 16 November King Leopold, speaking in English, referred to the time 'when Your Majesty rode into Brussels side by side with my parents that November day nineteen years ago'. He added: 'The celebrations that accompanied Your Majesty's coronation have given proof of the strength of the Empire and also of the stability of your royal house, which, as a French writer recently remarked, has something imposing about it, something comparable to the majestic operation of the laws of nature.'[12]

An invitation for the King and Queen to pay a state visit to France was issued at the time of the coronation. This was accepted, and the visit was planned for June 1938.

Another invitation, which was of a less formal nature but which was to have more important consequences, was conveyed on 11 May 1937 to Anthony Eden by James W. Gerard, the United States Ambassador. Eden reported on this:

'In the course of a conversation which I had this morning with Mr Gerard, the latter said that he had been specifically asked by President Roosevelt to express the hope that if and when the King and Queen paid an official visit to Canada, they would find it possible also to pay a private and unofficial visit to President Roosevelt at Hyde Park. Mr Gerard said that were Their Majesties to pay such a visit, it would greatly gratify the President and would have an excellent effect in the United States. I explained to Mr Gerard that there was no question of the King visiting Canada in the immediate future.'[13]

The possibility of a royal visit to India, too, was discussed by the King and his ministers. In January 1937 the Marquess of Zetland, Secretary of State for India, asked Wigram whether the King would consider such a visit in the following winter. Wigram replied that the King was 'overwhelmed with the magnitude of the task which had been imposed upon him' and felt he could not undertake a visit so soon.[14]

Zetland invited the views of the Viceroy, Lord Linlithgow, and Governors of Provinces about a visit in the winter of 1938–39. After receiving these he wrote to Linlithgow on 20 October 1937: 'I admit that I have experienced great difficulty in making up my mind. The arguments are very evenly balanced. If the durbar went well it might be a tremendous asset: if it went badly it would be an equally serious set-back.' A new federal structure for India was being planned, and Zetland feared that a royal visit might be interpreted by a hostile Indian Congress as an attempt to sell this over Congress's head. The cost was also advanced as an argument against holding a durbar.

Government opinion had begun to harden against a visit during the winter of 1938–39 when on 15 November 1939 Zetland wrote to Linlithgow: 'A new factor in the case is the apparent desire of Their Majesties to visit India as soon as we are in a position to agree to their doing so.' On 9 December the King discussed the question of a royal visit with Zetland for nearly an hour and, according to Zetland, 'expressed incredulity at the necessity for spending so large a sum as a million pounds, which he declared to be out of the question.' Discussions continued into the next year, and at the end of January Chamberlain wrote a three-and-a-half-page letter in his own hand to Hardinge, stating that he had asked Zetland 'whether if the financial difficulties were removed, the political difficulties would still be so serious as to cause him to maintain the advice he had already given to the King against a visit next winter.' Zetland maintained that they were. The King did not conceal his disappointment, but on 3 February he accepted as final the decision that the visit must be postponed.[15]

In September 1937 the King and Queen entertained Neville Chamberlain at Balmoral. In his letter of thanks Chamberlain wrote: 'One makes more progress in getting to know a man who is staying in the same house and with whom one converses on any topic as it comes up than one does in fifty official interviews, and my four days at Balmoral have made me feel that my relations with yourself and the Queen will henceforth be on a new footing. I need hardly say how greatly I value this approach to intimacy and how helpful it will be to me in my position as head of Your Majesty's Government.'[16] It was the beginning of a relationship which was to be of growing warmth.

In the same month King George entertained at Balmoral both King Boris of Bulgaria and King George of the Hellenes. It was the first time these two kings of neighbouring states, which had very nearly gone to war twelve years earlier, had met for a friendly talk.[17]

For a novice King it had been a demanding year, during which his confidence and grasp of complex events had continued to grow.

CHAPTER ELEVEN

Paris and Munich

1938

On the evening of Sunday 20 February 1938 Anthony Eden resigned as Foreign Secretary. His reasons were deep-seated and complex. A disagreement over British policy towards Italy was the culmination of a number of differences of opinion he had had with Chamberlain. He was also influenced in his decision by the state of his health.

There had been a Cabinet meeting on the Saturday, an event unusual enough to arouse speculation in the press. Questions continued to be asked, and as a result the King first heard of his Foreign Secretary's resignation from unofficial sources. He found this unsatisfactory and instructed Hardinge to discover why it had happened. The question was referred to Sir Maurice Hankey, the powerful figure who then held the three posts of Secretary to the Cabinet, Clerk of the Privy Council and Secretary of the Committee of Imperial Defence. On 4 March Hankey wrote to Hardinge: 'The Prime Minister agreed with me that it was very difficult to say at what moment serious difficulties did arise. I do not think that either he or I thought that the late Foreign Secretary would resign until a meeting of a small group of Ministers at 7.30 on the Sunday, at which he announced his intention to do so.'

Hankey went on: 'What I have actually arranged with the Prime Minister is that if developments should appear to be taking an untoward turn I should remind him of his responsibility to inform the King, and it will be for him to decide how this shall be done.' If the Prime Minister had some inescapable engagement immediately after the Cabinet, it would be for Hankey to inform Hardinge.[1]

When Eden came to the Palace to hand in his seals he found the King, as he put it, 'a most sympathetic and understanding listener'. In answer to questions Eden explained at some length why he had resigned. 'I do not suggest that he agreed,' he afterwards wrote, 'but the circumstances of our meeting for some reason removed all restraint and we had a man-to-man talk.'

In recalling these events Eden also wrote: 'The Sovereign reads Foreign Office and other telegrams of importance and has full and impartial knowledge of all that passes . . . Having read the same documents, it is sometimes comforting to find one has independently reached the same conclusion.'[2]

Hankey himself retired in May. After a meeting of the Privy Council on the 16th the King expressed the hope that his successor would be General Hastings Ismay, Hankey's deputy in the work of the Committee of Imperial Defence. This was a shrewd assessment of character. In World War II Ismay was to serve Churchill with great distinction. Indeed it was largely due to his tact and understanding that Churchill's system of dividing responsibility in the conduct of the war between the Cabinet and the Chiefs of Staff Committee worked as effectively as it did.

In fact, and quite rightly so, no one man succeeded to all Hankey's posts. Ismay became Secretary both of the Committee of Imperial Defence and of the Chiefs of Staff Committee. Sir Edward Bridges became Secretary to the Cabinet and Sir Rupert Howorth Clerk of the Privy Council.[3]

In his reaction to another change in appointments the King gave further evidence of his increasingly sound judgment of men. This arose from the dismissal of the Air Minister Lord Swinton, formerly Philip Cunliffe-Lister. Although his contribution to providing the nation with a competent Air Force was almost certainly greater than that of any other politician in the inter-war years, to a House of Commons growing more and more concerned with the Government's defence policy the presence of an Air Minister in the House of Lords, and therefore unreachable, had become unacceptable, and Chamberlain bowed to the Commons's judgment. He was suffering badly from gout at the time and was unable to have his usual weekly audience of the King. The subject of Swinton's replacement by Sir Kingsley Wood was therefore dealt with between King and Prime Minister by correspondence. The King wrote: 'I saw Swinton this evening, and I was very sorry to have had to say good-bye to him as Secretary of State for Air. He has done so well in the Air Ministry I feel, and he will be a great loss to the country at this time.'[4]

Chamberlain replied: 'I have parted with Lord Swinton very regretfully. He has done wonders for the Air Force but I was fighting a losing battle in trying to retain him. The House simply would not have it.'[5] Rather more than a year after war broke out the King was to note in his diary that when the battle had been won 'men like Lord Swinton will be remembered'.[6]

Early in January 1938 Sir Eric Phipps, the British Ambassador in Paris, was asked for his comments on the invitation to the King and Queen to pay a state visit to France which had been issued at the time of the coronation. Phipps replied on 10 January: 'Not only have I no qualms about a state visit to Paris, but I think it would be an excellent move.' In a reference to recent street rioting in Paris, he even expressed the hope that the visit would have a 'healthy effect upon Hitler, Mussolini and Co., who like to think that the streets of Paris are running in blood or at any rate very dangerous to walk about in.'[7]

From discussions which he had with President Lebrun and ministers Phipps learnt that the French Government wanted to use the visit to call attention to Franco–British solidarity in the face of any likely aggression and, for this reason, to give it as much popular appeal as possible. Among the suggestions put to him were that the visit should coincide with the celebrations on 14 July and also with a large military review, and that one at least of the King's daughters should take part in the visit. The King did not want his daughters to be involved, and an internal Foreign Office note stated: 'The idea of attending a military review is not one which appeals to the King.'[8] The reasons for this were not given.

The visit was planned to take place at the end of June, but on 23 June the Queen's mother, the Countess of Strathmore, died suddenly. The Queen had a deep affection for her mother, and it was not thought appropriate for her and the King to indulge in lively festivities in Paris a few days after her mother's death. In reply to a letter of condolence from Neville Chamberlain the Queen, who had a talent for expressing herself happily in letters, wrote of her mother: 'She had such a good perspective of life – everything was given its true importance. She had a young spirit, great courage and unending sympathy whenever and wherever it was needed, and such a heavenly sense of humour.'[9] The beginning of the visit was postponed to 19 July, the problem of mourning being dealt with in an ingenious manner. This was for the Queen to be dressed in white throughout her visit.

The delay served to heighten expectations in France, and the President of the Municipal Council of Paris, Provost de Launay, spelt out clearly what he expected the citizens of the capital to do. He called on them to decorate their houses and ensure that the colours of the two nations were everywhere intertwined. 'Acclamez le Roi,' he declared. 'Acclamez la Reine.' Paris would express 'her respectful affection for the sovereigns, her fidelity to a dear friendship and her faith in the future.'[10]

The drafting of the speech which the King was to make at the banquet at the Elysée Palace occupied the personal attention of the Foreign Secretary, Lord Halifax, as well as that of a number of his senior officials. Their main problem was to decide how strongly the King should emphasise Britain's faith in democratic principles and, even more important, her readiness to defend them. The King was dissatisfied with the first draft. In the final version, which he delivered in French, he emphasised that the defence of democratic faith demanded of all, to a high degree, courage and wise and determined strength.[11]

A military review of some 50,000 troops did take place at Versailles; the King unveiled the Australian war memorial at Villers-Bretonneux; a royal gift of 100,000 francs to the poor of Paris was handed over by Hardinge at a garden party given by the municipality. But the principal impact, by far, was made by the presence of the King and Queen in the streets of the capital.

Sir Eric Phipps, an experienced and able diplomat, described the scenes as 'a manifestation of such enthusiastic warmth that, by general consent, no celebration since the Armistice has evoked so profound a sense of unity, irrespective of Party and class, among the people of France.' The climax, he wrote, was reached 'when, on the evening of July 21st, the cordons were at last relaxed and many thousands of people gathered outside the Quai d'Orsay Palace to acclaim Their Majesties.'[12]

Such manifestations of anglophilia are rare in France and are normally associated with joint victory in battle. To the French Government the royal visit was a welcome response to its almost desperate search for allies. In spite of the confidence felt in the Maginot Line there was probably a more acute awareness in French than in British governmental circles of the threat presented by Hitler's Germany. The French policy of containment by alliances with the countries of central and eastern Europe was already almost in shreds, and shortly before the royal visit the French foreign minister, Georges Bonnet, by way of reinsurance, sent a message of goodwill to Count Ciano in Italy. He used as his intermediary the film star Madeleine Carroll.[13]

It was also significant that among the guests invited by the French Government for the royal visit was Winston Churchill, who at that time held no official position. And the response of the French people to the visit was no doubt a confirmation of the hopes and fears of their government.

With the new Foreign Secretary, Lord Halifax, the King had a closer personal *rapport* than he was ever to have with Eden. Indeed there was probably no political figure to whom the King felt more drawn in the course of his reign than Halifax. In the summer and early autumn of 1938, however, Halifax was in practice little more than a deputy Foreign Secretary, for after Eden's resignation Chamberlain took even closer control of foreign affairs than before.

While conducting his personal diplomacy Chamberlain was scrupulous in keeping the King informed of developments and of his own intentions. They had lengthy discussions at Balmoral, and after Chamberlain returned to London early in August he regularly sent the King long letters written in his own hand. In these, interspersed with accounts of his own unsatisfactory state of health, are to be found expressions of his aspirations for the peace of the world.

On 13 August he wrote: 'Since I have been back, the sinuvitis [sic] from which I have been suffering has improved slightly . . . I am still liable to sharp bouts of pain . . . Meanwhile I get some consolation from the fact that I have been able to get some valuable talks with Halifax about the Czecho-Slovakian situation which continues to give me a good deal of anxiety. The reaction of the German Foreign Office to our latest effort appears to have been bad, but of course it is Hitler's and not Ribbentrop's reaction that matters. I am not sorry to be in London next week when I can deal properly with any developments. I hope, Sir, that you had a good day with the grouse yesterday and that you are not being troubled with such violent thunderstorms as we had here.'

In the same letter he wrote that he continued 'to get echoes of the Paris visit' and added: 'Your Majesty evidently impressed everyone greatly with your speeches in French, while the Queen's smile as usual took every place by storm.'[14]

On 6 September Chamberlain wrote: 'Developments seem very slow and I am afraid that we may have to wait another week or even more before we can speak in confidence about the issue. All the same I have a "hunch", as J. P. Morgan says, that we shall get through this time without the use of force. Hitler cannot say that no progress is being made.' This letter followed another visit to Balmoral, and in it Chamberlain also wrote: 'I am more grateful than I can say to you, Sir, and to the Queen for all your kindness to me at Balmoral. I must confess to having arrived there in rather low spirits, but it did not take long to disperse the clouds.'[15]

A week later, after Hitler had made yet another threatening speech directed against Czechoslovakia, Chamberlain wrote to the King: 'I have been considering the possibility of a sudden and dramatic step which might change the whole situation. The plan is that I should inform Herr Hitler that I propose at once to go over to Germany to see him. If he assents, and it would be difficult for him to refuse, I should hope to persuade him that he had an unequalled opportunity of raising his own prestige and fulfilling what he has so often declared to be his aim, namely the establishment of an Anglo–German understanding, preceded by a settlement of the Czecho-Slovakian question.'

Later in the letter Chamberlain made it clear that this plan, of which he was informing the King in detail, had been discussed with Halifax, but had not yet been considered by the cabinet.

In all his negotiations and journeyings, which ended with the settlement reached in Munich at the end of September 1938, Chamberlain had the King's unstinted support and approval. The King even offered, on the morning of Chamberlain's departure for Berchtesgaden on one of his abortive trips, to send a letter to Hitler as one ex-serviceman to another expressing the hope that the peace would be kept. Neither Chamberlain nor Halifax favoured this proposal, as they feared an insulting reply might be received.

On his return from Munich in September Chamberlain received a letter from the King delivered to Heston airport expressing admiration and gratitude. To Halifax the King wrote thanking him for his untiring support of the Prime Minister 'in his search for a peaceful solution of the recent European crisis'. Both letters were written in the King's own hand.

In his response to the Munich settlement the King was certainly in tune with the great majority of the nation and with much opinion overseas. So many people came to greet Chamberlain on his return that the roads to Heston airport were almost impassable. The American Ambassador in London, Joseph Kennedy, conveyed a telegram to Chamberlain, which read: 'You're a great man. Franklin D. Roosevelt.'[16] Even the ex-Kaiser sent Queen Mary a letter for the first time since the outbreak of war in 1914, in which he wrote: 'I have not the slightest doubt that Mr N. Chamberlain was inspired by Heaven and guided by God.'[17]

The doubts in general came later, though one of the early doubters, Duff Cooper, went so far as to resign from the Government in protest. In recalling the occasion he wrote: 'I saw the King the same afternoon. He was frank and charming. He said that he could not agree with me, but he respected those who had the courage of their convictions.'[18] Duff Cooper and his wife began, after a time, to classify people they knew as either 'sound' or 'unsound' according to their readiness to resist German aggression. Both The Times and the Daily Express were, in their judgment, unsound. The King was one of those they considered sound.[19]

Another state visit took place in 1938, that of King Carol of Roumania. His visit had originally been planned to take place in the spring, but reasons were found on both sides for postponing it. German troops invaded Austria in March in order to effect the so-called Anschluss, and in consequence King Carol felt he could not properly leave his country at that time. The British government, for its part, was disturbed by some of the anti-Jewish decrees of the Roumanian government. One of these forbade Jews to employ Roumanian women under forty on the grounds that many Jews had engaged young servants for 'the traffic in live flesh'. The British fear was that King Carol might be subjected to hostile demonstrations during his visit.

The anti-Jewish Roumanian Government fell in February 1938 and was replaced by a non-party administration headed by the Orthodox Patriarch. A state visit was therefore agreed, and King Carol arrived at Dover on 15 November to be met by the Duke of Kent. The King and the Duke of Gloucester, Neville Chamberlain, Lord Halifax and Sir Samuel

Hoare, who was now Home Secretary, greeted him at Victoria station.

The normal pattern of state visits was varied slightly to enable King Carol to visit the RAF station at Odiham and army units at Aldershot.[20] The intention was of course to impress him with British military strength. In a memorandum on the visit Sir Orme Sargent wrote: 'The only way we could influence any of these countries of South East Europe is by making them effective offers of material assistance and by a display of superiority as against the forces, both military and economic, which Germany arrays against them.'

The Treasury evidently thought differently. When King Carol enquired about the possibility of obtaining arms he was told that 'His Majesty's Government have at present no power to give export credit guarantees in respect of armaments.'[21]

Under a new Roumanian constitution the powers of the King had been considerably increased. This situation was not to last for long. The pact made between Germany and the Soviet Union the next year reduced him to a mere puppet. He agreed to cede large areas of Roumanian territory to the Soviet Union, to Hungary and to Bulgaria, became increasingly unpopular in consequence, and in 1940 fled the country. He took with him his faithful red-headed mistress Mme Lupescu and nine railway-cars filled with treasures. He did however leave behind him a son, Michael, who towards the end of the war would briefly play a role of some importance.

When the 1938 visit was being planned Sir Reginald Hoare, the British Minister in Bucharest, wrote that the young Prince Michael was 'becoming difficult'. He added: 'The impression has been growing on me that King Carol makes him appear much too frequently in public . . . I wonder whether it would be possible for someone to convey to King Carol that children require careful handling.' He suggested Queen Mary as 'the obvious person'.[22] In fact it was King George VI who spoke to King Carol on the lines suggested.[23] It was the beginning of his concern for the young prince to whom he was later to give much helpful advice and guidance.

King Carol was invested with the order of the Garter. This and rumours of export credits to Roumania seem to have aroused some envy in Bulgaria. On 21 November 1938 the British Minister in Sofia, Sir George Rendel, wrote: 'The King and a number of leading Bulgarians are still very anxious to be friends with us, and the mass of the people distrust and dislike the Germans.' He added: 'If by any chance the possibility of an official visit to England could be contemplated . . . I think it might still make an enormous difference.'[24]

No official visit took place, but King Boris did stay with George VI at Balmoral in September. In the course of his visit to Britain he offered to mediate with Hitler, and did indeed attempt negotiations shortly afterwards. Sir George Rendel later thanked him for this in a letter which stated: 'In speaking as he did to Herr Hitler and other leading members of the German Government His Majesty showed himself a true friend of Europe.' According to his biographer, Pashanko Dimitroff, King Boris often showed this letter to close friends and said that if he were to be led to the gallows he could prove by the letter that he had done something worthwhile in his life.[25]

In November 1938 Lord Halifax had an audience of King George VI. An Anglo–Italian agreement (short-lived and ineffective) had recently been signed, and the King put forward the suggestion that he might write a letter to the King of Italy expressing satisfaction at the restoration of good relations. Halifax considered the suggestion closely and consulted the British Ambassador in Rome, Lord Perth. The Italian Government was at that time putting out certain feelers, and it was known that Count Ciano, the Italian Foreign Minister, Mussolini's son-in-law, craved a British decoration. Nevertheless it was thought unwise for the King to take the initiative so clearly.

The King's suggestion, though well-intentioned, was perhaps a little naive. Clearly he was still feeling his way in foreign affairs. Evidence of his inexperience had also been given when, on 10 August 1938, the Australian High Commissioner, Stanley Bruce, had put forward for the King's consideration a suggestion that either the Duke of Gloucester or the Duke of Kent should be appointed Governor-General of Australia. At his audience Bruce found the King noncommittal, preferring to discuss the suggestion with the Prime Minister before venturing an opinion.[26]

The Australian Prime Minister, Joseph Lyons, was strongly in favour of the appointment of one of the royal dukes. Lord Gowrie, who was due to retire shortly as Governor-General, took the same view. The Duke of Kent expressed himself in a private conversation with Lord Stanley, the Secretary of State for the Dominions, as extremely keen and said he believed the Duke of Gloucester felt the same.[27] The King however still demurred.

Admittedly Princess Elizabeth was still a minor, and if the King died the Duke of Gloucester would become Regent. The Duke of Kent, on the other hand, would probably have made an excellent Governor-General. He had the best mind of all King George V's sons. He was a man of charm and taste and, after a somewhat strenuous early sex life, had married the beautiful Princess Marina of Greece, sister of Princess Olga, the Yugoslav Regent's wife. Yet neither he nor the Duke of Gloucester was appointed. The decision was the King's. He felt he needed the presence of his brothers in Britain to support him.

CHAPTER TWELVE

In North America
1939

In January 1939 a draft speech was prepared by Stephen Tallents of the BBC for the King to broadcast on the subject of national military service. Among those to whom the draft was shown were the Archbishop of Canterbury and the Governor of the Bank of England. After much discussion the broadcast was never made. Such a speech, it was thought, might create the impression that war was imminent, and it was feared there might be panic selling on the stock exchange.[1] The decision not to ask the King to broadcast was consistent with much government policy in the first six months following the Munich settlement. Some preparations for war were made, including the increased manufacture of armaments, but in a manner which would minimise alarm both at home and overseas.

Chamberlain continued with his attempts to woo Fascist Italy away from Germany. In a long hand-written letter dated 17 January he informed the King of meetings he had had with Mussolini in Rome. 'Both Halifax and I,' he wrote, 'were personally impressed by Mussolini. In spite of daily efforts to keep himself fit by physical exercises, boxing, etc., he is putting on weight and judging by photographs his face has coarsened considerably. But he is still extremely alert both mentally and physically.'

Chamberlain went on: 'Talking with him is a much pleasanter affair than with Hitler. You feel you are dealing with a reasonable man, not a fanatic, and he struck us both as straightforward and sincere in what he said.'[2] A number of cordial meetings were held, but the political benefit derived from them was negligible.

The policy of trying to keep the peace by offering limited concessions to Hitler, of which the Munich settlement was the climax, was effectively destroyed in March 1939, when German troops marched into Czechoslovakia and Hitler announced that the country had ceased to exist. To Chamberlain the King wrote sympathetically on 18 March: 'I feel I must send you one line to say how well I can appreciate your feelings about the recent behaviour of the German Government. Although this blow to your courageous efforts on behalf of peace and understanding in Europe must, I am afraid, cause you deep distress, I am sure your labours have been anything but wasted, for they will have left no doubt in the minds of ordinary people all over the world of our love of peace and of our readiness to discuss with any nation whatever grievance they think they have.'[3]

A little more than a week after the German invasion of Czechoslovakia the French President, Albert Lebrun, and his wife arrived in Britain for a return state visit. In a speech at Dover the President declared that the people of France had been 'conquered by the grace and charm of Her Majesty the Queen and the eminent qualities and prestige of His Majesty the King.'[4] The usual pageantry was staged, and at a reception in India House the French guests were entertained by the BBC choir and by John Gielgud and Peggy Ashcroft performing the balcony scene in *Romeo and Juliet*. But behind the facade the talks which Georges Bonnet, the French Foreign Minister, had with Chamberlain and Halifax were concerned mainly with the guarantees Britain and France might give to the countries most clearly threatened by German aggression. These were Poland and Roumania.

The Polish Foreign Minister, Colonel Józef Beck, was invited to visit Britain in April, and in preparation for the talks they would have Halifax spent a Saturday with some of his principal advisers in the Foreign Office. The purpose, he explained in a letter to Hardinge, was 'to clear our minds as to the prospects of progress in the international approaches we have been making.' He added: 'I thought the King might possibly like to see the result.'[5]

The most important paragraphs in the paper enclosed were:

If Poland or Roumania are attacked directly or indirectly by Germany (e.g., in the case of Roumania, with connivance of Hungary) are they prepared to resist?

If so, Great Britain and France would be prepared to support them. (This is on the assumption that both Governments were, in fact, prepared so to pledge themselves.)[6]

These paragraphs were in effect the genesis of the guarantees which were later to be given to Poland and Roumania. As the Polish Government was determined to resist if Poland were attacked by Germany, they also meant a British and French decision to resist further German aggression. As there could now be little doubt in the minds of well-informed people that such aggression would follow, the guarantees were tantamount to committing Britain to an eventual declaration of war.

In reply to Halifax's letter Hardinge wrote on 27 March: 'The King is most grateful to you for your very interesting notes about the progress in the approaches which you are making to various countries in Europe. Poland certainly seems to be the crux of the situation, and it is also clear that a too open association with the Soviet may have unfortunate reactions in some of the countries whose support we are trying to enlist. His Majesty appreciates the great difficulty of these negotiations and sympathises with you in your responsible task.'[7]

A problem of lesser moment which was brought to the King's attention in March 1938 arose from a further visit to Britain by King Farouk of Egypt. King Farouk was now thought to be excessively under Italian influence, and low class Italian influence at that. In the words of Sir Miles Lampson he was 'frequently accompanied, particularly on nocturnal jaunts, by an Italian coiffeur, an Italian "masseur" and an Italian electrician, strange companions anyhow for an undemocratic Monarch.' It was also thought that 'an Italian midinette has been consoling His Majesty during Queen Farida's confinement'.[8] Once again George VI offered his advisory services, this time by speaking to Farouk's Chef de Cabinet, Ali Maher Pasha. Once again his offer was accepted with gratitude by the Foreign Office.

President Roosevelt was persisting with his plan to bring the King and Queen to the United States. This had first been put forward in May 1937, at which time Anthony Eden had replied non-committally. On 17 September 1938 the President wrote a letter which began: 'My dear King George.' In this he stated: 'When I was in Canada a few weeks ago Prime Minister Mackenzie King told me, in confidence, that there is a possibility that you and Her Majesty will visit the Dominion of Canada in the summer of 1939. If this visit becomes a reality, I very much hope that you will extend your visit to include the United States.' He suggested a visit to the International Exposition in New York and three or four days of 'simple country life' in the Roosevelts' home at Hyde Park. If the King decided to bring one or both of his daughters with him, the President undertook to arrange for some Roosevelts of the same age to be available to play with them.[9]

George VI's reply was guarded. 'I hope,' he wrote, 'it will not be inconvenient if I delay my answer until the plans for a visit to Canada are further advanced, and I am in a position to judge how long it may be possible for me to be absent from this country.' He made it clear that his children would not be coming to Canada, as they were 'much too young for such a strenuous tour', and wrote that the pleasure which he and the Queen would in any case take in the visit proposed by the President 'would be greatly enhanced by the thought that it was contributing in any way to the cordiality of the relations between our two countries.'[10]

The planning of the Canadian part of the King's North American tour posed some political difficulties. The Canadian Prime Minister, W. L.

Mackenzie King, was totally dedicated to its success. He was also in a strong position within his own parliament. As he put it in a letter to Roosevelt on 3 March 1939, 'Parliament will adjourn for a part of the time they [King George and Queen Elizabeth] may be here, but, in all probability, will carry on its proceedings over the greater part of the time. Fortunately, I have the best of colleagues and a large majority in the House of Commons.' He himself, he made it clear, would be totally occupied with the business of the royal visit.[11]

There was however a source of contention in the choice of the Minister or Ministers to be in attendance on the King. This gave rise to some rancour, a discussion of constitutional issues and even a temporary threat of a rift in Anglo-Canadian relations.

The King's original plan was that he would be accompanied on his visit to the United States by Mackenzie King, who was both Prime Minister and Secretary of State for External Affairs, and by Lord Halifax. Sumner Welles favoured this arrangement, but Roosevelt did not like it. Lord Halifax's presence might, he thought, arouse too much political speculation in the American press.[12]

Much of the planning was put in the hands of the King's Assistant Private Secretary. This was Alan Lascelles, who had served the Prince of Wales for a number of years and George V more briefly. He was also familiar with Canadian politics, having been Secretary to Lord Bessborough when he was Governor-General of Canada from 1931 to 1935. Nevertheless he seriously upset Mackenzie King, who at one point sarcastically expressed surprise that Lascelles did not refer to Canada as 'this colony'. Mackenzie King also took exception to the suggestion that President Roosevelt had the right to exercise any kind of veto on the choice of the Minister to be in attendance on the King, and on 14 March he sent a telegram of great length for the personal consideration of Neville Chamberlain.

In this he stated that 'owing to the exceptional significance of Their Majesties' visit and the many unforeseen as well as known questions which are certain to arise in the course of the Royal Tour' it had been decided that he himself should accompany the King and Queen throughout. No other arrangement would be acceptable, for, as he put it, 'my colleagues and I feel that we cannot, without permanent injury to Canada's present and future relations with the United States, afford to have our country, in the eyes of the American people and the people of other countries, subjected to a position in international affairs with its neighbour which we ourselves would regard as one of inferiority as compared with any other part of the British Commonwealth of Nations.' He also quoted Roosevelt, who in a letter to him had expressed the hope that the King would bring the Canadian Prime Minister with him as his ' "Minister in Attendance" or whatever they call it'.[13]

The decision of Mackenzie King and his colleagues was accepted. The King had privately expressed the feeling that 'it might be rather trying to have the same Minister in attendance throughout the whole of the royal progress of Canada and, incidentally, the United States.' There were Canadians too, particularly in the west, who questioned Mackenzie King's judgment. The Premier of British Columbia, for instance, was quoted as 'ridiculing a Prime Minister who never travels west of Toronto in the ordinary course of events but insists, even to the possible detriment of his health, in spending every moment he can with the King and Queen.'[14] But these were relatively minor criticisms, and in the event Mackenzie King's political instinct was to be proved right.

A bill was passed by the Canadian Parliament to enable certain royal functions to be performed in Canada, even though the royal seals remained in Britain, but in answer to an enquiry from Mackenzie King Hardinge telegraphed: 'The King has definitely decided not to bring the crown.'[15]

The planning of the visit to the United States was politically even more complex. Roosevelt was personally concerned with almost every detail, and in both concept and execution he showed masterly skill. At various stages he received valuable help from the British Ambassador, Sir Ronald Lindsay, who had an American wife and enjoyed a valuable relationship with the Roosevelt family. He was already due to retire, but it was decided that he should remain at his post until the end of the royal visit.

As soon as it was announced publicly in the USA that the visit would take place, doubts about its desirability were expressed. The distinguished columnist Walter Lippmann wrote that at a time when Congress was debating an unprecedented programme on rearmament the arrival of the King and Queen would 'revive suspicion of foreign interference and would disunite and distract American public opinion'. The Hearst press suggested bluntly that the visit was 'a manoeuvre to beguile the United States into something more than sympathy for Great Britain'.

Lindsay asked the President whether he had any misgivings about the wisdom of the visit. As he reported to the Foreign Office, the President's answer was 'an emphatic and unqualified negative'. Lindsay added: 'I myself concur. American rank and file has a very high sense of what is due to a guest and would never allow politics to be an embarrassment.'[16] In a letter to Sir Alexander Cadogan at the Foreign Office he wrote: 'I do not think that the King and Queen could have wisely proposed to come to the United States, making that the sole or main purpose of a journey. That would have given rise to every possible misunderstanding.' As an extension of the Canadian tour, however, the visit could be seen in a different light.

A complication arose from a visit which Anthony Eden paid to the United States late in December 1938. One of his purposes was to inform

Americans that Britain was readier to resist aggression than was commonly supposed. A broadcast speech of his reached a wide audience, and his good looks and dress style made a considerable impact. Unfortunately, this induced Senator Reynolds, a new member of the Senate Foreign Relations Committee, to declare: 'From Great Britain its handsome, broad-shouldered, fine-voiced Anthony Eden is sent to the United States to curry favour with full-blooded Americans, to blaze the way and to carpet the path that will be traversed by the King and Queen of England when they come to America to curry favour with the United States, all of them on bended knee, if not literally so, figuratively so.'

Irish opinion was also in places vociferous. A leaflet produced by Clan-na-Gael was printed in huge quantities for dropping from aircraft over Detroit. Its heading was 'THINK – AMERICANS – THINK.' Among the statements it contained was: 'As a result of English propaganda we were involved in a world war. No one questions this. Why should America extend the hand of welcome to England's crowned heads, when Americans groan under the burden of billions of dollars of defaulted payments on loans.'

Roosevelt accepted these as expressions of minority opinion which, for the purposes of planning the visit, he could ignore. A more delicate question was that of exactly where the royal couple should spend the rather limited time at their disposal.

Lindsay was at first in favour of a visit to Chicago, but accepted that this must be ruled out because of time and the facts of geography. Roosevelt favoured the spending of as much time as possible at Hyde Park. How much he was influenced by his desire to give the royal couple some time to rest and relax after the rigours of their Canadian journey, and how much by his own inclination to have them almost exclusively to himself, is debatable. In personal letters he submitted more than one draft programme to the King, and although the visit to Hyde Park remained a central feature of all of them, in the itinerary finally agreed rather more time was given to Washington than Roosevelt had envisaged.[17]

The Admiralty had made HMS *Repulse* available for the voyage of the King and Queen to Canada. But the King thought it unwise to take a battle-cruiser out of the fleet at a time of such international tension, and instead the Admiralty chartered the Canadian Pacific liner, *Empress of Australia*. Fog and the presence of an ice-field delayed the passage of the liner, and, as the King informed his mother by letter, there were those on board who had seen fit to remind the captain how near they were to the position where the *Titanic* was struck.[18] Quebec was eventually reached on 27 May 1939.

The 6000-mile journey across Canada was made by special train. One car contained the bedrooms, dressing-rooms, baths and sitting-room of the King and Queen. In another were the dining-room, offices and staff rooms. It was a form of accommodation with which the King and Queen were to become increasingly familiar in the course of World War II.

The visit was the first ever paid by a reigning sovereign to one of the self-governing dominions. As such it was certainly expected to arouse popular enthusiasm, but in fact the reception given to the King and Queen surpassed all expectations.

The Governor-General of Canada at the time was Lord Tweedsmuir, better known as novelist John Buchan. In a letter to his sister he described the visit to Ottawa, where, among other events, the King unveiled a war memorial. 'The Queen told me,' Tweedsmuir wrote, 'that she must go down among the troops, meaning the six or seven thousand veterans. I said it was worth risking it, and sure enough the King and Queen and Susie and I disappeared in that vast mob – simply swallowed up. The police could not get near us. I was quite happy about it because the veterans kept such admirable order.'[19]

This has been considered, perhaps correctly, as the genesis of subsequent royal walk-abouts. American press correspondents and Scotland Yard detectives appeared equally astonished. Giving his own impressions of the King and Queen, Tweedsmuir wrote: 'I have always been deeply attached to the King, and I realize now more than ever what a wonderful mixture he is of shrewdness, kindliness and humour. As for the Queen, she has a perfect genius for the right kind of publicity.'

In Dominion Square in Montreal, in the words of the *Financial Post*, 'the spontaneous acclaim of 100,000 French and English Canadians rose like a thunder-clap to the skies.' Of the warmth of this reception Sir Gerald Campbell, the United Kingdom High Commissioner in Canada, wrote that it was 'to some extent a surprise to well informed authorities', and that it 'gave the keynote to the rest of Canada.'[20]

'What started in Montreal,' the *Financial Post* correspondent who accompanied the royal party wrote, 'has reached a magnificent consummation across the western prairies. I believe the King has enjoyed more than anything else the informal spontaneity of these prairie celebrations. And little wonder! Think, of riding out of a prairie night into Melville, a town of under 4000 people in eastern Saskatchewan, and finding a teeming mass of 40,000 prairie dwellers assembled from distances of from 100 to 400 miles.' He went on to make the point that nearly everyone from an area as large as the province of New Brunswick had come, simply to catch a glimpse of their King and Queen.

Mackenzie King was understandably delighted. On his return to Canada, after accompanying the royal party to the United States, he wrote to the King: 'As never before, Canada has become conscious of its unity as a nation, and of the place it holds in the British Commonwealth . . . It has not been necessary to speak of loyalty – the nation has spoken for itself . . . What will perhaps please the Queen and yourself most is the added interest it has given everyone in all that pertains to the lives of Your Majesties and those of the other members of the Royal Family.'

A day earlier Mackenzie King had written to Sir Alan Lascelles. In view of their past differences it was indicative of his generosity, and of Lascelles's flexibility and tact, that he singled out as one of the great pleasures of the visit the opportunity it had given him of sharing responsibilities with Lascelles and of coming to know him better.[21]

Well-informed men who had been less personally involved than the Canadian Prime Minister, and who were therefore perhaps able to judge more objectively, were also much impressed by the visit itself and the impact it had made. The Chief Justice of the Superior Court of the Province of Quebec, R. A. E. Greenshields, declared that 'nothing has so stirred the people of Canada'. Sir Gerald Campbell, in a detailed analysis, wrote: 'The dominant feature has without doubt been the realisation by the people of the Sovereign and his Consort. Canada belonged to the King, but the King now belongs to Canada and I think that this attitude will last.'

The thoroughness with which an exhausting schedule had been carried out, the speeches given in French and English by both King and Queen and the contrast between their relaxed entourage and the heavily guarded presences of United States' and other European leaders all contributed, in Campbell's judgment, to the success of the visit. So did the fact that 'for some reason all classes appeared to expect them to be other than they are.'

'Cabinet Ministers of both races,' he went on, 'high military officers and judges have summed up their impressions in almost identical language. "If war breaks out now there will be no holding Canadians back," of French origin or otherwise.'[22]

On the evening of 9 June 1939 the royal party was greeted by Cordell Hull, the US Secretary of State, at the suspension bridge near Niagara Falls. It was the beginning of the first visit ever paid by a reigning British monarch to the United States.

Some three-quarters of a million people were estimated to have lined the streets of Washington the next day as the King and Queen were driven to the White House. There were visits to George Washington's tomb at Mount Vernon, to the Arlington Cemetery, to the Washington Navy Yard and to a Civilian Conservation Corps camp at Fort Hunt, Virginia. There was a drive too through the streets of New York. At the World's Fair the King and Queen visited the pavilions of the various Commonwealth countries represented. But it was at the Roosevelts' home in Hyde Park that the most important business was transacted. This was as the President had intended it to be.

Roosevelt's wife and son both published detailed accounts of the visit, and good facilities were afforded to the press at Hyde Park. The King made a favourable impression on the press corps by eating hot dogs and swimming in the grounds of the Roosevelts' home. The President, when offering the King a cocktail, said that his mother did not approve of them and thought he should have a cup of tea. The King, accepting a cocktail, said his mother did not approve of them either. Both King and President were too well-mannered to explain that the objections of their respective mothers to cocktails stemmed from wholly different prejudices – Queen Mary did not object to cocktails because alcohol was sinful, but because they were new and American.

The musical entertainment provided was, perhaps suitably, undemanding. Marian Anderson was the principal singer, the programme consisting mostly of negro spirituals, cowboy ballads and folk dances, with Schubert's 'Ave Maria' and Tchaikovsky's 'Pilgrim's Song' added for variety.

George VI was not the first British monarch to meet Franklin Roosevelt. George V had known him when he was Assistant Secretary to the US Navy in 1918 and had described him as 'a charming man'.[23] The charm also captivated his son. And after his return to Canada Mackenzie King wrote a letter which explained to the President the extent to which it did so: 'My dear Mr President: I almost wrote "My dear Franklin" for so indeed I feel, but my Scotch reserve gets the better of me whenever I begin to press too strongly.' He went on: 'I shall never be able to tell you what the visit to Washington and to Hyde Park, in company with Their Majesties, meant to me. What, however, I am even more grateful for, if that were possible, is what the visit meant to the King and Queen.'

After describing how the King had asked him to join him in his room Mackenzie King wrote: 'He told me that he had enjoyed his talks with yourself more than he had his talks with anyone else, that he found it easier to carry on a conversation with you than with almost anyone else, and that he had appreciated beyond words the welcome you had given him and the frank and open way in which you had talked over many matters.'[24]

Among the subjects which the President discussed with both the King and the Canadian Prime Minister was the defence of the American continent. On this his plans were precise and far-reaching. He spoke in particular about American naval patrols and made it clear that for these patrols to be fully effective bases would be needed in both Trinidad and Bermuda.[25]

The acquisition of bases in the West Indies was to be one of the great American diplomatic triumphs in World War II. The King was an early and ready advocate of the President's policy. As such he might perhaps be considered to have swallowed rather innocently the bait which the

President skilfully extended towards him. He might alternatively be acclaimed for sound judgment in appreciating that the deal, which involved the transfer of British bases, could benefit Britain as well as the United States.

He made careful notes of his conversations with the President, especially on the subject of likely American action in the event of war. One sentence he recorded was: 'If London was bombed USA would come in.'[26] How fully the King, and indeed the President, believed this statement remains open to speculation.

The British Ambassador, Sir Ronald Lindsay, was cautiously optimistic about the immediate political consequences of the visit. He thought it had been well handled so that it had appeared to be 'a natural event'. In consequence suspicions of political motives had been dulled. It would not, he believed, deter 'that minority of the Senate who are opposing the amendments of the neutrality law desired by the Administration', but he thought that if the US Government remained determined, resistance would become less effective.[27]

One unexpected consequence of the visit arose from the presence at some of the functions of President Roosevelt's intimate friend and adviser, Harry Hopkins, who was at that time Secretary of Commerce. Hopkins was later to tell Churchill's Private Secretary, John Colville, that he had at one time been anti-British and strongly opposed to the institution of monarchy. But then, on the night of the state banquet at the White House, Hopkins's young daughter was ill in bed and forbidden by her doctor even to catch a glimpse over the stairs of the King and Queen. She was bitterly disappointed, so the Queen, wearing jewels, tiara and the Order of the Garter, went to see her instead. Colville recorded Hopkins as saying: 'And that is how I first came to think you people must have some good in you after all.'[28] Hopkins was later to become Roosevelt's principal adviser on Britain's capacity to wage war and on how that capacity could best be sustained.

In retrospect the visit of the King and Queen to the United States in 1939 may be seen as a watershed in the conduct of British foreign policy. Until then, while the maintenance of Empire and Empire links was always a primary consideration, British diplomatic initiatives were directed mainly towards the countries of Europe. Indeed, after the Russian revolution of 1917 they were largely confined to western and central Europe. When a major, albeit abortive, attempt was made to bring peace and stability to the world at Munich in 1938, the only countries whose presence at the meeting was deemed necessary were Britain, France, Germany and Italy.

Undeniably the isolationism of the United States, particularly their refusal to join the League of Nations, had to some extent encouraged this attitude of mind. But after June 1939 the main direction of British policy changed abruptly. Alliance with the USA became a principal require-ment, and in almost every major issue account had to be taken not only of the United States Government but also, as often as not, of American public opinion.

The visit of the King and Queen was not the cause of this change, but it can well be seen as its first clear manifestation. It was also early evidence of the skill which before long would enable President Roosevelt to influence not only American foreign policy but also, to a large extent, that of the country which was to become his nation's closest wartime ally.

Large crowds greeted the King and Queen on their return to England, and on 23 June the King made a speech in the Guildhall in London in which he recalled his impressions of the visit. Of his speech Alan Lascelles wrote to Mackenzie King: 'I have never heard the King – or indeed few other people – speak so effectively, or so movingly.' In the same letter he wrote: 'I think it is no exaggeration at all to say that every one of us, from the King himself down . . . will always look back on the last seven weeks as the most stirring and most momentous episode in his whole life.'[29]

CHAPTER THIRTEEN

Outbreak of War
1939

On the day on which the King spoke in the Guildhall about his visit to North America it was announced that he and the Queen had accepted an invitation from the King of the Belgians to pay a state visit to Brussels in October. In the weeks which followed it became increasingly clear that the visit was unlikely to take place.

Neville Chamberlain and his fellow Ministers had been forced into the opinion that what little hope there might be of preventing war lay in showing Hitler beyond all possible doubt that Britain would actively resist any further German aggression. The King concurred in this, and on 3 July he offered, as a personal initiative, to talk to Philip of Hesse, who had married the king of Italy's daughter and was said to have ready access to Hitler.

'Do you think it would be possible,' he wrote to Chamberlain, 'to get him over here and to use him as a messenger to convey to Hitler that we really are in earnest?' He added: 'I have met Philip of Hesse, though some years ago, and he seemed to me then to be sensible. That was in 1930!'[1]

Chamberlain replied that he had recently heard from three different sources, including von Dirksen, who had replaced Ribbentrop as the German Ambassador in London, that 'Hitler does understand that we mean business this time.' He and Halifax decided that little purpose would be served by using Philip of Hesse as an intermediary.

As a gesture in support of the new Anglo-Polish alliance the King suggested on 10 July that the president of Poland should be added to the list of presidents to whom he sent congratulatory messages on their birthdays. The list was at that time limited to the presidents of the United States, France and Turkey. The Foreign Office pointed out that if the president of Poland were to be added to the list, so should the president of Britain's oldest ally, Portugal. The King accepted this.

At the end of July the King was involved in an effort to counteract the effects of Japanese, German and Italian anti-British propaganda in Afghanistan. He agreed to offer a personal birthday gift to King Zahir Shah, and the British Minister in Kabul was instructed to enquire whether a Rolls-Royce would be acceptable or whether he would prefer some other present. The cost, it was decided, would be borne by the government of India.[2]

These were pitiful attempts to stem the approaching flood, and even so efforts to combat the threat from the Rome–Berlin–Tokyo axis did not extend to seeking the support of the Soviet Union. That such a policy was not envisaged was indicated by a curious episode which occurred in July 1939.

At a dinner party Queen Mary learnt from the Brazilian Ambassador, Regis de Oliveira, that he was about to be recalled. Oliveira was the doyen – the most senior member – of the Diplomatic Corps, and his departure would mean that the next doyen would be the Soviet Ambassador, Ivan Maisky. Queen Mary informed the King, and Hardinge wrote to Lord Halifax: 'This situation will, in His Majesty's opinion, be rather awkward; and he is wondering if you feel that, without interfering too much in the domestic politics of Brazil, anything can be done to convey to the Brazilian Government how much the departure of Senhor de Oliveira will be regretted.'

The attempt was made, but the Brazilian Minister for Foreign Affairs, while expressing his satisfaction that Oliveira's presence in London was so much appreciated, insisted that the time for his retirement had come. Maisky had to be accepted as doyen.[3]

Increasingly during the summer of 1939 the King was in effect preparing himself for the role he would play in the years ahead. On Sunday 2 July, after attending morning service in Westminster Abbey, he reviewed a parade of national servicemen in Hyde Park in the afternoon. Later in the month he paid a visit with his family in the royal yacht *Victoria and Albert* to the Royal Naval College at Dartmouth. Lord Louis Mountbatten was also present, as was his nephew, Prince Philip. Early the next month the King reviewed 130 warships of the reserve fleet in Weymouth.

The King did manage to begin his annual summer holiday in Balmoral. A feature that year was the holding of his boys' camp, the last to take place, in the grounds of Abergeldie Castle, a property near Balmoral which was leased to the royal family. But the holiday did not last long. Late in August news was received of the agreement reached between Germany and the Soviet Union which became generally known as the Ribbentrop–Molotov pact. This provided, in accordance with historical precedent, for yet another partition of Poland, the fourth. It was also an unequivocal signal to Hitler that he could make his planned attack on Poland safe from Soviet intervention.

The King promptly returned to London and received a letter from Neville Chamberlain dated 23 August. This stated: 'Briefly, following the disclosure of the pact . . . it was decided that some immediate announcement must be made indicating that what had happened in no way altered the policy of this country or our determination to fulfil our pledges . . . When Parliament meets tomorrow it is our intention to ask for the passage into law of the Emergency Powers (Defence) Bill . . . I have been glad to be informed of Your Majesty's immediate return to London, and shall welcome the opportunity of a full discussion of the position tomorrow.'[4]

The King took the view that the new agreement between Germany and the Soviet Union might weaken the ties between Germany and Japan and asked whether he might with advantage send a friendly message to the Japanese Emperor. The suggestion was not pursued, nor was a last-minute proposal by the Canadian Prime Minister that the King might make a final direct appeal to Hitler. Final appeals to Hitler were in fact made by a number of heads of states, but they had no perceptible impact.

On 1 September German troops invaded Poland. Two days later Britain declared war. That evening the King broadcast a message to the nation, in which he said: 'For the sake of all that we ourselves hold dear, and of the world's order and peace, it is unthinkable that we should refuse to meet the challenge.' In a restrained, unhistrionic style which fitted the mood of the time, he added: 'War can no longer be confined to the battlefield. But we can only do the right as we see the right, and reverently commit our cause to God.'

Australia and New Zealand declared war on the same day as Britain. In the Canadian Parliament the decision to declare war was taken without a division. In the South African Parliament the vote in favour of war was narrow but decisive, and as a consequence a new government, with General Smuts as Prime Minister, replaced the government of General Herzog.

The only country of which the King was the titular head to remain neutral was Ireland, but Irish links with the Crown were already tenuous. This had been shown during the King's visit to Paris in 1938, when the Irish Minister, Art O'Briain, had informed the French Government that he would be 'effectivement absent'.[5]

In Britain the King was faced with limited changes in the government. Two months before war broke out Chamberlain had written to the King: 'I hear there were anxious rumours in the lobby this evening to the effect that my audience this morning was for the purpose of submitting the names of Winston and Anthony for positions in the Cabinet. When told that these were only idle rumours much relief was expressed.'[6]

With the outbreak of war Chamberlain modified his position, and Churchill and Eden became respectively First Lord of the Admiralty and

Secretary of State for the Dominions. A somewhat half-hearted overture to the main opposition parties was rejected.

Government actions in the early weeks of the war were largely defensive, and much concerned with the threat of aerial attacks on London and other great cities. One of the most important measures was the establishment of a radar chain round the coasts, and early in September a demonstration of this was staged for the benefit of the King when he visited Fighter Command Headquarters. This was given personally by Air Marshal Sir Hugh Dowding, the Commander-in-Chief.

The screen which the King was watching showed a large number of aircraft approaching the English coast, and the King understandably wanted to know what was happening. It was then discovered, to everyone's embarrassment, that the aircraft were not over the sea at all, that they belonged to the RAF, and that they had been sent up to intercept an aircraft which also proved to be British.[7]

Other early measures included the drawing up of plans for the accommodation of leading members of the government in Worcestershire, should the bombardment of London become too intensive. The Prime Minister and key members of his staff were to go to Spetchley Park, near Worcester. The heads of the three Service Departments were to be sent to Worcester, Droitwich and Malvern, and the War Cabinet was to meet in Hindlip Hall, which was comparatively near all three towns. Four servants were in fact installed in Spetchley Hall in December 1939, bringing with them a number of supplies. These included considerable quantities of foolscap envelopes, tinned pineapples and prunes. In the emergency plans no special provision seems to have been made for the Royal Family.

A personal problem which concerned the King in the first weeks of the war was that of the whereabouts and future employment of the Duke of Windsor. On 6 September the Duke of Windsor wrote to Winston Churchill from Antibes: 'It would greatly facilitate the Duchess' and my return to England if you could send a destroyer or other naval vessel.' Even though this might have been thought an extravagant demand in time of war, the King concurred, and the Duke and Duchess of Windsor reached England on board a destroyer commanded by Lord Louis Mountbatten.

The King and his brother had a friendly meeting, but after it the King wrote to Chamberlain: 'He seems very well, and not a bit worried as to the effects he left on people's minds as to his behaviour in 1936. He has forgotten all about it.'

A post was found for the Duke of Windsor on the staff of the British Military Mission to France with the rank of major-general, but before long he was complaining to Winston Churchill of 'fresh evidence of my brother's continued efforts to humiliate me by every means in his and his courtiers' power.' In particular he complained of 'an order issued by the King behind my back, which in effect imposes a ban on my entering areas occupied by British troops in France.'[8]

Churchill replied on 17 November, pointing out that offence had been taken when the Duke had visited the British GHQ in France and himself taken the salute, although the Commander-in-Chief had been present. The Duke's proposal that he should visit the RAF in France in the uniform of an Air Chief Marshal was also objected to, and the Duke's conduct had even been considered at a meeting attended by the three Service Ministers and the three Chiefs of Staff. On that occasion, Churchill wrote, 'it was decided that Your Royal Highness, having accepted active employment as a major-general, ought to adhere to this uniform and rank.'[9]

In the diplomatic field in the latter half of 1939 the King was both active and effective. King Boris of Bulgaria had expected to pay one of his frequent visits to Britain in September 1939 and to stay at Balmoral. The outbreak of war prevented him from coming and instead George VI sent him a long and friendly letter which expressed the British Government's appreciation of the neutral attitude to which Bulgaria was adhering.

The King added: 'I sincerely hope that Bulgaria will, as I am sure she wishes to do, maintain that neutrality in all circumstances. You can, of course, rest assured that neutrality will be respected in the fullest degree by my Empire so long as it is not violated by others.'[10]

Sir George Rendel, the British Minister in Sofia, delivered the letter in person to King Boris on 22 September and described him as 'deeply touched'. King Boris, he wrote, 'went on to speak in the warmest terms of His Majesty the King, a subject to which he returned more than once later in the conversation.'

On the origins of the war, Rendel wrote, 'His Majesty agreed that Herr Hitler, whom he long regarded as having lost touch with realities, had probably never believed that we should come in against him.' King Boris replied to King George with a cordial letter, which was written in French and began 'Cher Bertie'.[11]

The maintenance of Bulgarian neutrality, which was clearly in British interests, was to remain the hope of King Boris and an objective which he pursued as long as he could. His efforts were more effective than might have been expected, though they had steadily diminishing prospects of success.

Late in September, after a treaty of alliance between Britain, France and Turkey had been initialled in London, a military mission from Turkey headed by a formidable soldier, General Mehmet Orbay, arrived with the object of purchasing armaments. Little could be spared from either Britain or France; Orbay did not conceal his disappointment, and since

Above left: Prince Albert and Prince Edward on the beach at Osborne, Isle of Wight

Above right: When very young indeed

Below left: Princess Mary watches her elder brothers salute

Below right: Family group: Prince Albert, Princess Mary, Prince Edward, Prince Henry, Prince John, Prince George

Above left: Naval cadet

Above right: With fellow cadets at Niagara, June 1913

Below left: Riding a motorcycle to lectures at Cambridge

Below right: Brooklands, 1922. The Earl of Athlone and Duke of York talk to S.E. Woods

Above left: Christening of future King Peter of Yugoslavia. He is in the arms of his grandmother, Queen Marie of Roumania. Others *left to right:* King Alexander of Yugoslavia, Queen Sophia of Greece, King Ferdinand of Roumania, Duke and Duchess of York

Above right: On honeymoon at Polesden Lacey

Below left: At the Wembley Exhibition, 1925

Below right: Partnering Louis Greig in the men's doubles at Wimbledon

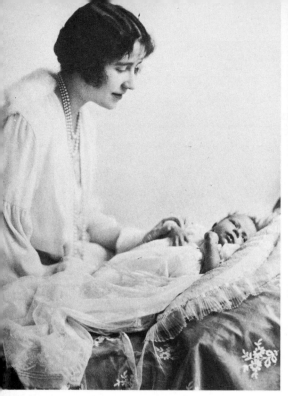

Above left: The Duchess of York with the future Queen Elizabeth, aged one month

Above right: The Duchess brings a teddy bear back from East Ham in 1926, the year of the General Strike

Below: Garden party at Glamis Castle, July 1931. Princess Margaret is in the pram

the British Government attached importance to maintaining his goodwill, not least because the Soviet Union also was seeking a pact with Turkey, the King was asked to receive him. This he did, with evident effect. After the meeting General Ismay wrote about Orbay's visit to Hardinge: 'One cannot but think that he would have gone away a disappointed man, if it had not been for the tremendous impression created upon him by his private audience with the King.'[12] The Anglo–French–Turkish treaty was duly signed.

In October a personal approach was made to King George by King Leopold, who asked in what form active help could be given to Belgium. King George consulted Lord Halifax, who pointed out that unless Belgium were willing to enter into discussions involving the military staffs of both countries little could be offered. In a memorandum which he sent to the King after their discussion Halifax stated that 'the Belgian Government were of the opinion that in the present circumstances there was little foundation for the hypothesis that Germany would launch an attack through Belgium.'[13]

The next month King Leopold appealed again to King George, this time in conjunction with Queen Wilhelmina of the Netherlands. The two sovereigns offered to act as mediators, their purpose to prevent the war from spreading further. The letter claimed that 'the belligerent parties have declared they would not unwillingly examine a reasonable and well-founded basis for an equitable peace.' In making this appeal King Leopold was influenced by the promptings of Germans opposed to the Nazi regime. Probably for this reason King George was disinclined to reject the appeal entirely, and he discussed with Lord Hankey the possibility of offering to discuss terms with the German people, but not with Hitler or his government. Hankey, not unreasonably regarding this suggestion as naive, advised the King to discuss it with Chamberlain.[14]

Chamberlain did in fact prepare a draft answer which might have implied that he was not entirely closing the door. It contained the statement that he would 'heartily welcome' any steps taken by King Leopold and Queen Wilhelmina 'which might avert or even postpone the outbreak of active warfare'. But this draft was shown to Churchill, who pointed out that it could be interpreted as authorising King Leopold 'to open another channel of negotiation with Hitler.'

Chamberlain, who was suffering badly from gout at the time, wrote back: 'I should not have thought that my draft would bear the interpretation you put upon it, but I don't attach any importance to the words as I am sure nothing could come of King Leopold's efforts.' A suitably uncompromising reply was therefore sent by the King, although twenty members of the Labour Party wrote to Chamberlain to express support for the Belgian-Dutch initiative.

On 23 October 1939 the King wrote a long letter to Mountbatten. Its

immediate purpose was to ask him to keep a friendly eye on a young
protégé, the Marquess of Graham, who would be serving under
Mountbatten. He went on: 'I saw Philip of Greece on his return here, and
I told him he had much better return to Dartmouth till Xmas, when we
can review his position again. Has he communicated with you lately?

'You never told me how David's trip went off. I only saw him on his
own while he was here, not a very pleasant interview but quite friendly. I
thought he had not changed one bit, but perhaps his behaviour was rather
forced. He did not seem to think he had done anything wrong . . .

'I have had an awful cold but have at last got rid of it. It was just through
getting over tired.

'I wish I had a definite job like you. Mine is such an awful mixture
trying to keep people cheered up in all ways, and having to find fault as
well as praising them.'[15]

The King made a practice of always wearing uniform when appearing in
public. The Queen, by contrast, having come to the conclusion that
uniforms did not suit her, sensibly decided not to wear them. Of the
numerous visits the King made to units of the armed forces late in 1939
perhaps the most important was that to the British Army in France in
December. Because it was widely reported in the French press it
considerably increased the awareness of people in France that there were
in fact British fighting forces in their country.

The King had discussions with the French and British Commanders-
in-Chief, General Gamelin and Lord Gort, as well as with political
leaders, and, in spite of the intense cold and other physical discomforts,
seems to have absorbed something of the general air of optimism. A visit
was later paid to General Alexander at his headquarters in a chateau at
Bersée, when, according to one of Alexander's biographers, the royal
party 'radiated the confidence which Alexander did not share'.[16]

When the King had been about to leave for France Chamberlain had
informed him of a conversation he had had with General Ironside, the
Chief of the Imperial General Staff. 'He gave me,' Chamberlain wrote, 'a
very reassuring account of the line which he believes to be impregnable,
but he says the ground is in a terrible condition. He never saw it so bad in
the last war.'[17]

Unlike the Army in France the Royal Navy was engaged from the
outset in active warfare, and in consequence the King had on 19 December
one of his more satisfying tasks to perform. This was an investiture, when
he bestowed the first naval decorations of the war, two DSOs, one DSC
and two DSMs. They were awarded for the recovery and detonation of an
unexploded mine which had fallen into the mud near Shoeburyness.[18]

In the latter part of 1939 the Queen, no doubt in order to learn more of
what Britain was facing, read Hitler's *Mein Kampf*. On 15 October she
sent a copy of the book to Lord Halifax with a note stating: 'I do not

advise you to read it through, or you might go mad, and that would be a great pity. Even a skip through gives one an idea of his mentality, ignorance and obvious sincerity.'[19]

The King found himself impressed by a poem, which was the work of a little-known writer named Marie Louise Haskins. In preparing his Christmas broadcast that year he had the help of Lord Baldwin, but he also decided to include some lines by Miss Haskins, which began: 'I said to the man who stood at the gate of the year, "Give me a light that I may tread safely into the unknown".' This broadcast, possibly because a few months of war had served to bring the King closer to large numbers of people, made a deeper impact, it was generally acknowledged, than any of the Christmas broadcasts he had given before.

CHAPTER FOURTEEN

The Prospect of Defeat
1940

On 3 March 1940 the King recorded in his diary: 'The war in its first six months has been one of words and propaganda. The Nazi regime is very good at it and preaches by this means of its greatness. There have been several "peace" moves and "scares" that Germany would invade Holland and Belgium, or else the Balkans.'[1]

The initiative remained wholly with Germany during this period, and British policy was a blend of largely passive resistance to the main threat and a search for action elsewhere, much of it ill-advised. At one stage plans were agreed for sending British volunteers to help Finland, whose territory had been invaded by Soviet forces at the end of November 1939. In France the Daladier Government advocated the despatch of four divisions to Finland. The overcoming of Finnish resistance in March 1940 prevented either intention from being carried out. Plans for offensive action in Scandinavia, in order to prevent supplies of iron ore from reaching Germany, were equally abortive.

Awareness of how little was being achieved led to divisions within the Government, and also to structural changes, which were discussed with the King early in 1940.

During his visit to the British Expeditionary Force in France in December the King had been made aware of the antagonism felt by Lord Gort and other high-ranking officers towards the War Minister, Leslie Hore-Belisha. Chamberlain decided that Hore-Belisha must go, and on 9 January Hore-Belisha came to Buckingham Palace to hand in his seals of office. The King was reported to have said to him that no man could have done more than he did.

Churchill was more specific. 'The outstanding achievement of your tenure of the War Office,' he wrote, 'was the carrying of conscription in time of peace.'[2] Hore-Belisha had also been a strong advocate of extending the Maginot Line as far as the coast.

In March Chamberlain decided to reshape his Government, largely in order to make control of the conduct of operations simpler and more efficient. He informed the King in advance of his proposals, and on 25 March the King wrote to him: 'Your intention of having a War Cabinet, whose members will be concerned with co-ordination rather than with departmental duties, seems to me a very sound one, and I hope also that the Opposition will accept your invitation to join.'

The opposition parties did not do as the King had hoped. The King also wrote in his letter: 'I cannot help feeling a little apprehensive of the criticisms which might arise if there were not a leavening of younger men in such a War Cabinet.'

The lack of fighting in western Europe in the winter of 1939–40 was due to the German High Command having decided that the best time to launch a major offensive was the spring. This was not generally understood in Britain, where the appearance of stalemate led the advocates of a negotiated peace to press their claims. An inordinate amount of Chamberlain's time was at this period spent in arguing by correspondence with the supporters of a peace settlement. To the King's slight embarrassment one of the more persistent of these was the Duke of Gloucester's brother-in-law, the Duke of Buccleuch, who was a Privy Councillor and before the war had been a prominent admirer of Hitler.

Such evidence as there was of successful British military action was understandably seized upon with enthusiasm by the British press and public. One such action occurred in February 1940, when Captain Philip Vian, commanding HMS *Cossack*, located the German ship *Altmark* near Bergen. The *Altmark* had 299 British prisoners of war on board. Vian sent in a raiding party, who succeeded in releasing all the prisoners.

The King sent a message of congratulation to Churchill, who replied: 'The knowledge which we all have at the Admiralty that Your Majesty watches every step we take with keen and experienced eye is a stimulus in the heavy and anxious work we have.'[3]

Towards the end of January 1940 information was received of the impending arrival of the first of the important visitors whom President Roosevelt was to send to wartime Britain. This was Sumner Welles, the US Under-Secretary of State. The Marquess of Lothian, the British Ambassador in Washington, telegraphed: 'I am sure I need not emphasize the desirability of every attention and courtesy being paid to Mr Sumner Welles, who, as you know, has distinct views regarding his own importance.' The American Ambassador in London, Joseph Kennedy, informed Halifax that the purpose of the visit was 'to place the President in a position to judge whether there was or was not the possibility of finding the way of settlement.'[4] By 'settlement' Kennedy clearly meant peace with Germany.

Sumner Welles arrived on 11 March. The next afternoon he had a meeting with Halifax, followed by an audience of the King and tea at Buckingham Palace. A brief was prepared for the King, the closing sentences of which were: 'Germany . . . hopes to dominate Europe if not the world, as Dr Goebbels admitted in his Posen speech. Public opinion in Great Britain is united in its firm resolution to defeat this aim but is prepared to lay down arms the moment this has been achieved.'[5]

Two important decisions affecting the King's family were made early in 1940. At the beginning of the year Princess Elizabeth and Princess Margaret were brought south from Scotland, Princess Elizabeth celebrating her fourteenth birthday at Windsor. The King had decided to continue the practice of educating royal children privately rather than in schools, but, unlike his father, he was determined that his own children should be instructed by people of true distinction. Princess Elizabeth's education was placed under the care of the Provost of Eton, Sir Henry Marten, from whom she learnt much of constitutional and imperial history.[6]

On 9 April 1940 German forces invaded Denmark and Norway. That afternoon the King visited the War Room at the Admiralty. It was an indication of the frustration he felt at not being an active member of the fighting services that in the evening he recorded in his diary: 'Everyone working at fever heat except me.'[7]

British naval forces were soon engaged, and at home there was an outbreak of optimism, which the press for the most part encouraged. The King was to some extent affected by this, and on 12 April he wrote to Winston Churchill, who was now not only in charge of the Admiralty but Chairman of the Coordinating Committee responsible for the general conduct of operations.

'I have been wanting to have a talk with you about the recent striking events in the North Sea, which, as a sailor, I have naturally followed with the keenest interest, but I have purposely refrained from taking up any of your time.' The King went on: 'I would like to congratulate you on the splendid way in which, under your direction, the Navy is countering the German move against Scandinavia.' Characteristically he ended his letter: 'I also beg of you to take care of yourself and get as much rest as you possibly can in these critical days.'[8]

The Scandinavian campaign was a swift and decisive victory for the Germans. The hopes aroused in Britain served to increase the shock felt once defeat had occurred. Nor was it forgotten that less than a week before the German invasion Chamberlain, in a direct reference to Norway, had said: 'Hitler has missed the bus.' Demands for a change of government became more insistent, particularly in the House of Commons.

Chamberlain was by then a tired and sick man. In fact he had little more than six months to live. His huge earlier following had derived largely from the public's image of him as a safe leader who could be relied on to preserve the country from war. As a war leader he had aroused no enthusiasm. Politically, a man exclusively of the Conservative party, by 1940 he had little following outside it. The Labour leaders did not like him personally, and he had none of the talent for cross-party camaraderie with which more flexible politicians are often endowed.

On 8 May forty-four Conservative members voted against the Government in a division. Although the Government still had a clear majority, this was taken as a call for Chamberlain's dismissal. Josiah Wedgwood, an Independent member, led the singing of 'Rule Britannia', and Leopold Amery quoted Cromwell's words to the Long Parliament: 'You have been here too long for any good you have been doing.'

For two days the question of who would lead the Government remained undecided, and before it was settled German forces invaded the Netherlands and Belgium.

Chamberlain hoped for a time to remain as head of a Coalition Government, but Attlee and Sir Archibald Sinclair, the leaders of the Labour and Liberal parties, made it clear they would not serve under him. Chamberlain then favoured Halifax as his successor. The King was distressed by the attempts to remove Chamberlain. In this he was influenced by characteristic, albeit excessive, loyalty. He too favoured Halifax as Chamberlain's successor, and indeed in his record of his discussion with Chamberlain he wrote: 'I, of course, suggested Halifax.' This was a serious error of judgment. Many years later Harold Macmillan was to tell the truth starkly when he wrote: 'The talk of Halifax as Prime Minister was absurd, not because he was a peer, but because he was absolutely unfitted to the task.'[9]

Fortunately Halifax was also a man of the highest integrity with no excessive ambitions. To this the nation owed, to a considerable extent, the appointment of its greatest war leader. Once Halifax had indicated his reluctance to take office the King had little choice other than to ask Churchill to form a new Government. This he did on 10 May. In doing so he was fulfilling the expectations of his first Prime Minister, Stanley Baldwin, who in 1935, after deciding not to appoint Churchill to office, had written: 'Everything he undertakes he puts his heart and soul into. If there is going to be a war – and no one can say that there is not – we must keep him fresh to be our war Prime Minister.'[10]

The Netherlands and Belgium were soon overrun. Queen Wilhelmina telephoned King George from the Hague to ask for help from the RAF. This had little effect, and soon afterwards she left Holland by destroyer for England, where a Dutch Government in exile was to be established. As an immediate measure she was given accommodation in Buckingham Palace.

King Leopold of the Belgians took a different decision. Admiral of the Fleet Sir Roger Keyes, sailor and politician, who had had a distinguished record in World War I, was serving as special liaison officer with him, and on 22 May he informed Churchill that the Belgian Government was trying to persuade the King to leave the country before the army capitulated. Keyes added: 'Of course he has no intention of deserting his army, and he considers he can serve his country better by staying there rather than as a fugitive with a Government which represents no one while outside the country.'

King George had already telegraphed King Leopold offering to look after his children in Britain. To this King Leopold replied that his children had already reached France. He added: 'Your thought has deeply touched me. I thank you both. My affectionate greetings.'

In the words of Sir Roger Keyes the Belgian Army 'was held together and fought bravely for seventeen days, under dispiriting conditions of retirement forced upon them, thanks to the inspiration of King Leopold.'[11] In the end the King felt compelled to surrender.

In Britain the overwhelming successes of the Germans against British and Allied forces alike caused profound shock. To assuage national pride some sections of the press looked for a scapegoat. In a peculiarly shameful manner King Leopold was chosen, one tabloid paper even seeing fit to describe him as 'King Rat'.

King George shared the view of the British Government that, with Germany in total control, the proper place for King Leopold as monarch was in Britain. He therefore made a thoughtful appeal to him on 25 May. 'I note,' he stated, 'that Your Majesty considers it to be your duty to your people and to your allies to remain with your Army in Belgium. In taking this decision Your Majesty will not have overlooked the extreme importance of preserving a united Belgian Government with full authority outside the territory occupied by the enemy, and while paying tribute to Your Majesty's devotion I and my Government must express our grave concern at your decision.'

He conceded that it would be 'presumptuous' to advise King Leopold on his duty to his people, but called attention to the possibility that he might be taken prisoner, 'perhaps carried off to Germany, and almost certainly deprived of all communication with the outside world'. This would leave the Belgian people 'bereft of their natural leader'.[12]

King Leopold did not change his decision. King George continued to respect him for this, while believing that he had failed to distinguish properly between his different functions as King and as Commander-in-Chief.

The defeat of the Dutch and Belgian armies was followed by disaster on a much larger scale in France. The French Army, which less than a decade earlier had been the most powerful military force in the world, was overwhelmed, and with it the much smaller British Expeditionary Force. For Churchill's new Government, policy and strategy consisted of salvaging what it could from the impending wreckage.

On 23 May Churchill was received by the King at 10.30 in the evening – during the extremity of the crisis his meetings with the King were more frequent than usual. He told the King that the BEF would probably have to be evacuated from France, and that this would mean the loss of virtually all its heavy equipment including tanks and guns. The next day, which was Empire Day, the King was to broadcast to the nation. The time had clearly come to abandon the facile optimism which had been so prevalent in Britain since the outbreak of the war. It was even more important to offer no suggestion of defeatism or despair.

One of the many great services which Churchill rendered in 1940 was unfailingly to find the right balance of realism and hope when telling the nation what its prospects were. The King lacked Churchill's power of oratory, but he was able to strike an equally appropriate note. 'Let no one think that my confidence is dimmed,' he said, 'when I tell you how perilous is the ordeal which we are facing. On the contrary, it shines in my heart as brightly as it shines in yours. But confidence alone is not enough. It must be armed with courage and resolution, with endurance and self-sacrifice.'

The Commander-in-Chief, Lord Gort, did not believe that a high proportion of the British troops would be successfully evacuated from France. His doubts were shared by the Chiefs of Staff in London, and with hindsight it is clear that the German forces could well have prevented the escape of large numbers. Nevertheless at Dunkirk and elsewhere British and French troops continued to be embarked, and day by day the King noted in his diary the numbers. On 3 June he wrote: 'The last of the BEF have been evacuated.' The next day he wrote to Churchill: 'I wish to express my admiration of the outstanding skill and bravery shown by the three Services and the Merchant Navy in the evacuation.'

For a time the intention was to land British forces in France to continue the struggle, but during the first half of June it became clear that effective resistance in France would soon cease. Various expedients were tried to sustain a spirit of defiance. One of them was suggested by a junior French general and minister in the Government, Charles de Gaulle, who had escaped to Britain to continue the fight. This was a proclamation of union between France and Britain. A document to this effect was prepared in Downing Street, John Colville, the Prime Minister's Private Secretary, noting in his diary: 'Meanwhile the King does not know what is being done to his Empire.' Neville Chamberlain, as Lord President of the Council, went to the Palace to tell him.[13]

This startling departure from centuries-old national policy never in practice came into effect, and its proclamation had no influence on events. On 16 June Marshal Pétain formed a new Government and began to sue for armistice terms. Less than a week earlier Italy had entered the war on the German side.

With the defeat of France, suggestions that Britain should make peace came in from a number of quarters. In Britain the National Peace Council, headed by C. E. M. Joad, wrote to Lord Halifax that 'His Majesty's Government should invite the German Chancellor to indicate in precise terms the character of the peace which he desires.' Monsignor William Godfrey, the Apostolic Delegate in London, also wrote to Halifax, informing him that 'the Holy Father . . . has in mind, of his own initiative, to approach the Governments of Germany, Italy and England, appealing to them to make an effort of common agreement to bring this conflict to an end.' On this Churchill commented: 'I hope it will be made clear to the Nuncio that we do not desire to make any enquiries as to terms of peace with Hitler.'[14]

To the King Churchill's policy seemed self-evidently right. 'How can we talk peace with Germany now,' he wrote in his diary, 'after they have overrun and demoralised the people of so many countries in Europe?' As just one small expression of his own attitude he had a shooting range set up in the grounds of Buckingham Palace, where he and members of his family and his staff practised with various small arms.[15]

The King's personal safety was nevertheless a cause of concern to the Government. On 19 June the Lord Chancellor, Lord Hailsham, wrote to Churchill to propose that the King's daughters should be sent to Canada. 'I observe,' he wrote, 'that the Nazis both in Norway and Holland made a desperate attempt to capture the Royal Family; no doubt they will do the same in this country if they can . . . So far as the King himself is concerned, I have looked into the question and I think that the Regency Act passed in 1937 gives sufficient protection to enable us to put the royal power into Commission in the event of his being captured; and I think you will agree that it would be disastrous to suggest that he should leave the country – and probably he would not go!'

The King indeed had no intention of leaving the country. Nor had the Queen, and they decided that their daughters should stay in Britain too. A special unit was however formed from the Brigade of Guards to provide protection for the royal family against German parachutists.

The President of the United States also was personally concerned about the safety of the King. He and Cordell Hull had a number of talks with Mackenzie King in Ottawa on the action to be taken if Britain were to be overrun. In that event Roosevelt hoped that the centre of what he called 'imperial as distinct from domestic authority' would be in Ottawa. In a discussion on 26 May he said that he did not know much about the British constitution, but added that 'the Empire had done so many strange constitutional acrobatics in the past that it should not be difficult to separate the "Imperial Council" from the local United Kingdom administration.'

It was with some hesitation that the President suggested the King might come to Canada, and Hull intervened to say this would have an adverse political effect in the United States. He and the President then agreed that it would be used by their political opponents to accuse the President of 'establishing monarchy on the North American continent'. Bermuda, it was felt, would be a more suitable temporary refuge.[16]

Churchill was little concerned with such refinements. What he wanted from the United States was active help, particularly through the provision of destroyers, and he instructed Lord Lothian in Washington to try to obtain these. 'If Great Britain broke under invasion,' he telegraphed, 'a pro-German government might obtain far easier terms from Germany by surrendering the fleet, thus making Germany and Japan masters of the new world. This dastard deed would not be done by His Majesty's present advisers, but if some Quisling Government was set up, it is exactly what they would do, and perhaps the only thing they could do, and the President should bear this very clearly in mind. You should talk to him in this sense and discourage any complacent assumption on United States' part that they will pick up the debris of the British Empire.'[17]

At this lowest point in British fortunes both the King and Churchill found themselves spending an inordinate amount of time trying to solve problems presented by the Duke of Windsor. As the German armies advanced, the Duke somewhat precipitately left his post in Paris to join the Duchess in Biarritz. From there they made their way to Madrid. Fearing they might be captured and exploited by the Germans, Churchill wanted them to return to Britain as soon as possible. The King shared Churchill's feelings. So did Hardinge, who, after reading some documents concerning the Duchess, wrote to one of Churchill's Pivate Scretaries: 'This is not the first time that this lady has come under suspicion for her anti-British activities, and as long as we never forget the power that she can exert over him in her efforts to avenge herself on this country we shall be all right.'[18]

The Duke refused to return unless the Duchess were accorded what he considered suitable recognition. 'My wife and myself,' he telegraphed Churchill, 'must not risk finding ourselves once more regarded by the British public as in a different status to other members of my family.'

The suggestion was then put forward that the Duke might be appointed Governor-General of the Bahamas. Lord Lloyd, Secretary of State for the Colonies, discussed this with the King and reported that the King had said: 'Tell him to do what he is told.' The offer was therefore telegraphed to Sir Samuel Hoare, who was now Ambassador in Madrid, and the Duke accepted, informing Churchill on 31 July: 'I naturally do not consider my appointment as one of first-class importance.'

Until their actual departure the danger that the Duke and Duchess might fall into German hands remained. To inform the Prime Ministers of the Dominions of the appointment Churchill personally drafted a telegram, which contained the sentence: 'The activities of the Duke of Windsor on the Continent in recent months have been causing His Majesty and myself grave uneasiness, as his inclinations are well-known to be pro-Nazi and he may become a centre of intrigue.' The sentence was omitted from the telegram as sent.[19]

There was indeed a German plan to capture the Duke and Duchess but, like much else which the Germans did or tried to do in clandestine warfare, it was bungled.

During the months of almost uninterrupted disaster in the summer of 1940 Churchill and the King established an excellent working and personal relationship. The King, like most other people, quickly appreciated that as the leader of a beleaguered nation Churchill was incomparable. Churchill, for his part, revered the institution of monarchy and had a personal liking for the King. He was conscientious in keeping the King informed of policy and events, upsetting him only by periodic lapses into unpunctuality.

When the new Government was being formed the King questioned the appointment of Lord Beaverbrook to ministerial office. This was not unreasonable, for Beaverbrook's record as a politician was erratic and somewhat disreputable. Nor could the King see any reason, other than his personal loyalty to Churchill, why Brendan Bracken should be made a Privy Councillor. Churchill stood by his original recommendations. Bracken before very long was to be a successful Minister of Information, and there were advantages in securing the wholehearted commitment to the Government of such a brilliantly successful newspaper proprietor and dedicated propagandist as Beaverbrook.

Churchill's Government was to differ greatly from its predecessor in both its method of functioning and its composition. Churchill himself had the immense advantage of having held responsible office in an earlier world war, and he knew how different the conduct of government has to be in war and in peace.

To exercise supreme control of operations he worked directly with the Chiefs of Staff rather than the Service Ministers. He was also constantly in touch with those aspects of foreign affairs which directly affected the conduct of the war. Home affairs he left largely to the other members of the Cabinet, apart from periodic sorties into particular events which took his fancy.

In its composition the Government was a true coalition, but with one curious emphasis. The three most important ministers concerned with home affairs were all members of the Labour Party. As Deputy Prime Minister Attlee was chairman of a number of coordinating committees. The Home Secretary was Herbert Morrison. The Minister of Labour was Ernest Bevin. During the winter of 1940–41 home affairs were to be the King's principal preoccupation as the war began to involve civilians in a manner without precedent in the nation's history.

CHAPTER FIFTEEN

Civilians' War

1940

The King shared the belief held by a number of senior members of his armed forces that the Germans would try to invade Britain in the late summer of 1940. Hugh Dalton, the Minister of Economic Warfare, recorded in his diary that the King had told him the date fixed for the invasion was 1 August.[1] On 5 August the King wrote to Neville Chamberlain, who had recently undergone an operation: 'From what I have seen lately "that man" will receive a hot reception if he does try and come here. But I feel that he must make the attempt this summer.'[2]

The preliminary to the planned invasion was a massive air attack which began in the middle of August. The main targets were, first, Channel shipping and ports, then fighter airfields, and then London. During this period the King visited a number of stations of Fighter Command. Soon after he arrived at Northolt, where a Polish squadron was stationed, his inspection had to be called off to allow the squadron to go into action. On that day alone the RAF made 417 sorties.[3]

On 24 August the King visited another Allied unit, the so-called Free French forces commanded by General de Gaulle. Recalling the occasion later, de Gaulle wrote: 'King George VI came to visit our little army. To see it, one could well believe that "the stump of the blade" would be toughly tempered. But heavens! how short it was!' The King he described as 'exemplary and always informed'.[4]

On 9 September a bomb was dropped beside Buckingham Palace, but did not explode. Three days later the King was working with Hardinge in the palace when they saw two bombs fall some thirty yards away. Windows were shattered, two great craters were formed in the quadrangle, and the chapel was wrecked. The King and Queen immediately made a tour of the whole basement, where they learnt that none of the staff had been hurt. In reply to a message from the War Cabinet the King stated: 'Like so many of our people, we have now had a personal experience of German barbarity which only strengthens the resolution of all of us to fight through to final victory.'

In Churchill's words, 'the King, who as a sub-lieutenant had served in the Battle of Jutland, was exhilarated by all this, and pleased that he should be sharing the dangers of his subjects in the capital.'[5] This was almost certainly an accurate, rather than a romantic assessment. Even as sophisticated an observer as Harold Nicolson, after lunching in the company of the King and Queen and Lord Gort, wrote in his diary: 'What astonished me is how the King has changed. He is not like his brother. He was so gay and she so calm. Gort was simple and modest. And those two resolute and sensible. We shall win, I know that. I have no doubts at all.'[6]

A new offer to mediate in search of peace was rejected in August almost with disdain. This came from King Gustav of Sweden. On it Churchill commented uncompromisingly: 'The intrusion of the ignominious King of Sweden as a peace-maker, after his desertion of Finland and Norway, and while he is absolutely in the German grip, though not without its encouraging aspect, is singularly distasteful.' King George's reply was courteous, but ended: 'No useful purpose would be served by a meeting such as Your Majesty contemplates between representatives of Great Britain and Germany.'[7]

By October German plans for the invasion of Britain had been abandoned and the Battle of Britain, the first major contest of the war in which the British achieved any success, had been won.

Early in October the King received a letter from Neville Chamberlain informing him that because of the state of his health he had placed his resignation in Churchill's hands. In it Chamberlain wrote: 'I cannot contemplate the termination of my relations with you, Sir, as a Minister, without a good deal of emotion. Broadly speaking, I was your first Prime Minister and I shall always recall with gratitude the confidence which you have been good enough to give me and the increasing intimacy of our conversations which were so encouraging and helpful to me during one of the most anxious and difficult periods which have ever faced a Minister in all our long history.'[8]

Late in October 1940 Churchill came to the conclusion that in concentrating attacks on London the Germans had made a mistake. They were trying, he wrote to Chamberlain, 'to intimidate a people whom they have only infuriated.' A wiser policy, he thought, would be to bomb factories. This the Germans very soon did, and on the night of 14–15 November a devastating raid was made on Coventry. The King decided to go there without delay. He arrived on the 16th, to be met by, among others, Herbert Morrison, the Home Secretary. He spent more than five hours among the ruins. For years afterwards Morrison spoke with admiration of the effect of the King's visit.

Visits to other bombed cities, including Birmingham, Bristol and Southampton, soon followed, and the effect of the King's visits was much as it had been in Coventry. As sovereigns the King and the Queen did not, and were not expected to, share the deprivations of those who suffered from poverty, unemployment or other social afflictions. But they did share, and were seen to share, the consequences of enemy action. This brought them closer to the nation as a whole than almost any other circumstance could have done. Churchill expressed the feeling which was evident in the country when he wrote to the King: 'This war has drawn the Throne and the people more closely together than was ever before recorded.'[9]

In recognition of the nature of the war the King decided that two new awards should be instituted. The subject of medals and other decorations interested him deeply. He had a considerable collection at Windsor, and the design of the new awards was largely his own work. These were to be known as the George Cross and the George Medal, and they would be conferred for acts of conspicuous courage in circumstances of extreme danger. They were intended primarily for civilians, but members of the armed forces might receive them for appropriate actions of a kind which would not normally qualify for military honours. The new awards, which would rank immediately after the Victoria Cross, were announced by the King in a broadcast on 23 September.

In the autumn of 1940 the intervention of the King was called for in delicate negotiations which were being conducted with the Government established under Marshal Pétain in Vichy. While de Gaulle's Free French movement was accepted in Britain as a rallying-point, importance was attached to maintaining some form of contact with Pétain's government – especially since reports had been received that the Vichy Government was considering handing over the French fleet to the Germans.

On 25 October the King sent a personal message to Pétain through Sir Samuel Hoare in Lisbon. It began: 'At this serious juncture in the life of the British and French peoples I send you a message of goodwill.'

After pointing out that French ports and airfields were being used by the Germans to attack Britain the King stated: 'These tragic events have not weakened in British hearts the sympathy and sense of comradeship which have grown up over many years of peace and war between the British and French nations.' He then referred to reports of 'an attempt by the German Government to secure from you undertakings that would go far beyond the terms accepted by you at the time of the Armistice.' He finally expressed confidence that the Marshal would 'reject proposals that would bring dishonour to France and grave damage to a late ally.'[10]

The French reply, which came more than a week later, was discouraging. The people of France, the King was told, 'after having fought at the side of the British people, deeply resented the repeated acts of aggression perpetrated by the British fleet against France and the support given by His Majesty's Government to Frenchmen who had rebelled against their own country.' No undertakings were given except 'to respect in an honourable manner the interests of the French nation'.[11]

Nevertheless there was some evidence that the King's message was not without effect. At the end of October the Portuguese Minister in Vichy was officially informed that 'there was no idea of hostility to England on the part of Marshal Pétain and the French Government in endeavouring to come to an arrangement with Germany. The arrangement contemplated was purely of an economic and social character.' The delay in replying to the King's message, the Portuguese Minister learnt, had been due to the temporary absence of the notoriously anglophobe Foreign Minister, Pierre Laval. The effective Portuguese ruler, Dr Salazar, thereupon offered to act as intermediary between the British and Vichy Governments. This offer was duly accepted.[12]

Neville Chamberlain died of cancer on 9 November. The funeral service took place in Westminster Abbey on the 14th, Churchill, Lloyd George, Baldwin and Halifax acting as pall-bearers. Churchill personally ordered that the date of the funeral service should be kept secret in order not to attract enemy action. The King was represented by the Duke of Gloucester.

Among the changes which the King introduced in the autumn of 1940 was a new arrangement for his talks with the Prime Minister. Instead of a weekly meeting at 5 pm the King invited Churchill to lunch with him every Tuesday. After a few months the King decided that no servants should be present, and he and Churchill helped themselves and each other to the relatively meagre rations available. It was an expression of a growing intimacy which, Churchill was to declare, had had 'no precedent since the days of Queen Anne and Marlborough during his years of power'.[13]

Whereas the King had begun his letters to his previous Prime Minister 'My dear Mr Chamberlain', he now began to write 'My dear Winston'. He was also able to express to Churchill with some freedom the feelings of gloom to which everyone at the centre of affairs was at that time periodically subject. On 29 October he wrote to Churchill: 'I am so sorry that everything nowadays is so worrying for you. There is not a bright spot anywhere.'[14] A month later, by contrast, he was writing to Halifax about post-war economic policy.[15]

Among those who now looked to the King for help in promoting their own ideas for the better prosecution of the war was Lord Louis Mountbatten. On 18 October he described in a letter to the King how, when commanding the destroyer HMS *Javelin* he had been attacked by two British Blenheim bombers. He asked the King to keep this a secret but added that he would recall it when the time came for the Royal Navy to renew its claims for control of Coastal Command.[16]

Towards the end of the year the King was closely involved in the making of an appointment of major importance. On 12 December Lord Lothian, the British Ambassador in Washington, died suddenly. Churchill's immediate choice for the post was Lloyd George, who declined the offer after consulting his doctors. Churchill then thought of Halifax, who was hesitant. Before making up his mind Halifax went down to Windsor to consult the King, who told him he believed that the appointment of Ambassador to Washington at that time was perhaps more important even than the post of Foreign Secretary. Halifax seems to have accepted the King's advice, and he agreed to Churchill's request.[17] In announcing the appointment Churchill wrote to Roosevelt: 'It is my duty to place at your side the most eminent of my colleagues, and one who knows the story as it unfolds at the summit.'[18]

The King's voice, when he gave his Christmas broadcast that year, was described as 'tired and rather lifeless'.[19] As a Christmas present Churchill gave the King the kind of coverall thought appropriate for wearing in air raid shelters and known as a 'siren suit'. He gave the Queen Fowler's *Modern English Usage*.[20]

CHAPTER SIXTEEN
Extension of War
1941

In the early months of 1941 the persistent bombing of major British cities, known as the Blitz, continued. So too did the visits by the King and Queen to the areas which had been attacked. Their journeys were normally made by the royal train, the drivers of which were told their destination only at the last moment. Inside, an office was set up, where the King, after his day's visiting, could go through his despatch boxes in the evening. When night came the train was usually stopped near a tunnel, which could provide some protection should an air raid take place.

Other visits were made by car, and after one such visit the Queen wrote to Lord Halifax on 23 April: 'This morning we went down to East and West Ham, where the whole place is flat, and everywhere we stopped the people were magnificent. Words fail me – you know this spirit – it is unbeatable.'[1] In similar vein, with reference to the continued threat of invasion, the King wrote of the British people a week later to Roosevelt: 'Their resolution and their confidence are supreme.'[2]

In the autumn of 1940 the King had been provided with two partly armoured staff cars, which were considered proof against normal small arms fire. Early in February 1941 he enquired whether thought could be given to producing a fully armoured car which he could use to perform his duties in the event of an invasion or an exceptionally heavy air attack. But the decision was taken, with Churchill's assent, that the Ministry of Supply staff should be 'relieved from the job of designing a new type of armoured car for such a limited purpose'.[3]

Since there was no adequate air raid shelter in Buckingham Palace and the King was told that it would take four months to construct a suitable one, for a time he was persuaded to spend nights in Windsor. This meant that he had to travel fairly regularly to London. Among the inconveniences of the arrangement was the absence, to which Churchill personally called attention in February, of a secure telephone line to

Windsor Castle. The objections raised to installing one were based on cost, and it was not until August that the Treasury agreed to foot the bill. Soon afterwards the King decided that the general inconvenience of commuting between Windsor and London was excessive, and he returned to Buckingham Palace.[4]

Fortified by his reelection in 1941, President Roosevelt continued his practice of sending emissaries to Britain who could advise him personally on the British capacity to resist. The receiving of these visitors was to be among the more important of the King's wartime tasks.

The first of the emissaries to come to Britain in 1941 was Harry Hopkins, who arrived on 8 January. He bore a letter from the President to the King, which stated: 'Mr Hopkins is a very good friend of mine in whom I repose the utmost confidence.'[5] Hopkins was an idealist, who had been engaged in welfare work in the poorest quarters of New York, and Churchill was unstinting in the trouble he took to establish with him a relationship of mutual regard.

An American visitor of a different kind, whom the King also entertained early in 1941, was the unsuccessful Republican Presidential candidate in 1940, Wendell Willkie. A report later submitted to the British Foreign Office by the Hon. T. H. Brand, who accompanied Willkie during most of his visit, stated that he arrived in London with the belief that Churchill's position was insecure, that the Labour party would probably soon take control, that the discontent of the working population was acute, and that there were continual strikes. At the end of his visit, Willkie told Brand his impressions were that 'the Prime Minister has the confidence and faith of at least 99% of the population, the government are united in their purpose to pursue the war, and the people of the country are determined to see the struggle through.'

A new American Ambassador was appointed in 1941 to replace Joseph Kennedy, much to the relief of virtually everyone in authority in Britain, including the King. Hugh Dalton recorded in his diary how the King spoke unusually harshly of Kennedy, and in particular of the fear he had shown of being bombed the day the war began.[6] Kennedy's successor was John G. Winant, who bore a strong physical resemblance to Abraham Lincoln. The King took the unprecedented step of meeting Winant at Windsor railway station, an action which, Halifax reported, made a most favourable impression on the American President and public.[7]

Among the contentious issues to which both the British and American administrations had to give attention was that of the military bases in the Western hemisphere, which, it had been agreed, the United States should acquire in parts of the British Empire.

The Bermuda House of Assembly appealed directly to the King, expressing concern that 'some new conception of American hemispheric defence' might affect Bermuda's status as 'an integral part of the British Commonwealth'.[8] The King noted in his diary: 'I told Alec H that there was no question of my giving consent to hand over the sovereignty of these B.W.I. as I am the custodian of my subjects.' At a meeting of the Privy Council on 28 February he asked Lord Cranborne, the Secretary of State for the Dominions, to remain behind at the end to discuss the whole question of the bases.

Cranborne was himself strongly critical of the American conduct of the detailed negotiations surrounding the acquisition of a number of bases in the Western hemisphere, and Churchill felt it necessary to issue a general instruction to those involved. 'The condition into which this matter is drifting,' he wrote, 'is becoming very dangerous to the life of the State. Since the arrangement was made about the bases and the destroyers, the President has introduced the Lend and Lease Bill which it is believed will be carried in the next few days. At the least four or five thousand million pounds worth of credits in one form or another will be granted to Great Britain without any real prospect of the debt being paid. . . Without this aid the defeat of Hitlerism could not be hoped for. It is therefore necessary to cultivate some sense of proportion in dealing with these local matters, irritating though some of them may be.'

He went on: 'The strategic value of these Islands is incomparably greater to the United States than to Great Britain. They were in fact chiefly valuable to us as a potential means of attacking the United States. As such an idea is not compatible with our outlook or position in the world, it is a direct British interest to have these Islands in part defended by the United States. We have long neglected these Islands. Their condition has been the subject of a very adverse report. The arrival of United States garrisons and the construction of important works will bring a great deal more money into them than they are likely to get in any other way.'[9]

Churchill's words were heeded, and on 31 March Halifax wrote to Roosevelt: 'Mr Churchill recently was able to settle the "bases" question by lifting it above the arguments and counter-arguments of experts.'[10]

The Lease–Lend Bill was also passed by the United States Senate in March, Churchill declaring in the House of Commons: 'The Government and people of the United States have in fact written a new Magna Carta.' Privately he expressed other opinions. After looking at the details of the new arrangements he wrote to Sir Kingsley Wood, the Chancellor of the Exchequer: 'As far as I can make out we are not only to be skinned but flayed to the bone.' As a policy he suggested to the Chancellor: 'I am sure we shall have to come to a "show down"; but I would precede it by a "lie down" and appear dumb and immobile. Let the difficulties mount up, and let things have a small crash. . . The power of the debtor is in the ascendant, especially when he is doing all the fighting.'[11]

As a guide to what was happening in the United States the King had, from 1941 until the end of the war, one particularly valuable source of information. This was the series of letters which Halifax addressed to him personally. The letters tended to be longer and more detailed than those Halifax sent directly to Churchill, for he evidently took the view that Churchill should be troubled only with matters of major importance or requiring his immediate attention. The great majority of his reports were of course also sent, in the ordinary way, to Eden, who had replaced him as Foreign Secretary.

Soon after his arrival Halifax wrote to the King about his reception by the President: 'Nothing could have been more charming than he was to us when we went to have tea with him in his yacht. He enquired a great deal after Your Majesties and said that he often looked back to what he hoped had been the two really comfortable days of your visit to the United States when you had been his guests at Hyde Park. . . He told me that he hoped that I should feel free at any time to ask to see him, and said that I should do this more easily if I didn't go through the State Department.'

Before long Halifax was telling the King that he had been struck by the bitterness of Republican opposition to the President. He even quoted one woman, described by him as 'intelligent and interested in politics', whose comments on the President had been: 'He fibbed at school, he lied at college, and was a crook in business, and I dare bet that no Senator would like to have an interview with him in his office without a witness.'

After a visit to Chicago and Kansas he wrote to the King at the time of the passing of the Lease–Lend Bill: 'A broad picture with which most people seemed to agree was that there were about 15 or 20% who want to get into the war at once; and another 15 or 20% who want to stay out at whatever cost, and a great middle group who want to give us all the help, and would do so quite happily regardless of consequences if they got what they consider a clear lead from the President.' In the same letter he wrote of the President: 'I was terribly shocked by how ill he looked. He was a shocking colour, and gave one the feeling of being a very sick man.'

In his replies to Halifax the King at times expressed himself with some freedom. On 4 April 1941, for example, he wrote: 'I did not feel too happy about the lease of the bases as the Americans wanted too much written and laid down. Everything was done in their interests, no give and take in certain circumstances. But no doubt when they get to know us better, as they will, we shall be able to settle things with them.' Of the Lease–Lend Bill he added: 'I do hope that the Americans will not try to bleed us white over the dollar asset question. As it is, they are collecting the remaining gold in the world, which is of no use to them, and they cannot wish to make us bankrupt. At least I hope they do not want to.'[12]

In the winter of 1940–41 the victories on land which the British were able to achieve were against Italians and Italian colonial troops, most of whom had little enthusiasm for the struggle. These successes, in North and East Africa, were none the less heartening, and on the 27 January 1941 the King received a personal expression of appreciation from the Emperor Haile Selassie of Ethiopia, who telegraphed: 'On setting my feet again on the sacred soil of my ancestors after my painful exile, I would like to renew to Your Majesty the expression of my profound gratitude for the sympathy and generous hospitality which was accorded me by your Government and your great people.'[13]

The Greek army too achieved considerable successes against Italian forces until, in the spring of 1941, Germany invaded Yugoslavia and shortly afterwards Greece. King George of the Hellenes and his Government were forced into exile, and on 14 April the Greek Minister in London put to Eden the suggestion that the King of the Hellenes might be allowed to exercise sovereignty over part of Cyprus and establish a government there. Eden took the view that this might establish a dangerous precedent, and after a stay in Egypt King George of the Hellenes came to London in September. King George VI, who was his cousin, met him at Euston station on his arrival from Liverpool and drove with him to Claridge's Hotel, where he and his party were accommodated. Before long criticism mounted among the large Greek colony in the Middle East of the decision to come to London, and the King of the Hellenes decided to make Cairo the seat of his Government in exile.

In Yugoslavia a coup d'état was staged towards the end of March 1941 which brought into power a new government, headed by General Simovič, pledged to resist German aggression. The coup had the support of the young King Peter and led to the overthrow of the Regent, Prince Paul, who had accepted a policy of conciliation towards Germany. A German invasion soon followed, and organised resistance did not last long. King Peter and his Government came to Britain. Prince Paul, who also escaped, was to find refuge in Kenya.

The Government which Simovič headed was one of the least satisfactory of the allied Governments in exile. Although inexperienced, King Peter had decided views on policy, and in a lengthy talk which he had with King George and Eden, from which all Yugoslav ministers were with difficulty excluded, he expressed his doubts about General Simovič. In particular he accused him of 'muddling' military affairs and propaganda. Both the King and Eden pointed out that Simovič had acquired a reputation as a symbol of resistance to German aggression and urged King Peter not to dispense with his services. King Peter agreed to make no changes for at least a month.[14]

George VI had a strong feeling of responsibility towards King Peter, who was his godson. Late in June he had a long talk with the young King's mother, Queen Marie, about his education, as a result of which it was decided that King Peter should go up to Cambridge. There were echoes of King George's own earlier experiences in a letter which Hardinge wrote to Sir Alexander Cadogan, the Foreign Office Permanent Under-Secretary, on 4 September. 'The King,' Hardinge stated, 'thinks it much better that he should live the life of an ordinary undergraduate, only going home for the week-ends.'

Cadogan found the arrangements satisfactory. 'We feel,' he wrote to Hardinge, 'that there is a great opportunity to ensure that the King is thoroughly Anglicized during his stay in England. At present, apparently, he appears to admire the United States of America above other countries.' It was also decided that during his vacations King Peter should be attached to a Brigade Headquarters of the Guards Armoured Division near Salisbury.[15]

By the summer of 1941 the likelihood of an invasion of Britain had clearly receded. British retaliatory air attacks on Germany had begun to take place. But military defeats continued, and no dent was made in the massive fortress of Europe which Germany had built up.

After her successes in south-east Europe Germany massed her divisions in Poland, Czechoslovakia and Roumania, and on 22 June 1941 German troops invaded the Soviet Union. To the British people this extraordinary decision of Hitler's provided the first reasonable assurance of their eventual victory.

Largely because of the German attack on the Soviet Union, and its possible consequences, Churchill decided in the summer of 1941 that he ought to have a personal meeting with Roosevelt. On 25 July the King formally gave permission for his Prime Minister to leave the country, Churchill explaining that he could, if an emergency arose, return from Newfoundland in a few hours by flying-boat. In fact he travelled aboard HMS *Prince of Wales* to Placentia Bay, where he telegraphed to the King on 9 August to announce his safe arrival. He bore a letter from the King to the President, which read: 'This is just a note . . . to say how glad I am that you have an opportunity at last of getting to know my Prime Minister. I am sure that you will agree that he is a very remarkable man.'[16]

During the series of meetings between President and Prime Minister which followed, the so-called Atlantic Charter was agreed upon. Consisting largely of platitudes, it nevertheless provided something of an answer to persistent public demands for a pronouncement of Allied war aims. Its most positive statement came in its first clause, which stated that the United States and Britain sought 'no aggrandisement, territorial or other'.

More immediate concerns were also discussed to Britain's advantage, the United States accepting responsibility for the protection of convoys as far as Iceland. The King noted in his diary that Churchill also took the opportunity to ask the President to consider America's position in the event of Germany defeating the Soviet Union by the coming spring and then renewing her attack on the West.

At the end of the discussions Roosevelt wrote to the King: 'I have had three delightful and useful days with Mr Churchill and the heads of your three services. It has been a privilege to come to know Mr Churchill in this way and I am very confident that our minds travel together.'[17]

It was soon evident to the British and American Governments that for the Soviet forces to resist the Germans successfully they would need large quantities of armaments, most of which would have to come from the United States and be transported from Britain to Murmansk in British ships.

As the chief administrator of Lease–Lend aid to Britain, Roosevelt had appointed Averell Harriman, a close political associate who had been Governor of New York. Before long Harriman was to take over Hopkins's role as Roosevelt's principal political adviser in Britain. He was also charged with estimating the supplies the Soviet Union would need, most of which could be expected to come in the first place from those earmarked for Britain. In the autumn of 1941 therefore Harriman set off for Moscow in the company of Lord Beaverbrook, who had recently been appointed British Minister of Supply. Before their departure they were received, together with their principal advisers, by the King and Queen. Harriman recorded afterwards: 'Our crowd was much impressed.' He also commented on the 'earnestness' and 'sincerity' of both King and Queen, which makes one wonder what else he had expected.[18]

The alliance into which Britain and the Soviet Union had in effect been forced by Hitler brought the King into closer contact with the Soviet Ambassador, Ivan Maisky, and other Soviet officials. One of his stronger earlier impressions was of the secrecy and suspicion which they seemed to carry with them. When R. A. Butler had an audience on his appointment as President of the Board of Education he found the King much less willing to talk about the affairs of Butler's new department than about those of the Foreign Office, where Butler had previously been a junior minister. In particular the King seemed to be much intrigued by a man described as 'a sinister figure of Mongolian appearance' who continually accompanied Maisky to meetings.[19]

In 1941 there was growing evidence of differences of opinion between the Government in Britain and those in some of the Dominions on how the war should be conducted.

After the French defeat in 1940 and the subsequent armistice the Canadian Government had been closer to the United States than to Britain in its attitude to Vichy France. A Vichy French Minister was accepted in

Ottawa, and a Canadian, Pierre Dufuy, was able, by holding the posts concurrently of Chargé d'Affaires in France, Belgium and the Netherlands, to visit Vichy and report back. In a sense therefore the King was represented in a country with which his Government in Britain had broken off diplomatic relations. The King was also one of the very limited recipients of the reports which Dufuy made.[20]

To Churchill, Canada's contacts with Vichy via Dufuy were an asset. Much less welcome were suggestions which came from the Australian Government that the War Cabinet in Britain should include representatives from the self-governing Dominions. On this he expressed his views in a telegram which he sent to the Australian Prime Minister, A. W. Fadden, on 29 August. 'We number at present eight,' he stated, 'and there has been considerable argument that we should not be more than five. The addition of four Dominion representatives would involve the retirement from the War Cabinet of at least an equal number of British Ministers.'

The inclusion of General Smuts in the War Cabinet in World War I was not, he argued, a relevant precedent, as he had been chosen for 'his personal aptitudes and not because he represented the South African or Dominion point of view.' The Prime Ministers of Canada, New Zealand and South Africa were, he concluded, satisfied with the existing arrangements, whereby they were invited, whenever they visited Britain, to sit with the War Cabinet and 'take a full part in our deliberations.'[21]

Further problems arose with the arrival in Britain in June of the New Zealand Prime Minister, Peter Fraser, whom Colville described as 'the embodiment of Scottish caution'.[22] Fraser had come via Egypt, where he had had talks with the distinguished New Zealand commander, General Freyberg. He shared Freyberg's view, formed after the Allied disaster which had followed the German attack on Crete, that unless adequate air forces were made available soon the Middle East, a theatre of war in which New Zealand troops were heavily engaged, would be lost.[23]

A few weeks earlier a distinction conferred on another Dominion Prime Minister had delighted the King personally. On 24 May he had a message conveyed to General Smuts stating: 'It gives me particular pleasure on this your birthday to appoint you a Field Marshal in the British Army.' The telegram described Smuts as 'the leader of a people whose fighting men have been playing a most brilliant part in the victorious campaign in East Africa'.[24]

During the period of heavy German air attacks, and in the months which followed, the Queen accompanied the King on his public engagements even more often than usual. When her own engagements were being considered, one of her Ladies-in-Waiting recalled, it was her regular practice to reply that the King must first be consulted.[25] Of the activities which she conducted independently of the King, one which was of some political significance was broadcasting.

On 24 January 1941 Eden wrote to the Queen: 'Last year Your Majesty graciously consented to broadcast a message to the women of France. This message created a profound impression in France.' He added that, after consulting Churchill, he was now asking her to broadcast again 'to express sympathy for the women of France in their present suffering and especially with those whose husbands and brothers are prisoners of war'. He offered to 'assist in compiling the message'.[26] She accepted his help and made the broadcast.

In June it was suggested that the Queen should broadcast to the United States an expression of thanks for private help given. Churchill and Brendan Bracken were at first opposed to this on the grounds that the broadcast might encourage complacency at a time when a great deal more help was needed. Halifax's opinion was asked, and on 10 July he telegraphed: 'To thank for private help, so far from impeding the development of public opinion in the direction we desire, would assist it, for thanks could be so worded as to make the emotional appeal, especially from Her Majesty, most telling.'

The Queen agreed to make the broadcast and sent Churchill a draft of what she intended to say, writing: 'I fear it is not very polished – a good deal of my own; but I do want to thank the women of US for their help and sympathy and encourage them to further efforts.' Churchill replied: 'I may say I think it is exactly what is needed, and it is only with great hesitation that I have suggested a few alternatives.'

In June the King had discussions with his youngest brother, the Duke of Kent, on plans which the Duke had for visiting RAF establishments in Canada, where men from a number of Commonwealth countries were undergoing instruction under the Empire Air Training Scheme. In proposing his visit the Duke wrote to Air Chief Marshal Sir Charles Portal, the Chief of Air Staff, that some of the men seemed 'to be very discontented, as apparently the scheme has been misrepresented to them, and they have been coming over here as observers when they wished to be pilots.' He added that the King considered his visit 'a very good idea'.

A suggestion that the Duke of Kent might take the opportunity of also visiting the United States was agreed more hesitantly. The Duke of Windsor was due to arrive in the country about the same time on his way from the Bahamas to visit his ranch in Alberta, and Halifax recommended that the Duke of Kent should do no more than visit the President at the White House or Hyde Park and fulfil one or two other routine engagements. Public opinion in the USA was very delicately balanced, and the anti-British lobby led by Senator Wheeler remained powerful.

'It would be a mistake,' he telegraphed, 'from the political point of view if the Duke were to stay for any longer period or to pay visits to other parts of the country... I have no doubt that Senator Wheeler and his friends would jump at any chance of representing longer stay by the Duke as an attempt on the part of His Majesty's Government to use the Royal Family for propaganda purposes.'[27]

Of the Duke of Kent's visit as a whole Mackenzie King wrote to Churchill on 30 July: 'It seems to have gone very well, and the impression left by it, as by the broadcasts made by His Royal Highness, has been a very good one.'

Halifax had shown similar caution in March when the idea of an official visit to the United States by the Duke of Windsor had been mooted. This led Churchill to telegraph to the Duke on 18 March: 'After much consideration and enquiry I have reached conclusion that Your Royal Highness' proposed visit to United States would not be in the public interest nor indeed in your own at the present time.' In the same telegram he voiced his objections to other aspects of the Duke's conduct. One was his proposed use of a yacht belonging to a Swede named Wenner-Gren in order to tour West Indian islands. 'This gentleman,' Churchill stated, 'is, according to the reports I have received, regarded as a pro-German international financier, with strong leanings towards appeasement, and suspected of being in communication with the enemy.'

Churchill's other objection was to a report in the magazine *Liberty* of an interview with the Duke. In this the Duke was quoted in a manner which, Churchill stated, 'will certainly be interpreted as defeatist and pro-Nazi, and by implication approving of the isolationist aim to keep America out of the war.'

The telegram ended rather sorrowfully: 'I could wish indeed that Your Royal Highness would seek advice before making public statements of this kind. I should always be ready to help, as I used to in the past.'

The Duke responded forcefully. 'I wonder,' he telegraphed, 'if Lord Halifax has been long enough in America to be able to predict that a visit of ours would become a show... In Miami last December ... our visit was most dignified and no harm was done to British interests that I am aware.' With evidently growing indignation he went on: 'The importance you attach to American magazine articles prompts me to tell you that I strongly resent and take great exception to the article in the magazine *Life* of the 17th March entitled "The Queen" in which the latter is quoted as referring to the Duchess as "that woman".'

After protesting yet again about 'the chronic anomaly of my wife not having the same official status as myself,' the Duke also ended his telegram sorrowfully with the words: 'I have both valued and enjoyed your friendship in the past but after your telegram ... and the tone of your recent messages to me here I find it difficult to believe that you are still the friend you used to be.'[28]

The Duke of Windsor did visit the United States later in the year, and on 4 October Halifax reported a conversation he had had with Roosevelt.

The President, he stated, had found the Duke 'very robust on war and victory and his attitude generally showed a great improvement on the impression the President had formed when he met him a year ago in the Bahamas.'

A curious incident which occurred in October 1941 illustrated the importance attached in certain countries to the exercise of the royal function in Britain. Two Swedish destroyers had been blown up as a result of some mysterious explosions. Sabotage was suspected, and it was thought that communists might be implicated. The number of countries which had escaped involvement in the war was diminishing, and in Europe in particular the Foreign Office wanted to retain as friendly relations as possible with the few remaining neutral powers. It was therefore decided to send a message of sympathy from the British government to the Swedish Government.

The British Minister in Stockholm, Victor Mallet, acted in accordance with the instructions he received, and on 20 September he reported to Eden that he had called on the Swedish Minister for Foreign Affairs to convey 'the sympathy of His Majesty the King on the disaster to the Swedish destroyers'. He added: 'M. Gunther was evidently much touched by this mark of sympathy and at once requested me to inform you of the gratitude felt by the Swedish Government. He would not fail to lay my note before the King of Sweden immediately.'

In fact it was an error in transmission that had caused the words 'His Majesty the King' to be substituted for 'His Majesty's Government', but the extremely favourable – if unintended – impression remained.[29]

On 11 November the King gave his formal speech on the prorogation of Parliament. It was the kind of task which he still performed with some difficulty, though with growing confidence. The speech was, as always, a concoction produced by his ministers, those who formed the King's Speech Committee in 1941 being Sir John Anderson, Eden, Arthur Greenwood and Sir Archibald Sinclair. The offices they held were respectively those of Lord President of the Council, Foreign Secretary, Minister without Portfolio and Secretary of State for Air.

In a review of the past year it was found necessary to state that 'the enemy has added to the number of countries temporarily over-run' and appropriate to express the hope that 'under Providence, and thanks to the unexampled efforts of the seafaring and farming communities, the food supplies of my people are assured.' The speech also welcomed 'as an Ally the great Union of Soviet Socialist Republics'.

Within a month of the delivery of this speech a new dimension was given to the war. On 7 December Japanese forces launched an attack on the United States base at Pearl Harbor. In doing so they followed the example of the German forces in Russia six months earlier by ensuring, through ill-advised acts of aggression, that the war would be lost by the Axis powers.

Only when she had gained powerful allies and the balance of material power had been reversed did Britain have any serious prospect of winning the war. That she had survived as a free country in the period between the fall of France and the involvement of these new allies was due to a variety of factors, one of the most potent of which was the extraordinary upsurge of spirit which began to occur in June 1940. Of this the King was far more than merely the outward symbol.

CHAPTER SEVENTEEN
Turning Points
1942

Acknowledging the receipt of a letter from Churchill to the King, Lascelles wrote to John Martin, one of the Prime Minister's Private Secretaries, on 17 January: 'It is a very great relief to know that you are all safe home – the greatest, I think, since that eventful Sunday when we heard they had established touch with the *Bismarck*.'[1]

Lascelles was referring to Churchill's return from the United States, when the last stage of his journey had been made by flying-boat from Bermuda to Plymouth. Soon after the attack on Pearl Harbor Churchill had decided that he needed another meeting with the President, and he had spent three weeks as Roosevelt's guest at the White House. They had agreed that Germany was to be considered the main enemy; there had been twelve meetings of the British and American Chiefs of Staff; and plans for an Allied landing in French North Africa had been considered.[2]

Churchill had described the American leaders as 'magnificent in their breadth of view'. On his return to England he gave the King an encouraging *résumé* of his talks, telling him that he was confident of ultimate victory.[3] An impression of American reactions to Pearl Harbor had also been conveyed to the King by Halifax in one of his long personal letters.

'I think one needed perhaps to be here at the time of the Japanese attack on Pearl Harbor,' Halifax wrote on 15 January 1942, 'to realize just how sharp was the effect of that. . . It has been rather surprising that there has not been a greater howl here for keeping everything they possess to defend the Pacific and the West Coast. There was a good deal of that in the first days, but since then there has been plenty of evidence that American opinion, speaking generally, was not at all inclined to let the Japanese business detract from the importance in their eyes of Hitler.'

He added: 'Looking at this picture in the big, I have no doubt at all that the fact of their entry into the war is having and will continue to have an immensely stimulating effect on production.'[4] On this the King commented in his letter of reply: 'It took us long enough to get our war production going under the most difficult conditions, so I wonder how long the US industry will take to get going.'[5]

In fact the first six months of 1942 were to be a period of almost continuous military disaster for the Allies, mainly in the Far East and, to a lesser extent, in the Middle East. For the British the most humiliating of all the defeats came with the surrender of Singapore on 15 February.

One consequence of the entry of Japan into the war had been the renewal of demands for greater participation in decision-making by the governments of the Dominions, particularly of those Dominions directly threatened by the advances of the Japanese armies. In fact, no fully satisfactory method of involving all the King's self-governing Dominions in the formulation of war strategy was ever evolved.

On 24 January a telegram was sent by the Dominions Office in London to the Australian Government confirming the Australian right to be heard in the War Cabinet for the formulation of policy. The establishment of a Far Eastern War Council in London, with representatives of Cabinet status from Australia, New Zealand and the Netherlands, to be chaired by Churchill, was also proposed. On this the New Zealand Prime Minister, Peter Fraser, commented pertinently that as responsibility for the Pacific theatre of war was being assumed by the United States, a War Council which met in London would serve little purpose.[6]

On 30 May it was therefore formally agreed that Stanley Bruce, the Australian High Commissioner in London and former Australian Prime Minister, should be accepted as 'the accredited representative of the Commonwealth Government in the War Cabinet and the Australian representative on the Pacific War Council'. But he did not find his position an easy one, and in a memorandum on 2 September he wrote: 'The impression has been created by the Prime Minister here and the Prime Minister in Australia that I am a member of the War Cabinet. Owing to that impression I am regarded in many quarters as sharing responsibility for decisions taken by the War Cabinet. . . It is asking a good deal to accept this responsibility when I am given so little information and consulted so little.'

He went on: 'The Prime Minister stands so far above all his colleagues that he is obviously the man in whom the supreme authority should be vested. The trouble is that while the Prime Minister is assuming that supreme authority, he is not utilizing his colleagues in the War Cabinet in a way calculated to provide him with the maximum assistance they can render.'

Similarly the Maharaja of Jammu and Kashmir and Sir Firoz Khan Noon were accepted as the Indian representatives in the War Cabinet, but on 7 September Churchill wrote: 'Though I shall naturally invite them to

Above left: **The New Zealand Tour, 1927**
Inspecting Guard of Honour, New
Zealand Rifles, Auckland
Above right: The Duke of York lands a
ground-shark in The Bay of Islands
Below: Deck tennis on board HMS
Renown

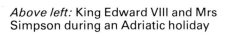

Above left: King Edward VIII and Mrs Simpson during an Adriatic holiday

The Coronation of George VI, 12 May 1937

Above: The Windsors approach Berchtesgaden

Below left: The meeting with Hitler

Below right: Neville Chamberlain arrives in Munich. Ribbentrop is on his left

State visit to Paris, 1938

The last of the boys' camps associated with the name of the Duke of York. It was held at Abergeldie near Balmoral in 1939

attend our Monday meetings, it must not be assumed that I shall feel able to invite them when Indian affairs are to be discussed. . . It will of course follow that they will not receive all papers circulated to War Cabinet Ministers.'[7]

An imaginative decision was to be made later when, in recognition of the fact that Cairo had become a kind of Allied capital city for the purposes of prosecuting the war, the Australian, Richard Casey, was established there with the title of Minister of State, a role he filled with distinction. But the Pacific War Council never became an effective body. When it first met in London on 10 February Churchill emphasised that it would not deal with the detailed conduct of the war, for which task General Wavell had been appointed Supreme Commander, but would 'review the broad fundamental policies'. This meant in practice that it would do so only after the event.[8]

Unsurprisingly, the sequence of defeats which caused the Chief of the Imperial General Staff, General Sir Alan Brooke, to say that 'we seem to lose a new bit of the Empire almost every day,'[9] gave rise to mounting criticism at home. Some of this was directed at Churchill, and the King wrote anxiously in his diary: 'There is a growing feeling that owing to his innumerable preoccupations there may well be aspects of defence which do not get all the attention that they should.'[10]

Churchill personally was irritated by the criticism, as he made clear to the King when he lunched with him on 17 February. Nevertheless two days later he effected a reorganisation of his Government, reducing the number of members of the War Cabinet from nine to seven. Five were already members. They were, in addition to himself, Attlee, Eden, Bevin and Sir John Anderson. Oliver Lyttelton, who had been Minister of State in Cairo, entered the War Cabinet with responsibility for production. The other new member, Sir Stafford Cripps, a Labour lawyer and churchman for whose intellectual powers Churchill had great respect, was made leader of the House of Commons, an appointment which further strengthened the Labour Party's influence over the political life of the nation.

Commenting on the reorganisation, the King wrote to Halifax on 1 March: 'I have been having a worrying time of late with all the criticism of Winston and his methods. I know the country is solidly behind him as their leader in these difficult times before us. The reorganization of the Government which he has done should have a good effect, if only the press would play fair and give them a chance to get results. I hope Winston will let Cripps, Eden and Lyttelton help him. He has confidence in them. Cripps has got a great opportunity to make good.'[11]

In Parliament the criticism culminated in a vote of censure on the Government, which was moved on 1 July. It was easily defeated, and the Government was at no time in serious danger, but relief was provided when a Member of Parliament, Sir John Wardlaw-Milne, made the extraordinary suggestion that the Duke of Gloucester should be appointed Commander-in-Chief. This was greeted with loud laughter. The Duke did take his military duties seriously, but even his widow, in a most discreet book of memoirs, was later to admit that when he had been at the Staff College she had had to help him with his homework.[12]

With the greater active involvement of Britain's armed forces, albeit for the greater part of the year still largely defensive and frequently unsuccessful, the King's role changed somewhat in 1942. No longer did the public see him, in the flesh, in cinema newsreels and in the popular illustrated news magazines of the time, primarily engaged in walking amid rubble and smoking ruins of bombed cities. More of his time was spent instead with service units, and he was increasingly involved in decisions affecting senior commanders. One such was General Sir John Dill, who had been superseded as Chief of the Imperial General Staff by Brooke and appointed the senior British representative with the Combined Chiefs of Staff in Washington. Halifax, now the British Ambassador in Washington, liked and respected Dill and wrote of him to the King on 15 January: 'He will be of immense help, and all the Americans like him very much.'[13]

A few months later Halifax had an important visitor from Britain. This was Lord Beaverbrook, of whom he wrote to the King on 9 May: 'I had a great deal of talk with him, which was all most entertaining and which got me to know him better than I had ever succeeded in doing before. His is a most extraordinary mind, and there is a great deal always at the back of it that does not easily come into view! I am quite certain he thinks that if the present Prime Minister was at any moment spirited away, the British public would clamour for Lord Beaverbrook to replace him. But here I suppose he deludes himself.'

Halifax added: 'Apart from what Lord Beaverbrook may do in the larger sphere, I was pretty satisfied that one of the principal things in his mind is to get his knife into Sir John Dill, and I hope Your Majesty will do anything you can to prevent this. Dill has made for himself a remarkable position here; he is completely trusted by the President and the American Chiefs of Staff.'

There was a suggestion that Dill might be sent to India, and Halifax ended his appeal to the King by expressing the hope that 'neither for that nor for any other reason will he be removed from what he is doing at this end.' Dill, of whom the King thought highly also, remained in Washington, where he died in November 1944. It was an indication of American appreciation of his efforts that he was buried in Arlington Cemetery.

The King served furthermore as final arbiter when ministers differed over appointments to the rank of Field-Marshal. On 20 August 1942

Wavell wrote to Churchill from the Middle East General Headquarters in Cairo: 'I have never before asked for anything for myself, but I am going to ask you now for promotion to the rank of Field Marshal. I have now over 1,000,000 under my command and am asked to assume wider responsibilities, so that I think I have fair claims to the rank.' Churchill passed this request to the Secretary of State for War with the comment: 'I am strongly in favour of this, and so is the CIGS.'

The Secretary of State for War was then Sir James Grigg, whose appointment had been an unusual one, as his career had been in the Civil Service. Colville described him as having 'a brilliant mind, a sharp tongue and a total inability to suffer fools gladly'.[14] To Churchill Grigg wrote on 15 September:

'Frankly I was very shocked that Wavell could have brought himself to ask to be made a Field Marshal. Moreover, I myself do not take a high view of his ability anyhow. He has, of course, any amount of brains, but I do not believe that he has any fire in his belly, or enough iron in his body. Further I still feel strongly that it would not be fair to Gort to do this. But having said all that I will put the proposal to the Treasury and to the King. I hope you will agree that the announcement must be carefully timed to synchronize with a victory.'

To this Churchill replied: 'I had no intention of publishing Wavell's baton till the New Year's Honours, but I do not agree that his case stands on a level with that of Gort. Lord Gort was pushed up by Hore-Belisha in a manner most detrimental to the Service and himself. I have the greatest regard for him, but I do not think that the grant of a baton is warranted by his service in this war. . . The King seemed very well disposed to the idea of making Wavell a Field Marshal in the New Year's list.'

Wavell appealed to Churchill again, asking in a personal telegram that his appointment should not be delayed until the New Year, but Churchill was able to make it clear that the final word rested with the King. In a note to Grigg appended to Wavell's telegram he wrote: 'I should like to meet his wishes. But H.M. wishes Lord Gort to have it too – no doubt at the same time. I think we must await the New Year.'[15]

The newer arms of the services increasingly occupied the King's attention in 1942. Shortly after the fall of France Churchill had made two characteristic decisions intended to demonstrate that Britain must soon cease to plan purely in terms of defence and move instead to the offensive. The first was to appoint Sir Roger Keyes in command of Combined Operations, whose first task would be to mount raids on the coast of Europe. The second was to create a new organisation to be known as the Special Operations Executive to foment active resistance in occupied countries. This he placed under the control of Hugh Dalton as Minister of Economic Warfare.

The command of Combined Operations was later entrusted to

Mountbatten, and in October 1942 the King paid its headquarters a visit. On 26 December he conveyed his opinion of Combined Operations in a letter to Mountbatten, in which he wrote: 'I do congratulate you very much on the success you have made of C.O. despite all the obstacles you have met and the heavy opposition you have fought both on the administrative side and in Active Operations! . . . Why should it be so difficult to get other people to understand the value of Combined Operations, after you have shown that it can, will and does work when properly organized and you have troops trained for it?'[16] As the principal activity of Combined Operations up to that point had been the raid on Dieppe four months earlier, which had been costly in lives, largely Canadian, and of little evident benefit, this was a generous appreciation.

When Dalton had spent half-an-hour with the King on 7 February 1941 they had discussed the affairs of the Ministry of Economic Warfare. Afterwards Dalton had noted in his diary that the King had not heard 'much, if anything, of the rest'. By 'the rest' Dalton meant the secret and subversive activities of SOE. By March of the next year, however, when Dalton was serving as President of the Board of Trade, he found that what the King now wanted most to talk about was SOE and, in particular, 'what sort of people they are whom we use'.[17] It was an interest which grew with the years.

One of the airfields used for air operations in support of SOE was Tempsford in Bedfordshire. After the King's Flight had been disbanded its captain, Wing-Commander E. H. (Mouse) Fielden, was given command of the Tempsford station. From there he regularly flew small Lysander aircraft which carried out pick-up operations in enemy-occupied France. On one of these he was presented by a grateful agent with a bottle of wine. This he later gave to the King.

That the King had become genuinely knowledgeable about both military and political affairs was becoming increasingly apparent to his Ministers. This was perhaps not surprising. Churchill was among those who noted how diligently he studied the papers sent to him. The range of subjects they covered was prodigious, and he was privy to the most important secrets, including the plans, which in 1942 became fairly advanced, for the production of the atom bomb.

It was significant, for instance, that when on 29 July 1942 the name of Attlee, as Deputy Prime Minister, was included in the list of those who automatically received copies of all telegrams exchanged between Churchill and Roosevelt, the list until then had been restricted solely to the King and the Foreign Secretary. In 1942, also, the King had dealings for the first time with the American military leaders. One of these was General George C. Marshall, the Chief of General Staff. In April Marshall arrived in London with Hopkins, one of their first engagements being to lunch with the King. They brought with them a letter to Churchill from the President, which stated: 'What Harry and Geo. Marshall will tell you all about has my heart and mind in it.'

This was an outline plan for an assault on western Europe. Emphasis was put on 'the unique opportunity to establish an active sector on this front this summer, through steadily increasing air operations and by raids and forays all along the coast.' 1 April 1943 was put forward as a tentative date for the main invasion, but it was admitted that lack of shipping might lead to a postponement until late summer.[18] Churchill described the plan as a 'masterly document' and told Roosevelt that, in principle, he and the Chiefs of Staff entirely agreed with it.[19]

On 28 October the General commanding the United States Army in the European theatre of operations, Lieut-General Dwight D. Eisenhower, received a letter from Buckingham Palace written by Piers Legh, the Master of the Household, which read: 'The King has expressed a desire to give an afternoon party at Buckingham Palace for officers of the United States Army, Navy, Red Cross and Nursing Corps, on the occasion of Thanksgiving Day on November 26th, 1942. It is suggested that the numbers should not exceed 250 in all. Would you therefore kindly inform me whether this proposal meets with your approval in order that the necessary details can be proceeded with.'

Eisenhower promptly replied: 'Please give my respects to the King and inform His Majesty that General Clark and I will be honoured to pay our respects on Thursday, October 29, at 11.30.'[20] It was to be the beginning of a friendship which both the King and the future American President would increasingly value.

One American visitor who arrived in Britain in October came in response to an invitation from the Queen. This was Eleanor Roosevelt, the President's wife, to whom the Queen wrote on 12 September: 'The King and I would be so pleased if you would care to pay a visit to England in the near future to see something of the varied war activities in which the women of Great Britain are now engaged. The work that they are doing would, I think, interest you, and I am sure the women themselves would be pleased and encouraged by a visit from you. If you think it possible to make the journey, we would be delighted if you would stay with us for a few days at Buckingham Palace. We would try to make your visit pleasant, and I need not say what pleasure it would give us to see you again. In order to get reasonably good weather and not too long a blackout, I suggest that the best time would be the last week of this month, or the second or third week in October.'[21]

Mrs Roosevelt's initial plans for her visit gave rise to some doubts and hesitations on the British side. On 20 September Churchill wrote to Eden: 'It seems to me it will be a pity for Mrs Roosevelt to end with two days in Dublin with De Valera. This would be widely criticized here by our own people. Surely something can be done to cushion her off it?'

Eden telegraphed accordingly to Halifax, who undertook to discuss the matter directly with Mrs Roosevelt. Earlier Halifax had written to Eden: 'She wants to see some formerly comfortable, or even wealthy house under wartime conditions. I don't quite know where she will find this, and she wouldn't get quite the picture as I daresay she wants from such a place as Arundel, which is, I believe, taken over by the soldiers with its owners living in two rooms.'[22]

In the end it was decided that Mrs Roosevelt should visit Queen Mary, who was then living at Badminton.

The aircraft in which she arrived was delayed for two days in Ireland by bad weather. When he heard of this Churchill was so keen to protect her from southern Irish influences that he was willing to send a fast car to take her to Belfast, where a destroyer would be standing by to convey her to Britain. The plan did not have to be put into operation, but in the course of her visit Mrs Roosevelt did spend two days in Northern Ireland, where American troops were stationed.

Mrs Roosevelt's visit was a strenuous affair. One newspaper reporter estimated that she walked 'fifty miles through factories, clubs and hospitals.'[23] After her return to the United States Halifax wrote to the King: 'It has been very refreshing to see what an impression England makes upon your visitors. Mrs Roosevelt and Mr Morgenthau have both returned thinking and, I am glad to say, saying they could not have imagined the atmosphere and the spirit there unless they had seen it for themselves. Mrs Roosevelt was very full of all Your Majesties had done for them and could not say enough about your kindness. She certainly does not seem to have wasted a moment of her time, and as she described one or two of her days' timetable to me I wondered how any human being could possibly have maintained the pace.'[24]

In a telegram which he sent to the President about the visit Churchill stated: 'Mrs Roosevelt proceeds indefatigably.'[25] Among Mrs Roosevelt's own most vivid and must quoted recollections of her stay in England was of eating meagre rations in Buckingham Palace off gold plate.

The entertainment provided for Mrs Roosevelt at Buckingham Palace included a showing of Noël Coward's new film, *In Which We Serve*. The King had a particular interest in this film. On 8 August, together with the Queen, the two princesses and Mountbatten, he had visited the studio to see the film being made. After their visit Coward noted in his diary: 'Altogether it was an exhibition of unqualified "niceness".'[26]

Mountbatten had made two hundred convalescents from the naval hospital at Haslar available for the film and had even written some technical material to be put into the mouths of naval officers.[27] When Coward encountered opposition from the Ministry of Information, one of whose officials thought that showing a British ship sunk was bad propaganda, he naturally turned to Mountbatten for help. Mountbatten in turn showed the script to the King and Queen, who supported Coward, and the sunken ship was retained in the film, together with a copy of the *Daily Express* of 1 September bearing the headline: 'There will be no war this year.'[28] That in such a matter the King was expected to serve as an unofficial court of appeal even in matters of censorship was an indication of the variety of roles he could be called upon to play.

On 25 August 1942 the King suffered the greatest personal loss he was to experience in the whole of World War II, when his youngest brother, the Duke of Kent, was killed in a Sunderland flying-boat which crashed in Scotland on a flight to visit RAF units in Iceland. There was only one survivor. The Duke and the other ten on board were thought to have been killed instantaneously.

The King expressed something of what he felt when writing to thank Edwina Mountbatten for her letter of condolence. 'It really is a tragedy,' he wrote, 'that he of all people just when he was coming into his own should have been taken from us. I shall miss him terribly as he was such a great help to me, and I found him so trustworthy and he never found anything too much trouble if it would help. I never saw enough of him since the war started as we were both so busy. I felt I had to make a pilgrimage to the place where he met his death and it did me good. We shall all miss him all our lives.'[29]

Among the arrangements which the King made following his brother's death, two in particular were evidence of the consideration he so often gave to the problems of others. It was decreed that although there were to be four weeks of Court mourning, the Lord Chamberlain's Office in Windsor Castle should announce that 'The King has graciously intimated that owing to the difficulty of obtaining material His Majesty does not wish officers not in possession of mourning bands to obtain them.'

And then, on 31 August, the King put to Churchill a proposal which, he hoped, would help the Duke of Kent's widow, Princess Marina. 'I would be glad to know,' he wrote, 'whether it would be all right for Princess Olga to come and be with her sister the Duchess of Kent, as I will then send her a cable at once. My sister-in-law is terribly lonely, and the presence of her sister will I know ease her pain.'[30]

The Foreign Office's advice was that there was no objection to Princess Olga's travelling from Kenya, provided her husband, the former Yugoslav Regent, Prince Paul, did not accompany her. Prince Paul was at that time interned in Kenya and suffering from depression. Smuts, who happened to be flying to Britain, offered to take the Princess in his aircraft, but her lady's maid fell ill, and she refused to travel without her. When the lady's maid recovered Prince Bernhard of the Netherlands also came forward with an offer of a lift.

Of the King's two remaining brothers, the Duke of Gloucester had

already performed a valuable service in 1942 in the country now known as
Iran but still at that time known to westerners as Persia. The country was
then undergoing the unusual experience of an Anglo–Soviet occupation,
an expedient which served to eliminate German activities over a large area
and facilitated the despatch of armaments to the Soviet Union. As a
consequence of the occupation, Riza Shah had abdicated in September
1941 in favour of his son, but even after Riza Shah's departure, Soviet
leaders distrusted the royal family, and at the time of the abdication
Maisky informed Eden that, in his Government's view, 'even if one
representative of the present royal family of Persia has to remain . . . all
the others should be sent away.'[31]

The British Government thought otherwise, and in May 1942 the Duke
of Gloucester was despatched on a diplomatic mission to Teheran. From
there he telegraphed to the King: 'Have been most warmly received by the
Shah and the inhabitants of Teheran. I wonder if you could give him the
GCB during the next few days. It would have a great effect on him and
would contribute enormously to removal of difficulties that still exist.
Harry.' The King promptly agreed.

On the Duke's departure the British Minister in Teheran, Sir Reader
Bullard, telegraphed: 'Visit has been a very great success and the
population have on every occasion turned out to welcome and acclaim His
Royal Highness's progress through the streets. From political point of
view it could not have been better timed and it has been noticeable that
within the last week Persian Government have been far more accommodating in settlement of outstanding questions. . . His Royal
Highness's success in establishing such warm personal relations with the
Shah should create a most favourable effect among the younger elements,
particularly in the Army, who naturally take their cue from His Majesty.
Informality on 12th May after a ride in the country was such that the Shah
drove His Royal Highness back to the Legation in his own racing car.'[32]

The Duke's success in Teheran was to be followed the next year by a
more exacting appointment, that of Governor-General of Australia. That
the King could now accept his departure with apparent equanimity shows
how greatly his confidence had grown. Early in his reign, when such an
appointment had been mooted, he had felt he needed the presence of two
brothers at home to support him. Now, for a time, there would be none.

There was no likelihood of a return to Britain of the King's older
brother, the Duke of Windsor. People who were close to the King have
stressed how fond he remained of his elder brother, but he did not let this
affect his judgment of where the Duke's obligations lay. In a letter to
Halifax on 3 March 1942 he wrote: 'I am so glad you were able to have a
talk with my brother when he was in Washington. The real fact of the
matter, which he does not realise, is that having occupied the throne of
this country he can never live in this country as an ordinary citizen. We

know this, so does Winston, but we can never tell my brother so in so many words.'[33]

On the condition which the Duke of Windsor had himself laid down for his return to Britain, the 'restoring' (his word) of a royal title to his wife, the King gave his final judgment on 8 December 1942 after the Duke had raised the subject once again in a letter. The King's decision was laid out in a formal minute to Churchill, which began, not 'My dear Winston', but 'The Prime Minister'. It was marked 'private and confidential': 'I have read the letter from my brother with great care,' the King wrote, 'and after much thought I feel I cannot alter a decision which I made with considerable reluctance at the time of his marriage.

'The reason for his abdication was that he wished to marry a lady who, having already two husbands living, was not considered by the country to be a suitable Queen of England. When he abdicated, he renounced all the rights and privileges of succession for himself and his children – including the title "Royal Highness" in respect of himself and his wife. There is therefore no question of his title being "restored" to the Duchess – because she never had it.

'I am sure that there are still large numbers of people in this country, and in the Empire, to whom it would be most distasteful to have to do honour to the Duchess as a member of our family. Everything has settled down so well in this unhappy affair, that to bring the matter up again at this moment would be a tragedy. I know you will understand how disagreeable this is to me personally, but the good of my country and my family comes first. I hope you will agree with me that this decision is right.

'I have consulted my family, who share these views.'[34]

Early in 1942 the King found himself with a new principal spiritual adviser. In December 1941, while staying at Windsor Castle, the Archbishop of Canterbury, Cosmo Gordon Lang, had informed the King of his decision to retire. In his place a churchman of a rather different kind, William Temple, who was in the Christian Socialist tradition, was appointed.

The King felt a considerable obligation to Archbishop Lang, one of his father's closest friends, not least for his handling of both abdication and coronation, and he was glad to offer him the use of a grace-and-favour house on Kew Green. It was known as York Cottage, but to avoid any possible uncertainty the King wrote to the Archbishop: 'It is not a cottage but a roomy Georgian house.'[35]

While the Anglo–American alliance in the year following the attack on Pearl Harbor grew steadily in strength, Britain's relations with her other principal belligerent ally, the Soviet Union, remained based on little except the desire to defeat a common enemy. The relationship was the subject of a letter to Halifax from the King on 9 May 1942. 'I am afraid,' the King wrote, 'Anthony Eden is having a difficult time with Maisky, and the exchanges of views seem unhappily reminiscent of Russian methods in 1939. I hope he may succeed in getting through with it in a form that will not be too distasteful to opinion here.'[36]

The arrival of the Soviet Foreign Minister, Vyacheslav Molotov, in May engendered little warmth. One of his principal demands was for formal British recognition of the annexation of territories by the Soviet Union following the Ribbentrop–Molotov pact. Although these included large areas of Poland, the country in whose defence Britain had gone to war, Eden considered the proposition seriously, only to be told by Churchill that to accept it would be 'contrary to all the principles for which we are fighting this war'.[37] The King received Molotov and wrote in his diary: 'He looks a small quiet man with a feeble voice, but he is really a tyrant. He was quite polite.'[38]

Churchill was personally responsible for a major British attempt to improve relations when he made a journey to Moscow in August. He did so with some foreboding and was later to write: 'I pondered on my mission to this sullen, sinister Bolshevik State which I had once tried so hard to strangle at its birth.'[39] The visit was particularly difficult because Churchill was quite unable to promise the Soviet leaders what they were insistently demanding, the immediate opening of a second front in western Europe.

Nevertheless some progress was made in improving military co-operation and in establishing harmonious personal relations with Stalin. When Churchill reached Cairo in the course of his return journey to England the King telegraphed to him: 'I am delighted that your talks with Stalin ended on such a friendly note. As a bearer of unwelcome news your task was a very disagreeable one, but I congratulate you on the skill with which you accomplished it.'[40]

In October 1942 a British parliamentary delegation set off for China on a goodwill mission. It consisted of two peers, Lord Ailwyn and Lord Teviot, and two commoners, J. J. Lawson and H. J. Scrymgeour-Wedderburn, Lord Ailwyn being the effective leader. While the preparations for departure were being made Lord Teviot wrote to Sir Alexander Cadogan: 'I do hope that you will find some means of arranging that the King sends by us a message of goodwill. . . I understand Wendell Willkie conveyed some such message from Roosevelt.'

The King received the delegation and duly sent a message to the President of the Chinese republic, Lin Sen. 'It is my earnest wish,' he wrote, 'that this visit will contribute to strengthen still further the excellent relations existing between our two countries. Separated though we are geographically, we are at one in our determination to fight on until we have banished the spirit of aggression from the world. We here in England have known what it is to stand almost alone against a cruel aggressor, and it is for this reason that the hearts of my people go out to yours in admiration of their gallant resistance against the common enemy.' The letter ended: 'Your sincere friend, George R. I.'[41]

During his visit to Cairo in August Churchill reorganised the Middle East command, appointing General Alexander as Supreme Commander to replace General Auchinkleck. On 10 August he gave Alexander a clear directive: 'Your prime and main duty will be to take or destroy at the earliest opportunity the German–Italian Army commanded by Field Marshal Rommel, together with all its supplies and establishments in Egypt and Libya.'[42]

Considerable reinforcements reached Egypt that summer; intelligence was greatly improved by the increasing use of deciphered German messages; and there was a new air of confidence as Allied troops under General Montgomery's command moved on to the offensive. In November a decisive battle was fought at El Alamein, which resulted in a total Allied victory. Of this the King wrote to Churchill:

> I must send you my warmest congratulations on the great victory of the 8th Army in Egypt. I was overjoyed when I received the news and so was everybody else. In our many talks together over a long period I know that the elimination of the Afrika Corps, the threat to Egypt, was your one aim, the most important of all the many other operations with which you have had to deal. When I look back and think of all the many hours of arduous work you have put in, and the many miles you have travelled, to bring this battle to such a successful conclusion you have every right to rejoice. . . At last the Army has come into its own, as it is their victory primarily, ably helped by the forces of the air and of those that work under the surface of the sea.
>
> I am so pleased that everybody is taking this victory in a quiet and thankful way, though their rejoicing is very deep and sincere.[43]

In his reply Churchill wrote: 'No minister in modern times, and I daresay in long past times, has received more help and comfort from the King.'

Some time before the battle of El Alamein the King travelled to Liverpool to inspect the underground room where detailed plans of extraordinary complexity were being worked out for the first major amphibious operation of the war to be launched jointly by Britain and the United States. It was given the code-name 'Torch'. 'If "Torch" fails,' Churchill had told Eden, 'then I'm done for and must go.'[44]

It did not fail. On 8 November Allied landings began at Algiers, Oran and Casablanca. To make these possible 300,000 troops were transported over huge distances with virtually no effective interference from the enemy. Complete Allied control of the Mediterranean would follow the next year.

CHAPTER EIGHTEEN

Victory on the Southern Front
1943

The political and undercover preparations for the landings in French North Africa were largely an American responsibility. The decision of the United States Government to retain diplomatic contact with the Vichy Government had facilitated secret negotiations. So had an arrangement made by a State Department official, Robert Murphy, whereby badly needed supplies could be brought into the French colonial territories from the United States and distributed under the control of American officials.

One less agreeable consequence of this was that when the Allied commanders landed they frequently found themselves dealing with French officials who had earlier declared their allegiance to Vichy and who now expected to remain in office. Between such men and General de Gaulle there was understandably little affection.

The King regarded the situation with misgivings. Some time before the landings took place Dalton, after an audience, had noted in his diary: 'The King has no time for Vichy and is surprised that the Americans have so long had illusions on this.'[1] American military reverses in North Africa also struck the King as disturbing, and on 22 February he wrote to Churchill:

> I am not at all happy about the present political situation in North Africa. I know we had to leave the political side of 'Torch' to the Americans, while we were able to keep Spain and Portugal friendly during the time the operation was going on. Since then I feel the underhand dealings of Murphy with the French in North Africa, and his contacts with Vichy, have placed both America and this country in an invidious position. I know we had to tread warily at the start, but is there nothing we can do now to strengthen Macmillan's and Alexander's hand in both the political and military sphere, to make the two French sides come together?

The American reverses might, the King feared, delay the proposed landings in Sicily, to which the code-name 'Husky' had been given, and on this he wrote:

> It looks as if the US Forces have had a sound defeat last week, which will not help them in French eyes, and as if we shall have to do all the fighting there. . . Now I hear that from the American point of view the date of 'Husky' will have to be postponed. . . This fact will throw out all our careful considerations for convoys and escorts and will upset our import programme again.

Churchill was in bed at the time with pneumonia, and the King had therefore missed one Tuesday lunch with him and expected to miss another. He apologised for disturbing Churchill but wrote: 'I cannot discuss these vital matters with anyone but yourself.'[2]

It might be argued that it was importunate of the King to write to his Prime Minister at such a time, but it was also an indication of how concerned he was politically, for he was normally extremely solicitous about Churchill's health and aware of the danger of adding to his burden.

Churchill was much less disturbed by developments in North Africa than the King and much more sceptical of the benefits to be derived from whole-hearted support of de Gaulle. Some two months earlier, in a secret session of the House of Commons, he had confided his opinion of de Gaulle to members of Parliament with some frankness. 'I have tried,' he said, 'to work as far as possible with General de Gaulle making allowances for any difficulties, for his temperament and for the limitations of his outlook. . . However now we are in secret session the House must not be led to believe that General de Gaulle is an unfaltering friend of Britain. . . I think he is one of those good Frenchmen who have a traditional antagonism engrained in French hearts by centuries of war against the English.' He had sent a copy of this speech to the King, who had replied: 'I am sure the House now has a very clear idea of the political make-up of France.'[3]

On the subject of Robert Murphy's activities, and in particular his support for General Giraud as an alternative French leader, Churchill now wrote to the King: 'His aim is to uphold Giraud and to provide a quiet tranquil Government for the 16 million people living in North Africa. . . The irruption of de Gaulle or his agents into this field, especially if forcibly introduced by us, would cause nothing but trouble. De Gaulle is hostile to this country, and I put far more confidence in Giraud than in him.'

Of de Gaulle he wrote further: 'He now wishes to go on a tour round his Dominions, "mes fiefs", as he calls them. I have vetoed this, as he would simply make mischief and spread Anglophobia wherever he went. I cannot see any future for the Fighting French Movement while he remains at their head.'

'As to the battle,' he went on, 'I suspend judgment until we hear from Alexander. The 2nd American Army Corps suffered a heavy defeat, and apparently was deprived of about half its important weapons. . . They are brave but not seasoned troops, who will not hesitate to learn from defeat and will improve themselves by suffering until all their strongest martial qualities have come to the front. What a providential thing it was that I perpetually pressed for General Eisenhower to take the Command, as the defeat of the American Corps, if it had been under a British general, would have given our enemies in the United States a good cause to blaspheme.'

Churchill ended his letter: 'Although I have been hampered by a high fever from reading all the telegrams, I think I have the picture truly in my mind, and I wish indeed that I could have given this account to Your Majesty verbally at luncheon.'

He was nevertheless in a sufficient state of vigour to give expression to one of his antipathies by writing: 'That old humbug Gandhi is fasting much longer than we were assured was possible.' He also gave the King encouragement by writing of the forces under Montgomery's command: 'I suppose Your Majesty realises that these two corps of the Eighth Army comprising together about 160,000 men, are perhaps the best troops in the world.'[4]

Churchill's sanguine assessment of military developments in North Africa was justified by events. On 13 May Alexander telegraphed to him: 'It is my duty to report that the Tunisian campaign is over. All enemy resistance has ceased. We are masters of the North African shores.'[5]

On the same day the King sent a telegram to Churchill, which read: 'Now that the campaign in Africa has reached a glorious conclusion I wish to tell you how profoundly I appreciate the fact that the initial conception and successful prosecution are largely due to your vision and to your unflinching determination in the face of early difficulties.'[6]

On an occasion such as this it was natural for Churchill to indulge his taste for sonorous phrases and, no less, to express his dedication to the monarchy. 'My father and my grandfather,' he stated in his reply, 'both served in Cabinets of Queen Victoria's design, and I myself have been a Minister under Your Majesty's grandfather, your father and yourself for many years. The signal compliment which Your Majesty has paid me on this occasion goes far beyond my deserts but will remain a source of lively pleasure to me as long as I live.'[7]

The King expressed a wish to go to North Africa as soon as possible. It would be his first overseas visit to a victorious Allied force. His wish was the first item on the agenda of the War Cabinet when it met on 6 June. It was agreed that the visit would be kept secret until the King actually arrived in North Africa. At the end of the meeting Churchill wrote in a minute to Sir Edward Bridges, the Cabinet Secretary: 'If he should pay a visit to Malta as he wishes, there would be no harm in mentioning this after he had left the island.' A stop in Gibraltar on the outward journey, which could well have invited the enemy's attention, was ruled out. The whole visit was given the code-name 'Loader', and in correspondence the King was referred to as General Lyon.

On 11 June Churchill telegraphed to Eisenhower and to Admiral Sir Andrew Cunningham, the Naval Commander-in-Chief, Mediterranean: 'I consider it most desirable that "Loader" should not be overworked with programmes filling every day and all day. A few days' rest and bathing should be interspersed with programmes. I should advise against staying too long in any one place.'

Arrangements were made for the King to receive a short daily summary of military news from areas outside the Mediterranean theatre, items of foreign political interest and a daily press summary. As the King was expected to be out of Britain for only about ten days it was decided, after some discussion in Cabinet, that it was not necessary to appoint a Council of State able to act in his absence.[8]

Churchill's principal political adviser in North Africa was Harold Macmillan, who had been appointed Minister Resident at the Allied Headquarters. Together with the three supreme commanders, Eisenhower, Cunningham and Air Chief Marshal Sir Arthur Tedder, Macmillan met the King at an airport near Oran on the morning of Saturday 12 June. The weather was extremely hot and humid, and the King had been unable to sleep during the overnight flight. Macmillan described him in his diary as 'tired and feverish'. That evening the King gave a dinner party, of which Macmillan wrote: 'The King had had a bathe and a sleep and was in excellent form. He was very good with Eisenhower, who was himself in excellent shape . . . the real natural simple gentleman that he is.' After dinner there was a small ceremony, at which the King presented Eisenhower with the insignia of the GCB.[9]

The next day the King gave a lunch party, at which the guests included Generals Giraud and de Gaulle. There had been some doubt whether the lunch would take place and, if it did, whether de Gaulle would be present. Churchill had advised the King not to entertain the two generals unless they were behaving well, and Macmillan felt obliged to tell the King that they were not. The King then asked his advice, and Macmillan recommended that the lunch should take place, as it might do some good and was unlikely to do any harm.

Shortly before the visit de Gaulle had been threatening to resign from the French administration in North Africa, but, while still in doubt, had said to Macmillan: 'If I am no longer in the government, will General Lyon wish to invite me?' Macmillan satisfied de Gaulle that the King would wish to invite him on his own merits. Of the actual event Macmillan recorded: 'The King did very well and spoke in good French to both generals, who were on his right and left.'

The most spectacular event in the King's tour was a visit to Malta. At the dinner party he gave on the evening of his arrival the King told Cunningham how keen he was to go there.[10] Tedder was also pressed on the point and wrote to Portal, the Chief of Air Staff, that 'the King insists on going to Malta'.[11] A few months earlier both Service chiefs would no doubt have vetoed a visit to what had long been a beleaguered garrison, but they now decided that the risk was acceptable, and the King set off in the cruiser *Aurora*.

The cruiser approached Malta early on the morning of Sunday 20 June. 'At 8.15,' Macmillan wrote in his diary, 'the King came on the bridge; a special little platform had been erected for him, a little projecting from and higher than the bridge. Here he stood alone, in white naval uniform. As we steamed into the Grand Harbour, a slow passage lasting at least three-quarters of an hour, all the cliffs and forts filled with troops, sailors, airmen and civilians, thundered out a tremendous reception.'

After being welcomed by the governor, who was now Lord Gort, the King drove for two hours through the streets. Crowds with banners were drawn up outside churches, and flowers and confetti were thrown. 'Considering,' Macmillan wrote, 'that they had only been told in the early morning, I don't know where they found the flags and how they had time to decorate the streets – but it was done.'[12]

The King spent some four days with the Eighth Army in the Tripoli area. Montgomery, who was particularly proud of the fact that he was the first victorious commander in the field to be visited by the King, put him up in his private caravan.[13] The message which, at the end of his visit, the King sent through Eisenhower to the British commanders on 25 June read: 'Throughout my tour it has afforded me intense pleasure to see the war-hardened men of the three British Services, the veterans of the Libyan deserts as well as their comrades from the west, in such high spirits and good health – and to realise that they are working in the closest harmony, not only with each other, but with the forces of our Allies, both in and out of battle.'[14]

Although long delayed, Allied landings in Sicily finally began in the early hours of 10 July. In telegrams to the Dominions' Prime Ministers Churchill described them as 'our greatest venture so far'.[15]

In a little over two months the Allied victory in Sicily was complete. Meanwhile Mussolini had fallen from power; Marshal Badoglio had become Prime Minister, and King Victor Emmanuel assumed command of the Italian armed forces. The acceptance of the Allied terms for surrender, and the invasion of the Italian mainland followed.

The Allies found it convenient to continue to deal with a government headed by Badoglio, although the British tenderness towards King Victor

Emmanuel was, understandably in view of his record, found questionable in a number of American circles. By September the Italian king felt sufficiently secure in office to set out in a letter to King George some of his views on relations between Italy and the Western Allies.

'I think it advisable,' he wrote on 23 September, 'to lay before Your Majesty in a confidential and personal way some considerations inspired by the common interests of our countries.' The first two of these 'considerations' were to free as much Italian territory as possible from German control in order to prevent northern Italian industries from working for the Germans; and to liberate Rome to prevent the formation of a new Fascist Government. The third consideration was the rate of exchange. 'A more favourable treatment than that adopted in Sicily,' King Victor Emmanuel wrote, 'would have incalculable moral and political repercussions for the common cause.' He made a similar appeal to President Roosevelt.

King Victor Emmanuel's stratagem worked. In a telegram which he sent to General Marshall shortly afterwards Eisenhower announced that a rate of exchange of 80 lire to the dollar and 320 to the pound had been adopted instead of earlier rates, which had been equally arbitrarily fixed, of 100 and 400. In making his decision, as Supreme Commander, Eisenhower had successfully overcome the objections of the British Treasury.

Further developments in the Mediterranean theatre of war and the future possibilities which they suggested occupied much of the King's attention in 1943. Among those to whom he talked at some length was a man who had acquired first-hand knowledge of the actions of Greek resistance forces. This was Colonel E. C. W. (Eddy) Myers, the principal British liaison officer with the Greek guerrillas. In describing their meeting Myers wrote: 'I found His Majesty extremely well briefed and most interested.'[16] But the talks on strategy in the Mediterranean theatre which the King found most stimulating were those he had with Field-Marshal Smuts.

The King was fascinated by this ex-guerrilla leader, who became his country's Prime Minister and the principal architect of the League of Nations, and who found relaxation in reading the New Testament in Greek. Churchill too had an abiding respect for one whom he had admired as a colleague in World War I and sought his counsel on a variety of subjects. In November 1942, for instance, without preliminaries or explanation, he despatched a telegram to Smuts, which read: 'What do you think about Miles Lampson as Viceroy?' Lampson was then British Ambassador in Cairo, and Smuts sent a balanced reply recommending that he should stay where he was. Churchill concurred.

Smuts was a strong advocate of a British advance into the Balkans at the earliest possible moment, and in September 1943 he sent Churchill two long telegrams. In one of them he stated that 'to the ordinary man it must appear that it is Russia who is winning the war.' He added the forecast that 'a tremendous shift in our world status may follow and leave Russia the diplomatic master of the world.' In the second telegram he wrote: 'We should immediately take Southern Italy and . . . launch a real attack on the Balkans and set its resurgent forces going.'

In Churchill he found a sympathetic recipient of his views, but one who had to take American opinion into account and who had just attended the conference in Quebec at which future Allied strategy had been agreed.

Churchill replied to Smuts from Washington: 'Believe me, my dear friend, I am not at all vexed by your two telegrams of criticism.' He went on: 'I have always been most anxious to come into the Balkans, which are already doing so well. We shall have to see how the fighting in Italy develops before committing ourselves beyond Commandos, agents and supplies.' He instructed his Private Office in London to show copies of his reply to 'the King, Mr Attlee and Mr Eden'.[17]

Having received only limited satisfaction from Churchill, Smuts turned to the King, whom he found less difficult to convince. He even sowed doubts in the King's mind about the wisdom of making the main assault in north-west Europe. On 14 October the King wrote to Churchill:

My dear Winston, I had a long talk with Smuts yesterday about the Mediterranean theatre of war. He has discussed this with you, and wants us to go on fighting there and not to switch over to a new front like 'Overlord'.

I have thought about the matter a lot since then and am wondering whether we three could not discuss it together. I have always thought that your original idea of last year of attacking the 'underbelly of the Axis' was the right one, and you convinced President Roosevelt and General Marshall to carry out 'Torch'.

The present situation as we know has turned out even better than we could have ever hoped for last year and would it not be possible to carry on there? Look at the present position in the Mediterranean. The whole of North Africa is ours, we command the Mediterranean Sea itself, Sicily, Sardinia and Corsica. Half the mainland of Italy is ours. Italy is now at war with our enemy Germany: Roumania and Hungary are trying to get into touch with us. What we want to see is Greece and Yugoslavia liberated; then Turkey may come in with us and maybe we shall see the three great Powers, Great Britain, USA and USSR fighting together on the same front!!

Let this country be the base from which all bombing operations will take place in an ever increasing intensity on Germany.

I was so impressed by what Smuts said that I felt I must pass it on to you. I know there are many difficulties for a change of plan at this late hour, but you, F.D.R. and Stalin are to meet in the near future. I am alone for dinner tonight, and if there is any possibility of Smuts and you joining me, it would give us all a very good opportunity of talking these things over undisturbed.

Would 8.30 or 8.45 suit you best?

The dinner took place, as did the discussion which the King had asked for. But in accepting the King's invitation Churchill warned him that there would be no major change in policy. 'There is no possibility,' he wrote, 'of our going back on what is agreed. Both the US staff and Stalin would violently disagree with us.' By way of consolation he added: 'I think there are resources for both theatres.'[18]

The respect and confidence which Churchill felt for the South African leader did not extend to the Australian political leaders in 1943. In particular he resented Stanley Bruce's position in the War Cabinet, and on 12 February he wrote in a minute:

> The position of Mr Bruce is highly anomalous. The Australians have now moved their last troops away from the general war zone to their own affairs. Why then should Australia be represented on the War Cabinet when Canada, which has five divisions, and New Zealand and South Africa, which each have one, are not similarly represented?
>
> I hear that Bruce is writing a lot of hostile stuff to his Government, and some time ago he made serious demands to become a full working member of the War Cabinet of the United Kingdom. I think he should be brought up with a round turn.[19]

Bruce, for his part, remained sceptical of the workings of the War Cabinet, of which he wrote in the same month: 'It is not fulfilling its functions and the Prime Minister is not getting the help he should. Too much of the burden is being borne by the Prime Minister. It is true, as many people would contend, that this is due to the Prime Minister's temperament. The Prime Minister's temperament, however, is no justification for failure to act if action is necessary.'

A Labour Government was now in office in Australia headed by John Curtin, who made no secret of his belief, fully justified by the facts of the war in the Pacific, that it was to the United States that Australia must primarily turn for military help. Churchill invited Curtin to Britain and to take his place in the War Cabinet while he was there, but Curtin felt unable to leave Australia. Instead he sent his Minister for External Affairs and Attorney-General, Dr Hubert Evatt.

Before Evatt's departure the British High Commissioner in Canberra reported that 'Evatt is very disgruntled that grand strategy of war should have been settled without Australia being consulted and without a single Australian general being invited to attend. He says that it is only Stalin's threat that he might throw in his hand if he did not get what he wanted which gave him such powers in London and Washington, and that the only thing would be for Australia to follow his example. He complains that "men like Eisenhower, who had not even moved a whole division in peace time," should be Commanders-in-Chief when Australian generals with experience of more than one war were ignored.'

On arrival in Britain Evatt revealed an exceptional talent for antagonising British ministers of all political persuasions, but Anglo–Australian relations were improved by the visit in May 1943 of a combined parliamentary delegation from Australia and New Zealand. After driving through bombed areas in London the members of the delegation were received by the King at Buckingham Palace, where they also talked informally to the Queen and the Princesses.

In their report the parliamentarians stated: 'Members were much impressed by the friendly atmosphere of this visit to the King.' The tenor of the whole report was indeed extremely laudatory, and it concluded: 'On our return we will convey to Australia a message of admiration, and in the words of that great Australian poet, C. J. Dennis, when in his own composition, *The Sentimental Bloke*, he "dipped his lid" to Doreen, we also say to Britain and her people "we dips our lids".'[20]

The King's decision to appoint the Duke of Gloucester Governor-General was also welcomed in Australia, and on 5 November 1943 Curtin wrote to the Dominions Office in London: 'I do sincerely feel that the appointment of His Majesty's own brother will have excellent results and will show unmistakably, to any doubters, how loyal Australians are to the Empire and with what affection they regard the Royal Family.'[21]

In July 1943 Sir Alexander Hardinge informed the King that because of the state of his health he must resign from the post of Private Secretary.

The role of the Private Secretary to the sovereign is an exacting one, calling for a deep understanding of the functioning of the monarchy which can only be acquired by a combination of instinct and a thorough study of precedents.

In political matters the King acts on the advice of his Ministers. This brilliantly-conceived convention allows a nation to enjoy both a democratic form of government and the benefits of monarchy, of which there can be many. These include a head of state above party who can be a focus of both loyalty and affection as well as a source of continuity, dignity, and the pageantry and ritual which attach themselves more easily to monarchy than to elected leaders.

The political convention of acting only on advice requires subtlety in its application. The number of issues on which the monarch actually receives political advice from Ministers is naturally limited, and in practice a great deal of advice has to be assumed to have been given and taken. Just as every day numerous civil servants are writing letters stating that 'the Minister has taken note' or 'the Minister has decided' when they are fully aware that the Minister has no knowledge of the subject whatever, so the

Private Secretary must frequently state on his own authority that 'the King has learnt' or 'the King wishes'.

A deeply conscientious, conservative, somewhat rigid man, Hardinge knew the King's business intimately and served him devotedly. Perhaps he remained in office a little too long. This would help to account for the devastating comments to be found in Macmillan's diary records of the King's visit to North Africa.

The judgments of the people he met which Macmillan recorded in his diaries were nearly always generous, but Hardinge he described as 'beyond the pale'. He added: 'His whole attitude towards the visit makes me wonder why he advised the King to undertake it at all. . . He just doesn't seem to live in the modern world. . . He would have been out of date in the 1900s and King Edward would have sacked him as outmoded then.'

To another member of the Royal Household who accompanied the King to North Africa, Sir Piers Legh, Macmillan was more indulgent. 'Joey Legh,' he wrote, 'does his best, and, although looking half-witted, is not so.'[22] Peter Townsend, a future Equerry to the King, confirmed this judgment later. 'Joey,' he wrote, 'despite appearances, was far from gaga. His judgment was unerring, his reflexes lightning-fast. He was, moreover, a most lovable character.'[23]

The King's new Private Secretary was Sir Alan (Tommy) Lascelles, who was to remain in office until after the King's death. A man of exceptional ability, who acquired an encyclopaedic knowledge of constitutional issues, he was more flexible than Hardinge and readier to give responsibility to his subordinates. He also had an easier relationship with the King than Hardinge had been able to achieve.

Sir Edward Ford, who was to serve as Assistant Private Secretary after World War II, had a very high opinion of Lascelles's ability.[24] Townsend admired his 'dry, pungent wit', but stated that he 'did not adapt himself to the changing times nearly as well as the monarch himself'.

An instance of how the King's wishes, or at least the King's name, could be used by a Prime Minister to assert his own authority, occurred in 1943. On 3 August Churchill sent a message to Sir John Anderson, who was then in Washington, and who, as Lord President of the Council, combined such diverse duties as presiding over the Privy Council and having political responsibility for Britain's contribution to the development of the atom bomb. The message read:

'The King took it somewhat amiss that you had left the country without seeking his permission and making provision during your absence for your duties as Lord President, with which he is closely concerned.

'I explained that this omission was due to an oversight and the haste of your departure; but I think you should cable expressing your regret. I am sure you will be forgiven. I am so glad you arrived safely.'[25]

How disturbed the King in fact was by Anderson's oversight is questionable, but after four years of war and austerity there was an increasing and understandable tendency for ministers to find reasons for overseas travel, and Churchill intended to control this. Therefore, after consultation with the King, he issued a memorandum, which began:

'I believe that it may be useful to remind my colleagues that it is the established practice for a Cabinet Minister to obtain the King's permission to be absent from the United Kingdom, whether on duty or on leave, and to inform His Majesty of the arrangements which he proposes to make for the administration of his office during that time.'[26]

Churchill continued: 'Any such arrangements must have my approval.' From then on the procedure laid down was scrupulously followed.

Less than six months earlier there had been an occasion on which the King felt obliged to act on advice which he clearly did not welcome. This followed the death of Cardinal Hinsley, the Roman Catholic Archbishop of Westminster.

On 15 March Hardinge telephoned Anthony Bevir, whose responsibilities in Churchill's Private Office were concerned with patronage and therefore included ecclesiastical matters, to ask his opinion on whether the King should be represented at the requiem mass. He was told that it might be inadvisable to break with tradition and that to do so might lead to undesirable expressions of extreme Protestantism.

John Martin, another Private Secretary, than minuted the Prime Minister: 'The King (after consulting the Archbishop of York and Archbishop Lang) has decided not to be represented.' Yet in a letter to Queen Mary the King wrote: 'No one was more annoyed than I was when I was "advised" not to be represented at Cardinal Hinsley's funeral. . . I know how much he had done to bring his church into line with our churches here and . . . I feel it was a great chance missed when relations are definitely better.'[27]

The King continued to receive during 1943 a flow of informative letters from Lord Halifax. Some concerned the United States Government, one of them containing the comment: 'I doubt whether a good administration is one of the President's gifts.' In another letter a visit to the Negro University at Tuskagee, Alabama, was described. 'One had the impression,' Halifax wrote, 'that the Negroes were demanding some sort of bread and were really being given a stone. . . It was impossible for the President [of the University], a cultured man and a Christian, to eat his luncheon in the same room as us.'[28]

In November the King invited Halifax to become Chancellor of the Order of the Garter, an appointment which was later to give rise to what was probably the last letter the King ever wrote.

There was also what appears to have been the only recorded instance of use by the King of personal influence to obtain supplies which were not readily available in Britain. In a postscript to a letter to Halifax he wrote: 'We are getting short of a certain type of paper which is made in America and is unprocurable here. A packet or two of 500 sheets at intervals would be most acceptable. You will understand this, and its name begins with B!!!' Halifax replied on 13 November: 'I have not forgotten Your Majesty's personal request about the parcel that you wish me to send to you and I will have this done!'[29]

At the conference in Quebec attended by Churchill and Roosevelt in August it was decided that a new command should be set up in South East Asia. Its task would be 'conducting operations based on India and Ceylon against Japan'. On 8 August Churchill sent a telegram to Attlee stating that Leopold Amery had suggested that Lord Louis Mountbatten might be appointed to the new command. Attlee favoured Cunningham, who was not keen to undertake it. Churchill was not convinced, and he telegraphed to the King:

'I presume Your Majesty will already have seen the question I put to the Deputy Prime Minister and Foreign Secretary about Dickie... I am increasingly inclined to suggest this solution to the President.'[30] This he did, and the appointment was agreed.

Mountbatten chose Kandy as the site of his headquarters, and on 24 November the King wrote to him: 'I hope the King's house at Kandy will be handed over to you. I have told Oliver Stanley (Colonies) to arrange it with the Governor.'[31] In the course of his duties Mountbatten was to write a number of long and informative letters to the King, one consequence of which was that the King acquired a new and detailed knowledge of strategic problems in the Far Eastern war.

In the telegram in which he told the King of his intention to propose Mountbatten's appointment to Roosevelt Churchill also stated, following his stormy visit to Moscow: 'Your Majesty will also have noticed that I have heard from the Great Bear and that we are on speaking, or at least growling, terms again.'

One gesture whose purpose was to make the relations with the Soviet Union rather more cordial involved a personal gift from the King. The great Soviet victory at Stalingrad in February 1943, following the prolonged defence of the city, had understandably aroused feelings of admiration in Britain for the courage and tenacity of the Soviet armies. It was consequently very much in keeping with popular feeling when the King agreed to a suggestion that he should present a specially designed sword of honour to Stalingrad.

The sword was taken to Teheran, where in the course of the tripartite conference there Churchill presented it to Stalin. Describing the ceremony Churchill telegraphed to the King from Cairo on 3 December:

'Marshal Stalin kissed the sword and handed it to Marshal Voroshilov. On behalf of the citizens of Stalingrad he expressed his deep appreciation of Your Majesty's gift and asked me to convey their thanks.'[32]

Of the King's Christmas broadcast that year Halifax wrote to him from Washington: 'It appeared to me to achieve what I should have thought was almost so difficult as perhaps to be impossible; namely giving a new direction and expression to what was in all our minds. . . It was reprinted in full in the New York papers.'[33]

CHAPTER NINETEEN

The Main Invasion
1944

On 7 January 1944 the King was sent by Mountbatten a comprehensive survey of strategic plans and prospects in South East Asia. As its contents make clear, no copies of the document were sent to the Prime Minister or the Chiefs of Staff. The appreciation began:

> Please forgive a typewritten letter but I am anxious to keep a copy of what I have written and in any case it will be easier for you to read a rather long letter this way.
>
> I feel I owe it to you, who expected so much of me, to place on record what has happened since I took over this Command.
>
> I am certain that you must be familiar with all the various operations which I am supposed to have staged and as this is going by a safe route I do not propose to use the code name but to describe the actual localities.

The words 'safe route' meant simply that the document would go straight from Mountbatten to the King and not via other serving officers or politicians. After explaining why the plan to land a substantial force in Sumatra, of which Churchill had at one time been a strong advocate, had had to be abandoned because of lack of resources, Mountbatten wrote:

> I arrived out here on October 7th and within a week went on up to see the Generalissimo at Chungking. I must point out that hitherto he had absolutely refused to collaborate with the British but during this meeting I not only obtained his collaboration but he volunteered to place the Chinese–American Task Force at Ledo (20th, 22nd and 38th New Chinese Divisions) and the Yunnan Force, estimated at a quarter of a million Chinese, under my command. . .
>
> Thereafter the Generalissimo promised full Chinese support and co-operation for the conquest of North Burma and even went so far as to say that he would allow me to divert transport aircraft off the China ferry route over the 'Hump'.

Mountbatten went on to describe his plans to capture the Andaman Islands and 'make a good attempt at cutting the supply line to Burma'. This needed the presence of a strong force of aircraft carriers.

I had been promised 10 for this operation (2 Fleet Carriers and 8 Auxiliary Carriers) and this would have been enough but for the fact that the Japanese, as a result of all the publicity about the formation of the South East Asia Command, greatly strengthened up their forces, both naval, military and air, in South East Asia. Against this air threat we felt that it was necessary to employ 16 carriers and I am glad to say that Admiral King agreed to loan 6 more carriers from the Pacific Fleet.

After listing plans for the use of General Wingate's Long Range Penetration Groups Mountbatten wrote:

That was the position when I went to Cairo and I received the congratulations of the Prime Minister and the President on having succeeded in putting together a sound and large scale series of major operations. . . In addition to this it was made clear to me that vast resources were coming out to me as soon as Germany was defeated. . .

Then the President and Prime Minister went off to see Stalin at Teheran. As you know he promised to come in against Japan if we finished off Germany quickly. By this remark he knocked out the first prop from my carefully built structure, and bit by bit the whole lot just came tumbling down.

The Andamans operation had had to be abandoned, and

the President had telegraphed to the Generalissimo regretting that they had to take away most of my amphibious resources without giving me a chance to try and explain matters myself. . . On receipt of the President's telegram the Generalissimo went up in a cloud of smoke and positively refused to advance with the Yunnan Force. Unless this Force advances it is of course impossible to join forces with China.

Mountbatten had been ordered to send all his tank landing craft back to England and in consequence had had to call off all amphibious operations. He wrote:

I am left with virtually no operations through absolutely no fault of my own. . . How foolish all those who made this great 'South East Asia Propaganda' after Quebec will look when nothing worth while comes out of the new Command, and incidentally how unfair on all of us out here. . .

But worse is to come. . . I now hear rumours that the Combined Planning Staffs are planning to finish off Japan entirely through the Pacific and that they do not even intend to give me back the small force I had for the Andamans.

In what was in effect a direct appeal to the King, Mountbatten went on: 'I feel that the planners have completely overlooked the political repercussions which affect you so closely.' He added: 'Unless they will agree to move my boundary and to give me more resources this job is a pathetic farce and I wish to God they had let me go back to my aircraft carrier.'

. The document concluded:

I need hardly ask you to treat this with even more than your usual caution. I have now put you completely in the picture. In fact, I believe you know more about it now than the Prime Minister and maybe you will be able to guide his mind in the right direction, but I beg of you not to show him this letter or reveal the source of all your information.[1]

The first and unavoidable reason for depriving Mountbatten of resources had been the slowness of Allied progress on the Italian front. This led to the decision to make a further landing at Anzio, which could serve both to liberate Rome and to secure a line protecting airfields, such as those at Foggia, from enemy counter-attack.[2]

The Anzio landings, which needed a minimum of eighty-eight landing craft, took place on 21 January. Two weeks before, on the very day on which Mountbatten had written his lengthy appreciation, the King had written to him: 'I am very sorry that you have been thwarted in your plans for an early offensive owing to the stagnated conditions in the Mediterranean. I can well understand how galling it must be for you, but I do feel that we have got to finish the Rome battle first, and so really do you.' He added: 'I am not feeling too bright myself over the prospects here this Spring, as no fighting US division of any kind has yet arrived here for training or anything, and the divisions in the Mediterranean are already on their way here when the job there is not half finished.'[3]

In answering Mountbatten's document of 7 January the King wrote on 19 March: 'I have been very discreet over the contents of your long letter. . . I gather that the PM and A.E. are backing you for the later phase as we must get back our own property and not let the Americans do it for us. India is now looked upon as an operational theatre of war instead of a political battle ground, and your show SEAC must not be allowed to dwindle because of operations elsewhere. It is a pity Italy is so slow which has taken up a lot of your material which you need.'

The King went on: 'I have been trying to write to you for a long time but circumstances have been contrary like. Lack of time of an evening for instance. You must take good cover at once on an Air Raid Alert in London now. It is short but intense and our A.A. barrage is noisy and effective. Not a good moment for letter writing.'[4]

In their correspondence at this period the King and Mountbatten discussed from time to time the future of Mountbatten's nephew, Prince Philip of Greece. In January 1944 the King wrote: 'Philip spent Xmas with us. He is becoming No. 1 of a new destroyer.'[5] On 10 August in an evident reference to the possibility of an engagement between Prince Philip and Princess Elizabeth he wrote:

> I have been thinking the matter over since our talk and I have come to the conclusion that we are going too fast.
>
> I suggest your speaking to Philip in Ceylon first and finding out whether he wants to go on in the Navy, in which case he would have to become a British subject. This being so he would have to ask George of Greece's permission to cease being a Greek. You could draft a telegram to Georgie from Ceylon. Were you to see him in Cairo you could tell him what is likely to happen. . . If you mention it to Georgie do please only speak about his going on in the Navy and not say anything about the other matter as they are both much too young. I am sure this is the best way of doing this particular operation, don't you, although I know how you like to get things settled at once.[6]

A little earlier the King had written to Mountbatten: 'I like Philip. He is intelligent, has a good sense of humour and thinks about things in the right way.'[7]

In April Princess Elizabeth celebrated her eighteenth birthday. The King considered that she should now be qualified to serve as a member of a Council of State if the necessity should arise. He therefore asked for and obtained an amendment to the Regency Act of 1937.[8]

In January the Cabinet discussed a suggestion that on her coming of age Princess Elizabeth should be created Princess of Wales. A paper on the subject replete with learning was produced, with which the King and Queen were in general agreement. The essence of its argument was that 'no peerage in her own right has ever been conferred on any princess in the United Kingdom'.

Having sounded out opinion, Churchill minuted John Martin: 'You should tell Sir Alan Lascelles that the Cabinet thought that if the King was opposed to conferring this title, it would be better that the announcement did not emanate from Buckingham Palace, as undoubtedly there would be disappointment in Wales which had better be encountered by Ministers.' The title was not conferred.

During the first two weeks of May 1944 the Dominions' Prime Ministers had a series of meetings in London which gave them fuller opportunities for discussion with each other than they had had at any other time during the war. Those present from overseas were Curtin, Mackenzie King, Fraser, Smuts and Sir Godfrey Huggins of Southern Rhodesia. The King entertained them to dinner at Buckingham Palace on 1 May at the end of their first day of meetings.

Churchill took the opportunity to reveal much of his past thinking about the conduct of the war and his present thinking about the Europe of the future. He made it clear that his own inclinations had been in favour of advancing into Europe from the south-east, but that it had been impossible to persuade the United States to take this view. He also said that he felt it would be necessary to build some kind of entity in Europe.[9]

Among the documents produced by the British on the subject of relationships within the Commonwealth was one written by Lord Halifax on 2 February. It was addressed to Anthony Eden and was in reply to a paper which had been circulated. Halifax wrote:

> I hope that I may be permitted to call attention to one special aspect of the intra-Imperial relationship which, it seems to me, is of such importance that the omission of all reference to it must impair the balance of any picture of the Commonwealth. This is the position of the Crown. It may well be that the machinery for consultation between the Members of the Commonwealth is susceptible of improvement and the evolution of a common policy on matters of high political significance is obviously essential. I would also agree with those who feel that to ignore certain features of Dominion developments making for greater independence and less inter-dependence would be foolish.

He went on:

> But we should surely make a profound mistake if we were to underrate the present and perhaps increasing value of the Crown as in fact, if not the only, by far the most effective and important, common symbol of unity and common organism serving the whole Commonwealth. Its appeal to powerful sentiments and emotions, which are not transitory but permanent, invests it with a quality largely independent of the changes and chances of politics. These, however disquieting or reassuring at any particular time, are likely often to be fallacious as indications of the real forces affecting permanent relations.

After referring to the wisdom of the decision taken at the Imperial Conference in 1926 to describe members of the Commonwealth as 'united by a common allegiance ot the Crown', Halifax wrote:

> Would it not be true to say that since that date the value of the Crown as a link between the Members of the Commonwealth has progressively increased as it has been more deeply apprehended? The Crown has withstood the tension of an abdication, and would be held by many to have emerged the stronger from the strain. In the Dominion of Canada a Royal visit immediately before the war furnished a remarkable focus of personal loyalty and affection, of which the influence has been far-reaching.

Halifax went on to advocate a policy which had earlier been suggested by Malcolm Macdonald:

After the war, the King and Queen should be advised not merely to visit the Dominions in turn but to take up residence in them successively for a substantial period in perhaps every other year. No doubt the initiative would have, ostensibly at least, to come from the Dominion itself in each case, and I fully realize that the whole plan is not without political difficulties. These might indeed be so great as to make it impossible of achievement, as might be the case if and when India reaches full Dominion status . . . It would be of the essence of any such proposal that Their Majesties should not go to the Dominions as visitors, but should exercise all their Royal functions in and from the Dominions in turn.[10]

It was a document which showed prescience as well as perception. Neither the King nor his daughter ever took up residence outside Britain, but in the years immediately after World War II, when the remodelling of the Commonwealth was to be one of the principal concerns of ministers, more and more attention was given to the central position of the Crown in an association which in other respects became increasingly heterogeneous.

As preparations for the landings to be made in Normandy grew more intense the King spent more and more time in visiting units of the fighting services. Not all his visits were to those who would be taking part in the actual landings. The days from 10 to 13 May, for instance, he spent with the Fleet at Scapa. But on 19 March he wrote to Mountbatten: 'The coming events here are very much in my mind and I have been seeing troops every week who will be engaged in them. I went to see one of Vian's landing exercises early in the morning one day in February, and later I hope to see his personnel before they start.'[11]

Shortly before D-day the King dined with Montgomery, who presented him with a copy of his *Notes on High Command in War*. At the final briefing on the invasion plans, which took place in St Paul's School in Hammersmith, the King was present, and he took the opportunity to make an unscheduled speech. Of this Montgomery noted in his diary: 'Absolutely first-class, quite short, and exactly right.'[12]

Churchill made it clear that it was his intention to be present at the landings in Normandy, even saying to Colville: 'What fun it would be to get there before Monty.'[13] The King had a similar desire, for, like Churchill, he hoped to be aboard HMS *Belfast*, but he was able to show greater restraint. On 31 May he wrote to Churchill:

I have been thinking a great deal of our conversation yesterday, and I have come to the conclusion that it would not be right for either you or I to be where we planned to be on D-Day. I don't think I need emphasise what it would mean to me personally, and to the whole Allied cause, if at this juncture a chance bomb, torpedo, or even a mine should remove you from the scene; equally a change of

Sovereign at this moment would be a serious matter for the country and Empire. We should both, I know, love to be there, but in all seriousness I would ask you to reconsider your plan. Our presence, I feel, would be an embarrassment to those responsible for fighting the ship or ships in which we were, despite anything we might say to them.

So, as I said, I have very reluctantly come to the conclusion that the right thing to do is what normally falls to those at the top on such occasions, namely, to remain at home and wait.

Churchill was not easily dissuaded. The King enlisted the help of Service chiefs, in particular Admiral Sir Bertram Ramsay, the Naval Commander-in Chief of the 'Overlord' operation, and General Ismay. He then made a further direct appeal to Churchill. This was effective. In his reply Churchill argued that as Prime Minister and Minister of Defence he ought to be allowed to go wherever he considered it necessary. 'I must earnestly ask Your Majesty,' he wrote, 'that no principle shall be laid down which inhibits my freedom of movement.' Nevertheless he accepted the King's judgment. 'I must defer,' he wrote, 'to Your Majesty's wishes, and indeed commands.'[14]

The first assault took place in the early hours of 6 June 1944. On that evening at nine o'clock the King broadcast to the nation, saying: 'That we may be worthily matched with this new summons of destiny, I desire to call my people to prayer and dedication. We are not unmindful of our shortcomings past and present. We shall not ask that God may do our will, but that we may do the will of God.' With the King's agreement the text of the broadcast was sent in advance to President Roosevelt.

As soon as it became clear that a bridgehead had been successfully established on the Normandy coast, plans for a visit by the King began to be considered. Exactly one week after D-day Churchill informed the King that the Cabinet had discussed the subject. 'They authorized me,' he wrote a little discouragingly, 'not to advise Your Majesty against such a step.'[15]

On the same day Churchill, having himself already visited France, sent a message to Montgomery to inform him that he would shortly have two further visitors. The message began: 'I must inflict upon you a visit from General de Gaulle tomorrow. This is, on no account, to be a burden to you in any duties you have to discharge.' De Gaulle was no doubt delighted to be leaving England, and there was perhaps a particle of justification in the poignant sentence which he wrote to the King and Queen at the time of his departure: 'You are the only two people who have always shown me humanity and understanding.'[16]

The second part of Churchill's message dealt with the King's visit. The King, he wrote, 'should not be advised to go into danger except the incalculable dangers of chance. I think he is very much interested in the naval arrangements, and really I do not see how a better programme could be followed than that which was arranged for me.' He added that the King 'wished me to tell you that you were not to withdraw your attention from any necessary military duty.'[17]

The King embarked in HMS *Arethusa* at Portsmouth at 8 am on 16 June. At noon he came ashore in an amphibious craft on a beach where Canadian forces had landed. He was then driven to Montgomery's tactical headquarters, where in his caravan Montgomery explained his plans for the break-out from the bridgehead. The King decorated a number of officers and men and returned to England the same evening. A laconic naval account described it as 'a most interesting visit, among other things a good many acrobatic changes of ships and boats in quite a respectable lop.'[18]

On 11 July, at one of their weekly luncheons, the King told Churchill that he would like to pay a rather longer visit to the armed forces in Italy. His suggestion was that he should spend a week visiting troops and then have a day in Rome.

The next day Eden wrote to Churchill:

If the King goes, he should confine himself to visiting his troops; and above all he should not visit Rome where various embarrassing situations would arise since it will be impossible to keep the visit secret. His Majesty should not see King Victor or the Prince of Piedmont. . . On reflection I would also advise against a meeting with the Pope, since in view of His Holiness's very neutral record in this war I think that the British public, apart from the Catholics, would resent the idea of the King of England visiting the Vatican. Incidentally the Pope has sent a pastoral letter to the Bishop of Berlin sympathising with the Berliners in their suffering. I am not aware that the Cardinal of Westminster has received one.

Churchill in turn wrote to Lascelles:

Ought the King to see the Pope, and what should he say to him? Obviously if the King enters Italy, he does so as a conqueror and the Lieutenant of the Realm must visit him. What are they going to say? Would not embarrassment be created if the King received the new Italian Government, whose fundamental position is that the monarchical question is in suspense? . . . Would not there be a danger of the Americans complaining that the institutional question of republic versus monarchy might be prejudiced by the visit of the representative of the triumphant Monarchy of Britain? Ought the King to go incognito and could secrecy be maintained, as was done in the case of his visit to Tunisia until the very last stage of the proceedings?[19]

After advising Lascelles to discuss the whole problem with Eden Churchill wrote to the King on 19 July: 'The War Cabinet agree that a visit by Your Majesty to your troops in Italy would be of great value.'

It was decided that the visit should be kept secret for forty-eight hours

The Visit to North America, June 1939 A crowd, composed mainly of children, give a tumultuous welcome at Medicine Hat, Alberta
Left: Iroquois Indians from Caughnawaga Reserve near Montreal with their own style of greeting
Below: With President Roosevelt in Washington

Above left: The King announces the outbreak of war to the Empire

Above right: The family tour Sandringham Park, which had been turned over to food production

Below left: Together with Winston Churchill, inspecting damage done to Buckingham Palace, September 1940

Below right: Air-raid shelter in a London's underground railway station

With Prime Minister Churchill and Deputy Prime Minister Attlee in the grounds of Buckingham Palace

Below left: The King in North Africa, 1943. Immediately behind, *left to right,* are Generals Alexander, De Gaulle and Giraud

Below right: 15 October 1944: Montgomery shows the King his dog 'Hitler'

Above left: W. L. Mackenzie King, Prime Minister of Canada

Above right: Lord Halifax, British Foreign Secretary and Ambassador to USA

Left and below left: Two of Roosevelt's principal personal advisors, Harry Hopkins and Averell Harriman

Below: President Vincent Auriol of France

and that the King should be referred to as General Collingwood. The King, it was agreed, would not visit Rome and no meeting with the Pope or King Victor Emmanuel would be arranged.

The King arrived by air at San Angelo airfield between Verrafro and Caserta on Monday 31 July. Harold Macmillan, who was in the welcoming party, wrote of the first morning's programme: 'We followed the King's party to the parade ground – half an hour's drive. Troops were drawn up along the roads and gave the King a splendid reception. The parade itself was very fine – an old-fashioned drill parade.'[20] The troops were from the Canadian Corps, to one of whose officers, Major J. K. Mahoney, a former newspaperman from Vancouver, the King presented the Victoria Cross. The recommendation of forty-eight hours' secrecy had clearly been jettisoned.

In the afternoon, Macmillan wote, 'General Alex met us and explained the whole battle. This was a great treat, and His Majesty seemed very pleased. . . He was in excellent form and most genial.'

The King stayed with the Commander-in-Chief, Mediterranean, General Sir Henry Maitland Wilson, at the Villa Emma in Naples. Macmillan visited him there the next day and showed him telegrams and other papers on Greek, Yugoslav, Turkish and Italian affairs. 'As usual,' Macmillan wrote, 'I was impressed by his retentive memory and his detailed knowledge of what is going on. When he is talking quietly his judgment is good and sensible. (When excited by company, he is sometimes a little wild in his talk.)'

In the course of his stay the King visited naval units in Naples, the Eighth Army at Viterbo and the Fifth Army at Nettuno and Tivoli. He also met representatives of the Polish Corps.

Macmillan's final verdict was: 'It has been a really happy and successful visit.' John Wyndham, Macmillan's Private Secretary, whose ancestral home was Petworth, wrote in a slightly different vein to his mother: 'The whole programme was well arranged, from the initial luncheon party, for 80, in one of the great Baroque salons of the Palace of Caserta (a setting finer than that which any of the guest of honour's own houses could boast) to the al fresco meal in the country at the end.' When a chair collapsed under the formidable figure of General 'Jumbo' Wilson, Wyndham commented, 'the royal sense of humour came creaking into action.'[21]

There were no untoward political incidents. Crown Prince Umberto, whose wedding the King, when Duke of York, had attended in 1930, sent a message expressing 'warm wishes for the growing and victorious fortunes of the British Commonwealth of Nations, of which Your Majesty is such a noble symbol and leader.' The King asked for a message of thanks to be sent to the Crown Prince with the request that it should be given no publicity.[22]

In October the King paid yet another visit to Allied forces on the continent of Europe. Once again his principal host was to be General Montgomery, and once again supreme commanders had to make personal judgments of the degree of risk attending the visit.

Portal, the Chief of Air Staff, believed there was now no good reason to advise against arrival by air at Eindhoven, though he added that there could be no guarantee of immunity against a chance shell 'unless the visitor never left the back areas'. Reporting his conversation with Portal, Lascelles wrote to Martin: 'This last the King will never consent to do. I am quite sure that if he is advised against carrying out Montgomery's programme . . . he will prefer to abandon the trip, or at any rate postpone it *sine die.*'

Montgomery, who was by now quite experienced in the business of entertaining distinguished visitors, wrote to Churchill on 6 October: 'The visit is being made on the very distinct understanding that there are no formal parades or inspections and the visitor is coming to stay at my TAC headquarters as a soldier guest as it were. . . The only real danger might be to the visitor's health. I live a caravan and tent life in the country and it is very cold. I seldom wear less than four woollies and a fur flying jacket.'[23]

The King visited the British Second Army and the First Canadian Army, and on 14 October Generals Eisenhower and Bradley received him at the US First Army Headquarters in Liège. After the lunch which followed, Eisenhower, in a short speech, said he felt everyone present 'could best express their feelings and appreciation of His Majesty's visit by saying that if there was ever another war, pray God we had Britain as an ally, and long live King George VI.' In the official US Army report of the occasion the King was described as 'obviously deeply touched by the General's words.'

The King was accompanied by Lascelles and Legh and by a figure described in the official American report as 'the proverbial Scotland Yard "Dick", whom you could spot a mile away by the fact that his right hand was continually placed inside his coat jacket'. Later in the day the King made General Bradley an honorary KCB.[24]

A little more than a month after the King's return Eden wrote to Churchill: 'We have had an indication from a good British source on SHAEF that Eisenhower would welcome a little extra attention at this stage from us.' Churchill replied on 26 November: 'I consider that at the end of the winter campaign it would be appropriate for the City of London to confer its freedom upon this remarkable American General.'

Enquiries made of the Lord Mayor of London's office elicited the reply that if the City's freedom were to be conferred Eisenhower would have to swear a special oath of allegiance to the King. This obligation derived from the fact that the City of London was the only part of his Empire which the King could not enter without the Lord Mayor's permission. It was later discovered that both Foch and Pershing had been made honorary freemen of the City, and these precedents were deemed appropriate.[25]

After the ceremony, which did not take place until 12 June 1945, Eisenhower took tea with the King at Buckingham Palace. By this time they were enjoying each other's company in an increasingly informal manner. The King's relations with Montgomery were rather less easy. The King was a stickler for the correct wearing of uniform on all occasions and in all respects. Montgomery's unorthodoxy, and particularly his addiction to a Tank Corps beret, certainly irritated him at times. Lord Chalfont went so far as to write: 'The King . . . disliked Montgomery's manner even more than his beret.'[26] This is questionable.

Lady Airlie, on the other hand, quoted the King as saying, after a visit to Montgomery in France: 'I like that man. He has taught me more about the Army than anyone. . . He purposely doesn't confuse you with a lot of military terms.'[27]

No doubt the King took for the nonsense it was the assertion, which Montgomery made to him personally, that his beret, being part of his panache, was worth at least an extra army corps.[28] But clearly the King's attitude to this complex character and great commander in the field, with his craving for affection and talent for arousing antagonism, was ambivalent. His views on the relative merits of Eisenhower and Montgomery, however, were made clear in a letter to Mountbatten on 7 January 1944. In this he wrote: 'I am thankful that Ike has been appointed here and not M.'[29]

When the King lunched with Eisenhower, he had expected General George Marshall to be present, but Marshall had had to return to the United States. This upset the King, and on 4 November John Martin minuted the Prime Minister: 'Last night at your dinner party the King mentioned to Mr Attlee his complaint against General Marshall for not lunching with him. . . Sir Alan is worried by the King's continual references to this matter and proposes to speak to him about it, though he does not hope to convince the King of what he is sure is the case, viz. that there was no intentional discourtesy and that General Marshall, being under orders to return to report to the President, was unable to vary his time-table.'[30]

Why the King should have persisted in taking such an unreasonable attitude is not altogether clear. Perhaps his resentment was evidence of increasing strain.

In June the King had confided to Mountbatten his immediate impressions of Marshall and other American Service chiefs. 'I saw all three US COS when they were here,' he wrote. 'I thought King had mellowed somewhat though still very Pacific minded. Marshall has grown older with strain and Arnold looks exactly like one of the pre-pre-war footmen I knew here years ago. But they were all helpful and were full of admiration and praise about Overlord.'[31]

Strain was increased in the summer of 1944 by the Germans' attacks on London with the flying bombs which they called the V1 and the British called 'doodle-bugs'. The Guards Chapel near Buckingham Palace received a direct hit, and on 18 June the King decided to cancel an investiture which was to have been held in Buckingham Palace. Sensibly too he decided to stay for a time in Windsor and to come to London only when his duties required him to.

Like other members of his family the King had great physical courage. A number of first-hand observers described him as being exhilarated during times of bombardment from the air, just as he had been at the Battle of Jutland. But his courage was particularly evident in the manner in which he overcame his more irrational fears. He had a profound fear of heights, and a Lady-in-Waiting recalled how, feeling obliged to visit a lighthouse, he had braced himself to climb the exceptionally high tower.[32]

Nevertheless the tension which was felt throughout the London area during the period of attacks by flying bombs in 1944 increased the tiredness which he was beginning to feel.

This did not prevent the King, on 30 November 1944, from writing to Mountbatten: 'I have always visualised a visit to the troops of the 14th Army during this next cold weather period, and when I saw Oliver Leese and Bruce Fraser before they went out East, I mentioned to them that I might (repeat might) pay a visit in February or March, but I have never said in January. Now that F.D.R. has again been elected President he may deign to grace this country with a visit on his way to or from meeting Uncle Joe somewhere or his armies in Western Europe, but the date has not yet been settled. Towards the end of January after the great man's inauguration has taken place in W.D.C. has been suggested. So I must be here to entertain him when he comes.'

The suggestion of irritation with Roosevelt was followed by an expression of doubts about what might happen in India. 'The political situation in India,' the King wrote, 'does not seem to be very peaceful, and should I go out to visit the Armies as I have done elsewhere some people might construe the visit to have a political aspect as well. I have suggested it to Winston but at the moment he gives me little support to the idea. However I have not given up the idea and I will talk to him again about it before Xmas. In the meantime . . . I don't want anyone to know of my proposal, in case it does not materialise.'[33]

The King was kept well informed by the reports which Wavell, as Viceroy, was sending. In September, for instance, Wavell had written to Leopold Amery, the Secretary of State for India: 'India is quiet now, and can be kept quiet until the Japanese war ends, though there is much bitterness among political Indians, who have no confidence in the intentions of His Majesty's Government to secure political progress. . . I am clear that the post-war period will be one of great difficulty and even danger, unless we can beforehand provide an outlet for the political and administrative energies of the educated Indians.'

There were also political considerations at home which limited the chances of a visit to India by the King. These too he explained to Mountbatten. 'Politics,' he wrote, 'is beginning to loom largely on the horizon now that Labour has decided to leave the War Cabinet at the end of the German war, so that I shall have to be here while the election is going on.'

There was in fact to be no visit to the Fourteenth or so-called 'forgotten' Army, nor did the King ever visit India. This he continued to regret in the years ahead, when in conversation he would often mention his disappointment.[34]

The King's letter of 30 November 1944 to Mountbatten, in which he expressed his hopes of visiting India, is in many respects a revealing one. Expressions of annoyance of a kind rarely found elsewhere in his correspondence continually recur. All are suggestive of an underlying strain. 'Winston,' he wrote at one point, 'is very overworked sending cables all day and night to F.D.R. and Stalin trying to straighten out the tangles which their underlings in all parts of the world are successfully making.'[35]

Feelings of stress did not in any way interfere with the King's performance of his duties. Nor did they impair the decisiveness with which he now acted, a decisiveness which he had acquired through the years of war and which contrasted so strongly with his attitude of mind when he had come to the throne half-a-dozen years earlier.

CHAPTER TWENTY
The End of the War
1945

In the early months of 1945 the pattern which the victorious powers were to impose on post-war Europe became increasingly clear. It was determined largely by the extent of the advances the Allied armies made from east and from west and was given some semblance of legitimacy at successive conferences held in Teheran, Yalta and Potsdam.

The Allied country which became the most immediate victim of such imposed settlements was Poland. For two months in Warsaw in the late summer of 1944 the Polish Home Army, which had been organised in secret, had fought a continuous battle against the occupying German forces. The Soviet Army had by then been within striking distance of Warsaw, but it had refrained from giving any help to the insurgents. Inevitably the Polish forces were finally defeated, and when the Red Army made its delayed entry into Warsaw early the next year it found itself in occupation of ruins.

When news that Soviet troops had entered Warsaw reached London, discussions took place within the Foreign Office, the BBC and the Political Warfare Executive on how the Polish capital's liberation from the Germans should be officially recognised. As soon as Paris, Brussels and Luxembourg had been liberated the King or Churchill, or both, had sent messages of congratulation to the Head of State or Prime Minister of the liberated countries.

In Poland there was a Soviet-controlled body known as the Lublin Committee. In London the Polish Government in exile, now headed by a Socialist named Tomasz Arciszewski, who had been smuggled out of Poland, was unwilling to accept the concessions made to the Soviet Union at Yalta, and therefore was politically somewhat isolated.

On 17 January 1945 Denis Allen, a New Zealander serving in the Foreign Office, recommended that 'after all that Warsaw has gone through it would still be appropriate that the King should send his message' and that it should be addressed to the President of the Government in exile in London. Various other opinions were expressed until finally Sir Alexander Cadogan, the Permanent Under-Secretary, wrote: 'I should certainly rule out any message from the King to the President of Poland. Not only would it be a red rag to Stalin, but it would also look rather silly addressed to one who has little chance of resuming his inheritance.'[1] This was the advice on which the King was called upon to act, and in consequence, shamefully, no message was sent.

Poland was one of the two countries to which Britain had given a guarantee in the summer of 1939. The other was Roumania, and in Roumania too in 1945 the Soviet Union was in effective control. There was virtually nothing the British Government could do to help Roumania, nor did it have any obligation comparable with that which was clearly due to Poland, whose people had fought with exceptional distinction from 1939 onwards.

Churchill was however determined to do what he could to ensure the safety of the young King Michael and the Queen Mother, and on 11 April he wrote to Roosevelt: 'We have unhesitatingly said that if they have no other sanctuary they may come to us. But I hope you will take some of this weight off us, as you are taking the lead in Roumania.'

The answer came from Winant, the Ambassador in London, his letter stating: 'The American Government feels that as a practical matter we should not be too eager to offer protection.' This aroused Churchill, who replied that the American Government's policy 'may cost the lives of these people'. He added: 'We should certainly not stand by and see them destroyed like vermin if they sought our shelter, even though they are but King and Queen.'

Winant admitted that he had signed his letter after it had been put before him by his staff 'as a routine matter', and that it was the only letter he had ever sent to Churchill without first reading it.[2]

Initially King Michael, who had played an estimable part in the overthrow of the pro-German Roumanian Government of Antonescu, and his mother made their way to Switzerland. But they did indeed later come to Britain.[3]

In contrast with other countries in eastern and central Europe, Czechoslovakia seemed for a time to have retained a welcome degree of freedom. President Beneš of Czechoslovakia, who had spent the war in Britain, lunched with the King on 14 February 1945 before returning to Slovakia via Moscow. The Foreign Minister, Jan Masaryk, also saw the King before his return home.

According to Masaryk's own account, the King told him he would make a good Secretary-General of the United Nations, serving as the perfect bridge between East and West. Masaryk claimed to have replied: 'Sir, I don't want to be a bridge. Men march all over them and horses drop things on them.'[4] The post of Secretary-General would presumably have given him a more peaceful end than the one he was to suffer a few years later when, after a successful Soviet-inspired coup, he was thrown to his death from a window.

The eclipse of such monarchies as remained in central and eastern Europe was a source of disappointment to Churchill, and a month before the end of the war he expressed his opinions on the subject with some vigour in answer to a minute from the Foreign Secretary. 'This war,' he wrote, 'would never have come if, under American and modernizing pressure, we had not driven the Hapsburgs out of Austria and Hungary and the Hohenzollerns out of Germany. By making these vacuums we gave the opportunity for the Hitlerite monster to crawl out of its sewer on to the vacant thrones. No doubt these views are very unfashionable.'

In the early months of 1945 German attacks by the rockets known as V2s continued sporadically. As they could be heard only after they had exploded, they were less unnerving than the V1s, and the highest number of deaths recorded in one week was no more than 180.[5] Nevertheless the damage caused by any one rocket was usually extensive, and visits by the King and Queen to areas which had suffered were proposed. That such visits never took place was due to strong representations from British Intelligence.

All German agents in Britain were at that time operating under British control, and this had made it possible for misleading reports to be sent to Germany about where the V2s were landing. It was established, furthermore, through the reading of German ciphers, that these misleading reports were believed, and it was therefore decided to discourage any royal visit to an actual damaged area, since any such visit could well have been reported in neutral newspapers and thus got back to the German authorities, exposing the disinformation they were receiving for what it was.

In formally inviting President Roosevelt to visit Britain in the spring of 1945 the King felt obliged to call attention to the V2s. 'I am very glad to hear,' he wrote on 13 March,

> that it may be possible for you to make your long-promised visit to my country after the conclusion of the Conference at San Francisco.
>
> You may be sure that you will get a very warm welcome from the people of Great Britain, and I send you and Mrs Roosevelt a very cordial invitation to be our guests at Buckingham Palace.
>
> We are still under daily enemy bombardment at the moment but we hope and trust the situation will be a bit better in a few months' time.
>
> We shall do our best to make you comfortable here and it would be a real pleasure to the Queen and myself to have you with us to continue that

friendship which started so happily in Washington and at Hyde Park in 1939. So much has happened to us all since those days.[6]

On 12 April, just under a month after this letter was written, the President died suddenly. The next day the King wrote to Churchill: 'I cannot tell you how sad I am at the sudden death of President Roosevelt. The news came as a great shock to me. I have lost a friend, but to you who have known him for so long and so intimately during this war the sudden loss to yourself personally . . . must be overwhelming.'

Churchill replied: 'I am touched by the kindness of Your Majesty's letter. The sudden loss of this great friend and comrade in all our affairs is very hard for me.' He added that he had considered going to the President's funeral, but he felt there was too much happening at home which required his attention to permit this, and Eden would go instead.

'I think it would be a good thing,' Churchill continued, 'that President Truman should come over here at about the same time as was proposed by his predecessor. He could visit his armies in Germany, and he could be Your Majesty's guest. . . I am making this proposal to him and to Stettinius very strongly through Anthony.'[7]

A memorial service for President Roosevelt was held in St Paul's Cathedral on 17 April, which both the King and the Queen attended. Twelve days earlier the funeral of Lloyd George had taken place. At this the King had been represented by the Duke of Beaufort, Master of the Horse.

On 9 June Churchill wrote in a minute to the Minister of Works: 'I have already asked for proposals to set up a statue of President Roosevelt in the same plot of unused ground in which that of President Lincoln stands.' Grosvenor Square, where the American Embassy stands, was later thought to be a more appropriate site.

By the end of March 1945 it had become clear that German resistance must soon come to an end and that certain official steps would have to be taken to mark the end of the European war. One of these was the drafting of a speech by Sir Alan Lascelles for the King to make when victory was finally announced. Lascelles sent his draft to Churchill, who wrote: 'Tell Sir Alan Lascelles I will give this my most careful consideration in the next few days. I should think there is at least a month before the occasion will arise.'

Nine days later he wrote to Lascelles to tell him how much he liked his draft, but added: 'I think the last paragraph is unduly religious. . . If the King takes this view I will try to think of a few concluding lines.'[8] Churchill and the King discussed the draft when they lunched together on 1 May. The text of the speech, as finally delivered, makes it clear that Churchill had no success in his attempt to minimise its religious content.

Churchill felt strongly that the public announcement of the end of the war in Europe should not be made by the King. On 3 April he sent a note to his Private Office, which read: 'As the announcement that the war against Germany has come to an end involves many controversial and political issues, the responsibility for making this should not be thrown upon the King. He should speak to his subjects at 9 pm or whatever is the best moment for an empire and world broadcast. Whether I find it necessary to make any observations upon this particular event can be settled later. My present inclination is that it will not be necessary.'9

The inclination did not of course last. Because of the somewhat piecemeal nature of the German surrender the choice of the day to be known as 'Victory in Europe Day' – later foreshortened to 'VE Day' – was somewhat arbitrary. Churchill decided on 8 May. At 3 pm on that day he announced to the nation in a broadcast that victory had at last been achieved over 'the evil-doers who are now prostrate before us'. Before doing so he lunched with the King at Buckingham Palace.

The King's speech was broadcast at 9 pm 'Much hard work,' he said, 'awaits us both in the restoration of our own country after the ravages of war and in helping to restore peace and sanity to a shattered world.'

Earlier in the day he and the Queen and the two Princesses had been cheered so enthusiastically that they had had to reappear on the balcony at Buckingham Palace eight times to acknowledge the crowds' acclaim. The King had then encouraged his daughters, under the escort of some young officers, to go out and join in the celebrations outside.10

On 7 April *The Times* had published an account of how in November 1918 King George V and Queen Mary had gone to the Royal Gallery, where King George had thanked the two Houses of Parliament for their formal addresses on the conclusion of the war. Lascelles thereupon wrote to Martin: 'The King hopes that a similar ceremony may be arranged when the present war comes to an end, and thinks that it would be made more personal if the actual Addresses from the Houses could be presented to him and read in the Royal Gallery, rather than being sent to him in advance, as they appear to have been done in 1918. His Majesty would, of course, in any case deliver his reply to the Addresses at the ceremony in the Royal Gallery.'11

This procedure was followed. The King, in his reply, spoke of the efforts made by the fighting services and civilians and by Britain's allies. He then said: 'I have done my best to discharge my royal duty as the constitutional sovereign of a free people, and in this task I have been unceasingly helped by the Queen, whose deep and active sympathy for all my subjects in pain or peril and whose intense resolve for victory has comforted my heart never more than in our darkest hours.'

The King also expressed a wish that the Sunday following VE Day should be observed throughout the country as a day of national prayer and thanksgiving. He himself had decided to attend a special service at St Paul's and was surprised to learn that Churchill appeared to have no such inclination. On 11 May Martin minuted Churchill:

'I told Sir Alan Lascelles of your wish to be excused from attendance at the Service at St Paul's. He thought that would be a great mistake, and that people would imagine some very extraordinary reason for your absence.

'I have just heard that the Lord Chancellor and the Speaker proposed to the King that to do you honour on this special occasion they should waive their usual proceedings (*sic*) and give you and Mrs Churchill their usual seats in the front row, themselves sitting in the second row. The King has approved this, saying that he thinks it a happy idea.'

Churchill decided, on second thoughts, to attend the service.

On 18 May 1945, some three weeks before VE day Churchill wrote to the leaders of the Labour and Liberal parties asking them to continue in office until Japan had been defeated. His proposal was not accepted, and on 23 May he tendered his resignation as leader of the Coalition Government to the King. The King thereupon invited him to form what came to be known as the Caretaker Government until a General Election could be held.

Churchill sincerely wanted the Coalition Government to continue. Indeed in his long political career he had found adequate scope for his talents only in Coalition or Liberal Governments. He believed that in the General Election which would follow the Conservative party would be returned to power, not least because he was its leader. But he had seldom concerned himself during the war with promoting his party's interests, nor did he assume that Conservative politicians were necessarily the people best fitted for high office. All this was shown clearly in a letter he wrote to the King on 28 January 1945.

In this he renewed his recommendation that the King should appoint Eden as his successor if he were killed. If he and Eden were killed at the same time, he considered that the King should send for Sir John Anderson, who during the war had held the posts of Lord Privy Seal, Home Secretary, Lord President of the Council and Chancellor of the Exchequer. Anderson was a professional administrator, who had been Governor of Bengal, and was not a member of the Conservative party. He had been returned to Parliament as Independent Member for the Scottish Universities.

'A new situation would probably arise,' Churchill wrote, 'after a General Election had been fought. If a Conservative Party were returned with a majority perhaps as large as they have today, they might desire that Sir John Anderson should become a Member of their Party or they might choose a Leader of their own. It is very likely that there will be a substantial Conservative majority in the new Parliament; but it by no means follows that that majority would not accept Sir John Anderson with or without his acceptance of the Leadership of the Conservative Party. The Prime Minister therefore feels that Your Majesty would be acting not only in harmony with constitutional usage, but also with the practical needs of the time in sending for Sir John Anderson in the contingency referred to.'[12]

Polling day in the General Election was fixed for 5 July, but largely because of the complexities of recording the votes of men and women in the armed forces the ballot boxes were not opened until 25 July. The election was for the most part conducted in a dignified and good tempered manner. There was however an embittered dispute between Churchill and Herbert Morrison, into which the King's name was dragged.

At an electioneering meeting in Lewisham Morrison said that when a V1 had fallen in Lewisham there had been no advance warning, the reason being that Churchill had given an order that there should be no warnings for single V1s. Morrison added: 'The result was that the casualties, in my opinion, were double what they would have been. I cancelled an order which he ought not to have given on his own authority.'

Churchill, who was out of London at the time, thereupon sent a telegram to Sir Edward Bridges, the Secretary to the Cabinet, stating: 'I do not consider a Minister is entitled to reveal Cabinet matters without the permission of the King. The King would act on the advice of the Prime Minister. This has always governed ministerial disclosure. Of course in cases of resignation or the Minister himself being under attack on the subject in question, this would not be unreasonably refused.'

An examination of the papers showed no evidence that Morrison had countermanded an order. In fact he had asked Churchill's permission to submit to the Civil Defence Committee a modification of the original policy, and Churchill had agreed. Bridges wrote that in his opinion Morrison had committed a technical breach of the Official Secrets Act and added:

'The summary of facts ... shows that Mr Morrison had ample opportunities for protesting against the decision not to sound sirens for single flying bombs, but that he did not do so and thereby made himself a fully consenting party. The breach of the convention which he has committed is thus clear beyond all doubt. . . As the Prime Minister says . . . the King's permission should be sought for disclosure of discussions in Cabinet.' Bridges's recommendation was that Churchill should write Morrison a short letter pointing out that he had 'offended against the well-established canons and conventions'. In the heat of a General Election this was not much satisfaction.[13]

There had been a number of indications that a Labour victory was not only possible, but likely. A few wartime by-elections had shown pronounced swings against the Conservative party. Some opinion polls had given similar indications. Yet the prevailing view was that, with victory conclusively gained after such a long and demanding war, the electorate was most unlikely to dismiss the Government in power and, in particular, its immensely popular Prime Minister. This was the opinion held by the King, by Churchill and, indeed, by Attlee. In the event the Labour party received the abnormally high figure in a United Kingdom election of 47.5% of the poll. This gave it 392 seats out of a total of 623.

The King expressed his own reaction to this overwhelming victory most clearly in a letter to Smuts, in which he wrote: 'It was a great shock to me to have to lose Churchill as my chief adviser.' To Churchill himself, after thanking him for all he had done during the war, he wrote: 'For myself personally, I regret what has happened more than perhaps anyone else. I shall miss your counsel to me more than I can say. But please remember that as a friend I hope we shall be able to meet at intervals.'[14]

It soon became reassuringly apparent that the policies of the new Labour Government would serve for the most part to maintain continuity.

During the war an unprecedented degree of central governmental control over lives and property had been freely accepted. Men and women had been directed into various forms of employment in the armed forces, the auxiliary services, industry and the Civil Service with fairness and considerable administrative skill. Rationing had been firmly and conscientiously managed so that the privileges which the rich enjoyed over the poor were minimised. In barrack-room, warship and air raid shelter a new egalitarianism had come into being in spite of the authority which rank conferred. In voting into power a Labour Government the electorate had therefore, deliberately or subconsciously, expressed a desire for a continuation of a number of aspects of this new social egalitarianism.

Continuity was maintained too in foreign policy. The election had taken place while the Potsdam Conference, appropriately given the code-name 'Terminal', was taking place. To the puzzlement of the Soviet delegates a new ministerial team came out to represent Britain and to pursue policies which nevertheless were barely distinguishable from those of their predecessors.

For the King adjustment to the change in government was made easier both by this evidence of continuity and by the fact that most of the principal new Ministers had already held office in the Coalition Government. He did however have a problem of adaptation when confronted with a Prime Minister whose style was so markedly different from that of his predecessor.

The King had had most cordial relations with both Chamberlain and Churchill, yet neither's appointment as Prime Minister had been wholly welcome to him when it had occurred. He had understandably regretted the departure of Baldwin, who had provided such a steadying influence during the period of the abdication and its immediate aftermath. Churchill had come into office when his own personal preference had been for Halifax. Now Attlee was replacing a man with whom the King had established a relationship of exceptional intimacy and trust.

In time the King's relationship with Attlee was to become one of deep mutual respect and real, though not overtly expressed, affection. In the conduct of public affairs it was to be exemplary. Yet the two men did not at first converse easily, both being essentially shy men. One important link they had was the deep interest both had shown during their earlier years in affording opportunities for a fuller enjoyment of life to boys from poor homes.

There was a brief threat at the time of the election to Attlee's position as leader of the Labour party. On 24 July, the day before the ballot boxes were opened, Morrison wrote to Attlee: 'I have decided that, if I am elected to the new Parliament, I should accept nomination for the leadership of the Party.' He recommended that the Labour Members of the new Parliament should have an opportunity to choose their new leader and ended his letter: 'That I am animated solely by consideration of the interests of the party, and regard for their democratic rights, . . . I need hardly assure you.'[15]

According to Kenneth Harris, one of Attlee's biographers, Ernest Bevin effectively dealt with Morrison's ambitions by saying to Attlee, once Churchill had tendered his resignation: 'Clem, you go to the Palace straight away.'[16] This Attlee did at 7.30 on the evening of 26 July, when he was asked to form a Government. Among his nominations for high office was that of Morrison as Lord President of the Council and, effectively, Deputy Prime Minister. In a handwritten note he listed his choice of ministers. The first two entries in the list were:

PM CRA
Ld Pres. HM.[17]

Attlee had considered choosing Hugh Dalton as Foreign Secretary. The King advised him against this, his own preference being for Ernest Bevin.[18]

The extent to which Attlee was influenced by the King has since been debated. Douglas Jay, for instance, stated many years later that it had been largely on the recommendation of the Cabinet Secretary, Sir Edward Bridges, that Bevin had been appointed.[19] When more than one responsible individual gives identical advice it is always difficult to decide whose voice was the more effective. What is certain is that the King expressed an opinion in favour of Bevin and Bevin was chosen. Subsequent events suggested that the preference for Bevin over Dalton as Foreign Secretary was fully justified.

In words which have frequently been quoted Mountbatten described the King's relationship to the new Government in a letter in which he wrote: 'You will find that your position will be greatly strengthened since you are now the old experienced campaigner on whom a new and partly inexperienced Government will lean for advice and guidance.'[20] This was barely an exaggeration. By 1945 the King had been on the throne long enough to have acquired something of that reservoir of knowledge and depth of experience which conscientious monarchs share with the most senior of civil servants.

The King's personal inclinations were not in favour of socialism, nor were those of his normal entourage. Peter Townsend, who had been appointed an Equerry during the war, was later to write: 'There was not a single socialist – at least above stairs – in Buckingham Palace.'[21] But experience made it relatively easy for the King to share the concerns of a Government with whose policies he was not always in agreement.

There were ministers, too, in the new government to whom he was strongly drawn. One of these was Ernest Bevin, whose phraseology in particular appealed to him. He enjoyed, for instance, being told by Bevin, who had had to have a number of injections, that his doctor had 'treated his behind like a dartboard'. He also relished Bevin's statement that he relied for his judgment of people and situations on 'the hedgerows of experience'.[22] Like his father, George VI tended to be more at ease with Labour ministers of working-class origin than with those who, like Dalton, had been educated at establishments such as Eton.

In the summer of 1945, with the war in Europe ended, the King thought it would be right that, as head of State, he should meet both Stalin and President Truman. On 16 June Churchill sent a message to Stalin marked 'Personal and Top Secret. Also Private.' This read:

> During the progress of our Conference from July 15th onwards, King George will be travelling in France and Germany inspecting his troops and he will probably visit the American headquarters. He would like very much to have an opportunity of meeting you and some of the Soviet generals. He would therefore like to come to Berlin on one of the days when we shall all be together. He would of course take no part in the business of the Conference. He would stay in the British sector.

Churchill went on:

> He would be very glad if you invited him to come to luncheon with you at the Soviet headquarters. He would in the evening give a dinner in the British sector to which he would invite yourself and other Soviet leaders and also President Truman and other members of his delegation. If desired by President Truman, he would lunch with him on the next day. Thereafter he would resume the

inspection of his troops. During his visit he would no doubt confer British honours on British, Russian and American commanders, agreed upon through the usual channels. Anyhow I hope it might be an occasion of goodwill and rejoicing, which would be helpful in other directions.[23]

Six days later, after a further talk with the King, Churchill sent Stalin a revised and simplified programme for the King's visit. 'It might,' he telegraphed, 'be better if he ... simply gave a luncheon to you and President Truman, together with suitable guests, and then departed in the afternoon to continue his inspection.'

Stalin replied only to the second message. 'In my plan,' he stated, 'there was no provision for a meeting with the King and it had in view only a conference of the Three concerning which I have already exchanged messages with you and the President. If however you consider it necessary that such a meeting should take place, I have no objection to your plan.'

Churchill described this as a 'most kind telegram' which he 'greatly appreciated'. Nevertheless he informed Stalin on 1 July that the King's visit had been cancelled. 'The King,' he stated, 'now finds it impossible for him to make his tour in Germany at the present time, as so many detectives and special officers will be required for the Conference of the Three. He has now informed me of his wish to visit Ulster at this time.'

To Stalin a shortage of security officers may have seemed an improbable eventuality and certainly no reason for cancelling a visit by a Head of State. When he dined with Churchill in Berlin on 18 July he asked him what the real reason for the change of plan had been. Churchill held to his earlier explanation, and a remarkable exchange of cordialities then took place.

In Churchill's words, Stalin 'affirmed that no country needed a monarchy so much as Great Britain, because the Crown was the unifying force throughout the Empire, and no one who was a friend of Britain would do anything to weaken the respect shown to the Monarchy.' To this Churchill replied that it would be his policy 'to welcome Russia as a great power on the sea'.[24]

There had been an earlier occasion on which Churchill's strong opinions on the monarchy seem to have impressed Stalin. This had been in Yalta in February 1945, when Stalin had proposed the King's health in a manner which Churchill described as 'meant to be friendly and respectful, but not to my liking'. Stalin had taken the opportunity to express his objections to monarchy in general, and to prevent a repetition of this Churchill proposed that in future the toast should be simply 'the three Heads of States'. This was agreed.

Difficulties were also put in the way of the King's intention to meet President Truman, but these he was determined to overcome.

The first lengthy assessment of the new President by Lord Halifax was written on 14 April. 'Truman,' he stated, 'seemed to me to be honest, affable and politically both tactful and a man to whom principles mean much. His attitude on international affairs is, from our point of view, impeccable. His critics say that he is not privately acquainted with details of foreign affairs. While this may be true no one who knows him can doubt that his modesty and open-mindedness are sufficient to enable him to acquire an adequate grasp of essentials of foreign affairs, and to employ experts at his disposal to the best advantage both rapidly and fruitfully. . . Truman is warmly pro-British. . . Everyone seems to agree that on international affairs he is likely to follow closely Mr Roosevelt's general lines.'[25]

From the British point of view this was encouraging. On 5 July Halifax delivered a letter from the King to the President inviting him to Buckingham Palace, and on the same day Halifax reported that Truman had told him 'he certainly intended to visit London on his way back unless something unforeseen occurred which obliged him to return to America, but this he did not anticipate.' After this statement had been made to Halifax the British Government had some difficulty in discovering what the President's intentions concerning a visit to Britain were. This may have been because the President himself was in some doubt.

On 6 July, the day after his meeting with Halifax, he went by train to Norfolk, where he embarked for Antwerp. In the train he wrote to his wife Bess: 'Now I'm on the way to the high executioner. Maybe I'll save my head. Let's hope so. George VI RI sent me a personal letter today by Halifax. Not much impressed. Save it for Margie's scrapbook.'[26]

The President's next letter to his wife was dated 12 July. In this he told her that he had had 'a most restful and satisfactory trip.' At the end he reverted to the prospect ahead of him in Berlin and, once again, to the King's invitation. 'I sure dread this trip,' he wrote, 'more than anything I've had to face. But it has to be done. Lord Halifax brought me a long hand letter from George VI asking me to visit him and the Queen at Buckingham Palace. I thanked him and told him I would if I could. Think I'll come home as fast as I can when it's over though if you and Margie were along we'd stop.'

On 23 July Churchill sent the King a message from the Potsdam Conference, which read: 'The President of the United States informed me yesterday of the deep regret he felt that he would not be able to accept Your Majesty's invitation to visit England before returning to the United States. Mr Truman is sending Your Majesty a letter of regret.'

The King was not to be put off, and the next day Lascelles wrote to Colville:

'The King wishes the following suggestion to be put before Mr Churchill on his return tomorrow for his consideration: Assuming that

President Truman returns to the United States by sea in the *Augusta*, would it be possible to bring her into territorial waters so that the King might go out from – say – Portsmouth in a barge, board the *Augusta*, have a talk to the President going down the Solent, and leave the *Augusta* by barge somewhere off the Needles? The King feels strongly that it is highly advisable that he should have an opportunity of meeting the President, even for an hour or so, before he leaves Europe. If the President is returning to the United States by air, then, of course, this suggestion is stillborn.'[27]

The King's proposal was accepted, although the venue was changed to Plymouth. Here the President, accompanied by his Secretary of State, James F. Byrnes, and his Chief of Staff, Admiral William D. Leahy, lunched aboard HMS *Renown* as guests of the King. In the afternoon the King called on the President aboard USS *Augusta*.

Recording the event in his diary, Truman described the King as 'a very pleasant and surprising person.'[28] Both he and Byrnes were much impressed by the extent of the King's knowledge of international affairs.[29]

The King's own vivid recollection of the occasion was principally of the freedom with which some of the Americans present discussed the atom bomb, which was in fact to be dropped on Hiroshima four days later. The King, who had been privy to the secret for a long time, had had an abiding fear that in a delirium or some other unforeseeable physical condition he would disclose the secret. Now he found it being talked about in the presence of waiters.[30]

Outside the very small circle of those who knew that the Allies had an untried and devastating weapon which they were willing to use, there was a general expectation in the spring and early summer of 1945 that the war against Japan would be prolonged and costly in Allied lives. The dropping of the atom bomb, and the realisation that it could bring the war to an end immediately, was therefore greeted with immense relief, particularly by servicemen and their families. The King's reaction was similar. On 6 August Mountbatten dined at Windsor and recorded: 'Everybody was in good form as the atomic bomb had just fallen.'[31]

Four days later, on Friday 10 August, the Japanese made proposals of surrender to the major Allies. Consultation between the Allies took place the next day, and an agreed answer was sent through Switzerland by the United States Government acting on behalf of all the Allies.

In Britain the State opening of the new Parliament had been fixed to take place at 11 am on Wednesday 15th. The King's speech had to be prepared, and by 4 pm on the 14th no definite news of the Japanese acceptance of the Allies' terms of surrender had been received.

Two different versions of the King's speech were therefore prepared, one to be used if news of acceptance was already known, and the other if it was not. In returning the speeches to the Prime Minister's Private Secretary, Leslie Rowan, Lascelles wrote: 'I should think this is the only occasion in history when the Sovereign has thus signed two alternative versions of the King's speech; I trust that the signed copy of the version which is not used will be preserved with a suitable note of the circumstances.'[32]

Confirmation of the Japanese acceptance of the terms was not received in Britain until 11.30 pm on 14 August, and at midnight Attlee broadcast the news to the nation.

The King had already informed Attlee that he hoped to receive members of the Government 'as soon as convenient' after the announcement had been made. Attlee suggested that Churchill might also be invited and wrote to Churchill: 'His Majesty has indicated that this course would be most agreeable to him.' Churchill was unwilling to accept an invitation extended to him alone. To do so might, he wrote, suggest he was dissociating himself from his Conservative colleagues. He asked whether some of them might be invited too. Attlee thought this could give the impression that a Coalition Government was still in being. The King's invitation, he told Churchill, had been extended to him as 'an unorthodox and personal tribute to yourself as the main architect of victory'. In the end the King received Churchill alone after the members of the Government had left. The spirit of party had triumphed over that of coalition.

On 17 May 1945 Lascelles wrote to Attlee's Private Secretary, John Martin: 'On the evening of May 29th The King and Queen will go for a few days complete rest to their small house near Balmoral. . . I hope to take part myself in this very necessary restorative period, and shall be going with Their Majesties.'

With the ending of the fighting in Europe certain pre-war royal habits had been resumed. In July, for instance, the King, although he did not share the Queen's delight in the sport, attended Ascot races. But release from the peculiar demands imposed by wartime conditions was only gradual.

After attending the thanksgiving service held in St Paul's Cathedral in May 1945 Sir Henry (Chips) Channon, the diarist, noted: 'The King looked drawn; but he has the Windsor gift of looking half his age.' This was perceptive, for the King could indeed look both older and younger than he was.

When the war came to an end the King was only in his fiftieth year, but his physique was not altogether strong, and the effects of strain were sometimes physically apparent. He was however an addict of fresh air and exercise; he never allowed weather conditions to prevent him from shooting, and he continued to play squash and tennis strenuously when the opportunity offered, believing these practices kept him fit. No doubt to a limited extent they did, but the most important factor in relieving the stresses upon him was certainly the quality of the King's family life.

In *Time and Chance* Peter Townsend, who as an equerry saw the family life at close quarters, gave an attractive and convincing picture of it. 'What struck me most,' he wrote, '. . . was the astonishing affection generated by that small family. Perpetual currents of it flowed between them, between father and mother, sister and sister, between the parents and their daughters and back again.'

Yet even within the family circle it was the King on whom the others primarily depended. Elizabeth Longford quoted Lady Granville, one of the Queen's sisters, as saying of the King and Queen in wartime: 'The King was a rock to her, indeed to all of us. In fundamental things she leant on him.'

In the late summer of 1945 the royal family came as usual to Balmoral. These visits were to only a limited extent holidays. The King and Queen were normally free of public engagements, but the despatch boxes continued to arrive, even in Scotland, and so at times did Ministers of the Crown.

One who came in September 1945 was Clement Attlee, whose visit was a considerable success. After his departure Lascelles wrote to Rowan: 'I hope the Prime Minister enjoyed his visit as much as everybody here enjoyed seeing him. He seemed in excellent form and surprisingly well, considering the immense volume of work that he has had to cope with in the last few months.'[33]

The King's discussions with the Prime Minister during this visit were primarily concerned with Commonwealth affairs. In the course of them the first of the post-war royal visits to a Dominion was provisionally agreed. This was to be to the Union of South Africa.

CHAPTER TWENTY-ONE
Aftermath of War
1946

With the ending of the war the King and leading members of the Government had to turn their attention once again to the problems of the Duke of Windsor, in particular where he might live and how he might be employed once his wartime appointment as Governor of the Bahamas came to an end.

Lord Halifax continued to keep the King well informed on this and other subjects. Indeed he ended one letter to the King, which ran to ten closely typed pages, by apologising for its length, then adding: 'Your Majesty was good enough to say that I might give you my impressions from time to time.'

Summarising one talk he had with the Duke of Windsor about the Duke's post-war prospects, Halifax wrote:

> Though he intended to see the war out in the Bahamas he wondered how long the war would continue, and where they would live after it was finished. He said he didn't think France might be much of a place to live in, and thought that the New World might be all right, but it was very expensive! He said that he was very happily married and had got the most wonderful wife, with whom he could be happy anywhere.

Halifax went on:

> I told him that if he would allow me to speak freely too, I should like to do so. I said that I had always doubted whether he had fully realized how deep had been the feeling excited by his abdication and subsequent marriage. . . Many people had inevitably felt that by abdicating from the duty he had inherited, he had let the show down, and that this feeling with a great many people had outweighed the deep gratitude that they had felt to him for all he had done as Prince of Wales. And although people fully recognized that he had done his best to minimize the public difficulty created by his act, there was also a sharp feeling

of criticism about his marriage which naturally focused itself in criticism of the Duchess. . .

The upshot of it all as left in my own mind was that he, as I expected and as Your Majesty knows, feels very keenly the difficulty about returning to England to resume the sort of life he might have expected, but so long as these difficulties persist, he will not try to force the situation.

Halifax went on to describe how he had entertained the Duke and Duchess to lunch together with the US Secretary of the Navy, Frank Knox, and his wife. 'The Duchess's behaviour,' he wrote, 'was completely correct, and in one tiny detail I thought that she acted with considerable tact by making Mrs Knox go into luncheon in front of herself.'[1]

One reason why the Duke of Windsor kept in touch with Halifax was that when the war ended he hoped to be given a job within what he called the 'ambit' of the British Embassy. The word 'ambit' seems to have been first used in this connection by Winston Churchill, and the Duke seized on it avidly. The job which he sought was never very clearly defined, but he evidently envisaged himself as a kind of roving ambassador serving in a general way to improve Anglo-American relations.

The possibility of employing the Duke in this way was considered by Eden, and among others, by Duff Cooper. In the summer of 1945 the Duke came privately to Britain and tried to enlist the support of the new Foreign Secretary, Ernest Bevin.[2] Lascelles too gave much thought to the subject. None of them found the idea of employing the Duke as an auxiliary ambassador in the United States more than superficially appealing. Lascelles explained the general feelings in a letter to Halifax on 10 March 1946, in which he wrote: 'As I told the Duke last summer, many of us during the last nine years have spent hours in taking to pieces the clock of British imperial constitutional machinery, and trying to fit it together again with an extra wheel – the wheel of an ex-King. We have never succeeded in making it go.'

In the same letter Lascelles set out on paper, more clearly perhaps than anybody else ever did, the King's own opinions on how and where his brother should live in the best interests of all concerned.

The King, feels strongly – as I do myself – that the USA is the only place where he can live, and that he should be urged to make it his permanent home as soon as possible. He must not settle in the UK, and he definitely told me that neither of them wish to do this; France today, and still less France tomorrow, is no place for him; and there are obvious difficulties in the way of his going to any corner of the British Empire. The King, as a matter of fact, is strongly advising him to pack up and go to the United States as soon as possible; to make himself a permanent home there, and in *an unofficial capacity*, to do what he can for the 'betterment of Anglo-American relations,' which, he always declares, is the job for which he is best fitted, and which he has most at heart.

Lascelles went on to recount how he himself had suggested to the Duke that he should buy a house in one of the southern States and 'make it a centre of private hospitality, like a great English country house in the nineteenth century'. This had seemed to appeal to the Duke, who had also suggested that he could provide the Ambassador with private reports on personalities. Lascelles had cautiously replied that this might be possible 'so long as they were private'.

'Since then,' Lascelles went on, 'the "ambit" idea has possessed him. . . When he left the USA he rashly told the newspapermen that he was going to get a job; if he goes home without one, he fears that they will laugh at him. . . As I asked the King to point out to him in a letter that he is in process of writing, the American press would be far more excited – even hostile – and give him much more trouble, if it were announced that he was going back with some mysterious and ill-defined attachment to the British Embassy.'

'The "ambit" phrase,' he added, 'like so many pleasant-sounding phrases in history, has proved a will-of-the wisp, raising false hopes.'[3]

The King's wishes, as expressed by Lascelles, were not to be fulfilled. Without the status, and indeed the material benefits, which the job within the 'ambit' of the Embassy would have conferred the Duke and Duchess came to the conclusion that life in the United States was not what they wanted.

With the prospect of a lengthy visit to South Africa ahead of him, and other visits to Commonwealth countries likely to follow, the King thought that the existing arrangements for the exercise of royal functions when he was away from Britain needed a general overhaul. On 3 April 1946 he discussed the problem at length with the Lord Chancellor, Lord Jowitt. The next day Jowitt reported to Attlee on their meeting.

'The King,' Jowitt wrote, 'thought the whole business of Councillors of State rather cumbrous and unnecessary in these days of flying, wireless and the like. Could he not when in Cape Town, for instance, transact London business just as, conversely, he can conduct the business of the Union of South Africa whilst in London? He thought that this matter was one which might usefully be broached by you at the forthcoming meeting of Dominion Prime Ministers.'

Nor was the King altogether satisfied with the choice of Councillors of State. In particular he asked why Queen Mary, who had experienced much, was not included among them, whereas Viscount Lascelles, the husband of Princess Mary, was. The King also pointed out that in the event of his own death and his daughter's accession, the act, as it stood, would preclude his widow from being a Councillor of State when his daughter went abroad.

Jowitt admitted that the alteration the King suggested had much to commend it, but it required legislation and he hoped this could be avoided. Jowitt also discussed the question the King had raised with Lascelles, who made the point that 'when the King was in South Africa with many duties to perform he would, whatever he thinks, probably be glad to be relieved of the duty of signing documents from the United Kingdom.'[4]

After some discussion the Cabinet decided to take no action on the King's proposals concerning the Queen Mother, but the King did at least have it on record that in his opinion the Duke of Gloucester should always be in Britain when he himself was abroad.

A number of other questions concerning the royal functions or activities in which he was personally much interested were decided rather more to the King's satisfaction. In December 1946, at Attlee's suggestion, it was agreed that appointments to the Orders of the Garter and the Thistle should thenceforward be made by the Sovereign without advice from the Prime Minister.

In February 1946 a committee set up under the Army Council recommended that Army dress after the war should consist of battledress for service and training and a new blue uniform for walking out. This was what the King had wanted, and he approved the order while accepting that for economic reasons, and because of a shortage of textiles, the introduction of the new uniform would have to be postponed.

In the day-to-day conduct of business the King's relations with his ministers were for the most part smooth. In a letter to the Duke of Gloucester the King did write: 'My new Government is not easy and the people are rather difficult to talk to.' It was however a letter written in a mood of some depression. Earlier in the letter the King wrote: 'I have been suffering from an awful reaction from the strain of the war. . . I really want a rest, away from people and papers, but that of course is impossible.'[5]

The Government itself faced formidable difficulties. On 27 April 1946, some nine months after taking office, Attlee said in a speech in Newcastle-upon-Tyne: 'I remember some of our opponents saying to me before the Election: "Don't you hope you won't win?" ' He then listed some of the Government's major problems, beginning, perhaps surprisingly, with those overseas.

'The war,' he said, 'let loose a flood of hatred. . . Old landmarks have been swept away, there have been great movements of populations. . . It is difficult to build a stable community in conditions of want, scarcity and starvation. We have inherited from the past difficult problems. Outstanding among these are Palestine and India. . . We have to use shipping for troop movements and for the movements of displaced persons to the detriment of recreating our shipping trade.'

'On the home front,' he continued, 'we are faced with innumerable shortages . . . in particular a shortage of housing. . . There is inevitably a time lag in converting industries directed to munitions to satisfy the needs of the people in time of peace.'[6]

The shortage of housing was an issue on which the Government was frequently under attack. Government policy was to entrust the building of the great bulk of new housing to local authorities, with the Ministry of Health having responsibility for coordination and the general direction of effort. The Minister of Health was Aneurin Bevan, who also had the task of introducing a national health service of extraordinary scope.

The King took a liking to Bevan, a man of abundant vitality and intellectual power, whose background was that of of the Welsh coal mines. He too had suffered in boyhood from a stammer and openly expressed his admiration for the way in which the King had overcome his difficulties. Bevan himself had done no less, having already acquired a considerable reputation as a parliamentary debater.

On a number of occasions the King discussed housing policy with both Attlee and Bevan, taking the opportunity, when he did so, of stressing the importance of not stifling all private enterprise.[7]

In effecting something of a social revolution, for which not a little of the preliminary work had been done under a coalition government during the war, Attlee was determined not to be dependent on trades union tolerance. He was also willing, if necessary, to alienate a number of those who could be expected to be his electoral supporters.

One of the early decisions taken by his administration was to prolong for five years the Emergency Powers Act. In January 1946 a plan was drawn up for the use of members of the armed forces in emergencies. In April the Cabinet decided to send troops to unload food ships in Glasgow and to act thereby as strike-breakers.[8] In these and other actions directed towards maintaining essential services Attlee had the full-hearted support of the King.[9]

The King also welcomed the scrupulousness with which Attlee kept him informed and consulted him on matters on which he had a right to express an opinion. In September 1946, for example, Attlee sent him a long letter explaining his plans for reorganising ministerial control of the Service Departments. These, he told the King, he had already worked out when he had been a Junior Minister in the War Office in the first Labour Government. He himself would be Chairman of a new Defence Committee. A new Minister of Defence would be Deputy Chairman and the effective controller of the Committee. The three Service Ministers would not be members of the Cabinet but would attend when required.[10] It was an important step towards the eventual establishment of an effective Ministry of Defence.

The success which he and the King had in establishing a good working relationship gave Attlee considerable personal satisfaction. He was himself a strong advocate of monarchy and more than once made the point that the greatest advances towards democratic socialism had been made in such countries as Britain, Norway, Sweden and Denmark, and not in republics.[11]

On 7 November 1946 the Cabinet had a discussion on what should be done to celebrate the twenty-first birthday of Princess Elizabeth, which would take place the following year, when she was expected to be in South Africa. Attlee undertook to make enquiries of the royal family, and discussions continued in the months which followed. It was decided not to establish a precedent by a formal resolution in parliament or by a gift from the Government. The sending of a telegram to South Africa was considered, but in the end it was decided that a letter should be delivered to the Princess by hand on her birthday. This gave Attlee an opportunity to express his own feelings about the monarchy. 'The steadfast leadership and selfless devotion of the Royal Family,' he wrote, 'shines forth as one of the greatest blessings and surest bulwarks of this land.'[12]

The countries whose affairs seemed to the British Government in 1946 to be most complex and to call for the most clear-sighted judgment were no longer Germany or the USSR or the United States. They were, as Attlee indicated in his Newcastle speech, India and Palestine. As Palestine was a mandated territory and not a colony of the Crown, the King's role there counted for little. In Indian affairs, by contrast, it was to become of increasing importance.

The wartime policy of the British Coalition Government had been to make maximum use of the Indian regiments, maintain the peace internally and engage, up to a point, in exploratory talks about the future. Sir Stafford Cripps had led a wartime mission with authority to discuss the kind of government which India might have after the war, but it had been unable to break down barriers.

Attlee now decided that before his own government took any major decisions on the future of India another mission should be sent out. It was to be led by the Secretary of State for India, Lord Pethick-Lawrence. The other members were Cripps and A. V. Alexander, who had been First Lord of the Admiralty in the Coalition Government and held the same post in Attlee's administration.

On 4 March Pethick-Lawrence wrote to Attlee:

The King wishes to see the Ministers who are going to India and we shall have an audience with him shortly.

I think I heard you tell Sir Stafford Cripps that you had spoken to the King but I do not know how much you have told him of our plans in regard to India.

Clearly, however, he ought to be informed that we are prepared to contemplate a settlement on the basis that India will not remain within the

Empire, and as this will affect the King's title I presume that his approval is necessary.

If you have not already told him I imagine you will wish to inform him yourself before our audience. . . I should be glad to have a note of what you have said or written to him to guide myself and my colleagues at our audience. I presume that a formal written approval by the King will not be necessary until a later stage.

Attlee wrote by hand at the bottom of Pethick-Lawrence's minute: 'I told him that the basis of our negotiations was necessarily based on the Cripps offer which gave India the freedom to choose her future which might be independence. He did not dissent from this.'

Two days later Pethick-Lawrence sent Attlee a further minute. In this he wrote:

We discussed what we should say to the King. We (i.e. ministers going to India) think that we should make it clear to the King that if India does decide to become an independent state this will of course affect the King's position and title.

We also propose to tell the King that whether India after attaining self-government remains within the Commonwealth or not it will not be possible to maintain the existing relation between the Crown and the Indian States, since if British India is fully self-governing our ability to carry out our obligations to the Indian States will be considerably weakened and may ultimately disappear.

A draft directive was prepared for submission to the King 'to prepare His Majesty's mind somewhat for discussion of these matters', Pethick-Lawrence expressing the opinion that 'India would be more likely to remain within the Commonwealth if offered the chance to leave'.[13]

Pethick-Lawrence's judgment of what should be said to the King and how it should be phrased was perhaps a little patronising, but he and his colleagues certainly made their intentions clear to him before their departure.

The mission reached India in the last week of March 1946. About the same time the King received a detailed and discouraging report on its prospects. This came from Lord Wavell, who was now in his third year of office as Viceroy. When Lord Linlithgow's term of office as Viceroy had been nearing its end in 1943 both Churchill and Leopold Amery, the Secretary of State for India, had for a time favoured the appointment of Eden as his successor. The King had felt strongly that it would be unwise to remove Eden from the post of Foreign Secretary and had expressed this opinion at some length in a letter to Churchill. In his letter he had also made the pertinent comment: 'I cannot help wondering if the political situation in India, unsatisfactory as it undoubtedly is, will yield to treatment at the hands of any individual statesman for some time to come.'[14] After further discussion, and some two months later, Wavell was appointed Viceroy.

In his report to the King on 22 March 1946 Wavell wrote: 'Though it is not easy to be optimistic about the prospects of agreement, there is no doubt whatever about the grim results that would be the consequence of failure.' He went on:

> The last three months have been anxious and depressing. They have been marked by continued and unbridled abuse of the Government, of the British, of officials and police, in political speeches, in practically the whole of the Press, and in the assembly; by serious rioting in Bombay; by a mutiny in the RIN, much indiscipline in the RIAF, some unrest in the Indian Army; by an unprecedented drought and famine conditions over many parts of India; by threatened strikes on the Railways, and in the Posts and telegraphs; by a general sense of insecurity and lawlessness.

In Wavell's judgment virtually all the politicians were equally blameworthy. 'Nehru,' he wrote, 'is the most consistently violent in his speeches and the most irresponsible.' Gandhi he found to be an exception and 'on the whole fairly reasonable'.

The boycotting, for political reasons, of victory celebrations, when he had witnessed 'the most impressive parade and the finest body of men I have seen in 45 years service', particularly saddened him. He also recorded with regret his failure to prevent what he considered the folly of breaking off trade relations with South Africa, adding: 'The treatment of their countrymen abroad is a matter on which all politically-minded Indians feel very strongly and they are hardly open to reason on it.'[15]

The Pethick-Lawrence mission's attempts to bring about the formation in India of a representative interim government failed, as Wavell had expected they would. But in a further report to the King he expressed his admiration of the way in which the mission had at last convinced Indian leaders that the British Government really intended to grant India her freedom.

Then, in October, a report Wavell sent to the King contained evidence of political progress. Elections to a Constituent Assembly were held, and an Executive Council was formed. As the Muslim League refused to participate in the Council, it was dominated by Jawaharlal Nehru and his Congress Party. But, as Wavell reported, 'the new Government was sworn in under the shadow of the most savage and destructive communal disturbances that have taken place in India for very many years.'

As a soldier Wavell found the prevailing concentration on political infighting, when the breakdown of law and order was so evidently threatened, distasteful. Towards the end of his report he wrote: 'I am afraid that I have little else for Your Majesty beyond this dreary record of political ineptitude.'

To give the King some relief from the general tone of his report Wavell added: 'I will conclude with an episode rather typical of this illogical country. The Ministers of Bihar – possibly the most anti-British Ministry of all – recently decided that a mere flag on their cars did not give them enough distinction, so added large identification plates bearing the Royal Coat of Arms.'

Wavell now placed his hopes in the holding of talks in a different atmosphere, that of London. This was accepted, and he arrived there in December.

Four political leaders came with him. Two were from the Executive Council: Nehru and the Defence Minister, Baldev Singh, of whom Wavell had written: 'He has more brains and good sense than any other Sikh I have met.' The others, Mohammed Ali Jinnah and Liaqat Ali Khan, represented the Muslim League.

The King talked to both Attlee and Wavell on 3 December. On the 5th the political leaders from India lunched with him at Buckingham Palace. The King found Nehru uncommunicative and Jinnah informative, but his talks brought him to the conclusion that civil war between the Hindu and Muslim communities was more likely than any political agreement. Summarising his own opinions, he wrote in his diary: 'We have plans to evacuate India, but we cannot do so without leaving India with a workable Constitution. The Indian leaders have got to learn that the responsibility is theirs and that they must learn how to govern.'

Wavell believed in a more radical solution. He analysed in a report which he now submitted to the King a number of policies which might be adopted, and came to the conclusion that 'our own interests would probably best be served now by a definite decision to withdraw our control from India by a given date.'

Attlee told the King that the policy Wavell favoured was too suggestive of a military retreat. He also doubted whether Wavell had 'the finesse to negotiate the next steps'. He considered Wavell a rather silent soldier and was reputed to have said that he did not think silent people got on well with Indians.[16] From a man who was himself as sparing of speech as Attlee, this was a revealing comment.

Wavell was certainly tired, and Attlee came to the conclusion that a new Viceroy ought to be appointed. The King concurred, and the Viceroy chosen was Lord Louis Mountbatten.

Who first suggested Mountbatten for the post is not altogether clear. The King was certainly concerned to find the most suitable employment for him after the fighting in South East Asia had come to an end. A letter from Mountbatten to Charles Lambe, a future First Sea Lord, written on 19 February 1946, makes it clear, for example, that the King had suggested that Mountbatten should become 'a sort of Chief of Staff to the Minister of Defence'.[17] It would not therefore have been unreasonable for the King to suggest Mountbatten as Viceroy, and in a filmed interview, which was released after his death, Mountbatten stated that the King had told him this was just what he had done.[18] Attlee, on the other hand, is recorded as having hesitated before putting Mountbatten's name before the King.[19]

All that is certain is that both King and Prime Minister thought the choice a good one. The King also insisted that Mountbatten should be told clearly whether the Government's policy was to retreat from India or to work for reconciliation between Hindus and Muslims.

In 1946 the King had to refer to the Foreign Office for advice on his relationship with the Yugoslav royal family.

Reports had been received that the Yugoslav Government was considering making a demand for the return of Prince Paul in order that he might be tried as a war criminal. On 6 May Smuts wrote a letter to Lord Addison, the Dominions Secretary, in which he stated: 'I look upon him as a refugee who has found asylum in my country, and who is entitled to the usual rights of asylum unless under exceptional circumstances. The Union Government will certainly decline to hand him over as a war criminal unless a very strong case for his being such is made out to our satisfaction. The refusal of the Yugoslav Government to hear the USA officers who were prepared to give evidence at the trial of Mihailovich has raised grave doubts as to the fairness or impartiality of these trials of war criminals by particular countries.'[20]

Prince Paul, a man who was much more interested in museums than politics, had done nothing to resist German attempts to take over his country, but King George, who knew him as a staunch Oxford-educated anglophile, could not regard him as a criminal in any sense of the term. He was moreover the brother-in-law of Princess Marina, his own brother's widow. The King felt that the obligations of friendship required him, when he went to South Africa, at least to acknowledge Prince Paul's presence. He therefore asked for the Foreign Office's advice. This was duly given on 9 July. It read:

> It seems to us preferable that such a meeting should be avoided because it would be likely to give rise to unfavourable comment. It is just the sort of thing that the Russian press finds useful as a pretext for insulting propaganda against us and it might also be misinterpreted in some circles in England. The same would not, we think, apply to a meeting with Princess Paul, for which there are strong family reasons, but we suggest that any such meeting should be private and that steps should be taken to ensure that neither Prince nor Princess Paul be present at any public function which Their Majesties may attend.[21]

After such advice had been given any meeting with Prince Paul and his wife had of course to be in private.

The official view of Prince Paul did not affect the King's relationship with other members of the Yugoslav royal family, towards all of whom he had a feeling of responsibility. He was godfather not only to King Peter, but also to King Peter's younger brothers, Tomislav and Andrew, and during the war he had suggested to their mother that the two younger boys should be educated at Eton, where he hoped to be able to keep a friendly eye on them. His advice was not taken.

In later life Prince Tomislav expressed, in retrospect, surprise that the King should have given up so much of his time to the affairs of the Yugoslav royal family. He and his brothers regarded the King as a kind of father figure, and they were all slightly in awe of him.[22]

In October 1946 the King was on the receiving end of a pleasant act of international friendship. This was the delivery by the Military Air Attaché of the United States Embassy in London of a consignment of lemons. These were a rare commodity in Britain at the time. The donor was General Dwight D. Eisenhower, to whom Lascelles wrote that the lemons 'will be greatly appreciated by Their Majesties'.[23]

It was an indication of the state of the British economy in 1946 that a little more than a year after the total defeat of all their enemies the King and Queen of England should have been genuinely delighted by a gift of a few lemons.

CHAPTER TWENTY-TWO

South Africa and a Royal Wedding
1947

On 1 February 1947 the King and Queen sailed from Portsmouth for South Africa on board HMS *Vanguard*. For the first, and, as it happened, the only time, they were accompanied on an overseas visit by their two daughters.

The visit, which had been discussed from time to time with Smuts, was planned primarily as a means of bringing together conflicting elements among white South Africans, those of British and those of Dutch origin. Its second purpose was to thank those, predominantly though not wholly the British element, who had been responsible for the important contribution they had made towards winning the war. The likely impact of the visit on other sections of the population of South Africa and Rhodesia was given less consideration.

Press coverage during the visit soon became a source of contention. Some ten weeks before the royal party's departure from Britain the President and Vice-President of the Association of American Correspondents in London, Joseph Evans and Merrill Mueller, sent a telegram to Sir Alexander Cadogan, who was then the Permanent United Kingdom representative to the United Nations. It began: 'The Association of American Correspondents in London regret that the occasion of Their Majesties' royal tour to South Africa next spring necessitates urgent appeal to you to relieve official obstructionism in order that proper representation for American press can be achieved.'

The telegram continued: 'We feel American press entitled to three representatives aboard HMS Vanguard carrying Their Majesties to Capetown and ten representatives American press with royal train for duration Their Majesties' South African tour. Precedent for adequate coverage by all nationalities formally established on occasion Their Majesties' visit to Canada and the United States in 1939. Association also cabling Secretary of State Byrnes to similar effect with copies to South

The King and General Eisenhower in France, 1944. Behind are Generals Omar Bradley and Courtney Hodges

Below left: VE-Day, Buckingham Palace

Below right: The King greets President Truman at Plymouth, August 1945

Above: **The Tour of South Africa, February/March 1947**
Durban City Hall: 20,000 people crowded into the square

Left: The King and his daughters in Natal National Park

Below: Rifle shooting aboard HMS *Vanguard*

Above: The King with his Commonwealth Prime Ministers. *Left to right:* Dudley Senanayake (Ceylon), Lester Pearson (Canadian Minister for External Affairs), Liaqat Ali Khan (Pakistan), the King, Clement Attlee (UK), John Chifley (Australia), Dr Daniel Malan (South Africa), Peter Fraser (New Zealand) and Jawaharlal Nehru (India)

Right: The King and Queen with their grandchildren at Buckingham Palace

Below: Opening the Festival of Britain, South Bank 1951

Crowds outside Buckingham
Palace waiting to learn from
bulletins the outcome of the
operation on the King,
September 1951

Right: Four royal dukes in
the funeral procession: *Left
to right:* the Duke of
Edinburgh, the Duke of
Gloucester, the Duke of
Windsor and the Duke of
Kent

Below: The King's coffin
drawn along Piccadilly

African High Commissioner London and Buckingham Palace.'

In forwarding this communication to the Foreign Office Cadogan stated: 'Adequate coverage by the American press of this event is a matter of considerable political importance.'

Lascelles telegraphed in reply: 'Vanguard is already completely full and there are no newspaper correspondents on board except for usual Court representatives of agencies, Reuters and Exchange Telegraph. If there were room on board, British, South African and other Dominion correspondents would have prior claim and all these have already been turned down. Their Majesties wish to have as much privacy as possible during voyage.'

He was able to duck the problem of what would happen in South Africa by stating that this was the responsibility of the Union Government. There would, he thought, be three, or possibly four, American correspondents in the train. He concluded: 'You may perhaps be interested to hear that Mr Evans has made similar peremptory demands for special treatment for American correspondents at the House of Commons.'[1]

The American correspondents were not given all the facilities they wanted, but their *démarche* was some indication of the international interest which the visit was likely to arouse.

A further indication of the dangers of causing offence by omissions from the official programme of events came in a letter to the Foreign Office from the British Ambassador in Brussels, Sir Hughe Knatchbull-Hugheson. He had learnt that there were no plans for the King and Queen to receive the Governor-General of the Belgian Congo when they visited Livingstone, and he wrote: 'The Governor-General is a special emissary from the Prince Regent bearing greetings to Their Majesties. He will have travelled several thousand miles for the purpose. We are engaged in improving and tightening relations between the Colonial Empires in that part of Africa. Finally and not least, it appears that Monsieur Jungers is inclined to be fussy. There may easily be unhappy consequences if he feels he has been slighted.'[2]

Unlike those of the American press, the demands of the Governor-General were met. The King duly sent a telegram to the Regent, Prince Charles, to inform him that it had been a great pleasure to meet M. Jungers.

The royal family had the good fortune to escape from Britain at a time when the country was in a state of acute discomfort, the exceptionally severe winter of 1946 being accompanied by enforced cuts in fuel supplies and a continuation of food shortages. To the King, who had grown accustomed to regarding it as an essential part of his task to share the setbacks and misfortunes of his people at home, the escape was a cause of embarrassment and misgiving. During his voyage, as news continued to come through of what was happening in Britain, he seriously considered abandoning his visit. Attlee informed him firmly that this was not to be considered.

In other respects the King enjoyed his time on HMS *Vanguard*. A young naval officer, Peter Ashmore, a future Vice-Admiral, who a year earlier had been appointed an equerry to the King, was a member of the royal party and later recalled the almost boyish pleasure which the King took in being again aboard a battleship.[3] For the Princesses the visit was an opening into a new world, away from the very restricted home environment in which they had been kept by the circumstances of war.

HMS *Vanguard* reached Cape Town on the morning of Monday 17 February in brilliantly fine weather. Soon after disembarking the King received addresses of welcome from both houses of the South African Parliament. He took the opportunity to present the Order of Merit to Smuts, but was shocked to find the ceremony largely boycotted by the Nationalist Party. Of the 46 Nationalist Members of the House of Assembly only 11 appeared. There were no Nationalist Senators.

Later in the day the royal family lunched with the Governor-General, Gordon Brand van Zyl, the first holder of the office to have been born in South Africa. In the evening there was a state banquet, when the King thanked the people of South Africa both for their war effort and for the generous hospitality they had given visiting troops.

Boycotts or partial boycotts imposed by different sections of the community in Cape Province had some effect at first, but they were increasingly ignored as the days went by. Some three weeks after the arrival of *Vanguard* in Cape Town the British High Commissioner, Sir Evelyn Baring, wrote to Lord Addison, the Secretary of State for the Dominions:

> The move on the part of the Indian passive resistance movement to organise a boycott of the Royal visit to Durban appears to have failed, and there is a strong body of Indian opinion throughout the country which is opposing all suggestion of a boycott. A meeting of natives in Bloemfontein at the beginning of February decided not to welcome the Royal Family; a spokesman stated that 'the only natives who see the King will be those who will be working and those who will be in handcuffs. That will be good as the King will see the natives in their usual surroundings – the slaves of the land.' In the Eastern Province (of the Cape) large crowds of Africans have, however, given an enthusiastic welcome to the Royal party.

Baring went on:

> It is too early yet to judge the deeper effects of the Royal visit on the people of South Africa. But it is safe to say that the visit to the Cape was a very great success. Before the Royal Family arrived papers supporting the Government gave no more than restrained and rather official publicity to the coming visit.

By the end of the first day in Cape Town they could write of little and publish photographs of nothing else. On the first day the Royal Family were given a good reception by the crowd. Before they left Cape Town they were received with real enthusiasm wherever they went.

Not long after the royal family's arrival in South Africa, Smuts, addressing a gathering of about a thousand young South Africans on top of Table Mountain, said of the King: 'The effect of his arrival is already evident throughout the country; there is more gentleness, more unity apparent. . . All over the country the King, by his bearing and spiritual qualities, is having a healing and soothing effect. Because of it we are being given the right perspective. Because of this I must pay tribute to the royal family for what they are doing for us.'[4]

A large part of the journey through South Africa was made by the so-called White Train. This was a third of a mile in length and the longest and heaviest to traverse the South African railway system. There were ten coaches, all painted in ivory and gold. The royal family and their personal staff were in the forward part of the train. The rear carriages accommodated the Minister in attendance, South African civil servants, cipher staff, policemen, electricians and catering staff. A pilot train, which travelled half an hour ahead of the White Train, had a post office coach and a telegraph office. Finally, a third part of the procession, known as the Ghost Train, carried spare parts and repairing gear.[5]

Other stages of the South African-Rhodesian journey were made by air. Fielden, who was still Captain of the King's Flight and now an Air Commodore, established the Brooklyn Air Base near Cape Town. Aircraft of the Flight travelled 160,000 miles during the visit.

Of the organisation of the tour as a whole Baring wrote to Addison on 16 May:

To my mind there was only one unfortunate feature. The programme was not evenly balanced between provinces. The Cape Province and particularly Cape Town was generously treated. The Western Transvaal, the most nationalistic part of the former republic, was not included in the programme. The Rand, with its great population and key position in the future politics of the Union, received a comparatively short visit, and it is in Johannesburg and particularly the reef towns that a real resentment has been felt and expressed.

After paying tribute to the organisational skills of the South African police and railway authorities Baring went on:

Inevitably the proceedings at larger centres became stereotyped, but every effort was made to carry out the sound idea which underlay the arrangement of the tour – to enable the Royal Family as often as possible and as informally as possible to meet the South African man-in-the-street and, perhaps even more, the South African man-on-the-farm. From this point of view journeys by train, the use of a train as a base, and repeated stops at wayside stations, were all most useful. . .

A great impression was made by the action of the King, the Queen and the two Princesses in descending from the train at every wayside halt where people awaited their arrival. The occasions were numerous, and these meetings were among the most successful of the tour. At them it was possible for the typical farmer, usually an Afrikaner, to speak with the King and Queen and, especially when conversation turned on country topics, to realise how false was the Nationalist picture of a family of proud people remote from the cares of ordinary life and lacking all interest in the affairs of rural South Africa. 'But they are just like our own people' was the cry raised by a large crowd, including many members of the Ossewa Brandweg movement, as the King and Queen climbed back on the train at the small Free State station of Marseilles.

Baring continued:

The warmth of the welcome given by the Africans of the Union was great but not surprising. Most of them have for many years cherished their loyalty to the Crown and still associate the name of Queen Victoria with those ideas of freedom and justice for all races which gave their political principles to the Cape Province Liberals of the days before Union and which seemed by Africans to have been rejected by their European rulers at the time of General Hertzog's native legislation in 1936.

There was, Baring noticed, a striking difference between the arrangements made for the reception of the royal family by black Africans in the Protectorates of Basutoland, Bechuanaland and Swaziland and those in the Union.

In Basutoland, 'facing the Royal Family in a great semi-circle were between 70,000 and 100,000 Basuto from all districts of all types, dressed in a great variety of clothes. . . They demonstrated in almost unmistakable fashion their feelings against the transfer of Basutoland to the Union, since they believe, however incorrectly, that the assumption of control of Basutoland by the Union would imply a lessening of the link with the Crown.'

Similarly, in Bechuanaland 'some 25,000 Africans and 2000 Europeans were present. Considering that the country was suffering from shortage of water and foot-and-mouth disease (both of which are impediments to ox transport, which is the usual means of travel of these people) the numbers were very satisfactory. . . The orderliness of the African crowd was most impressive. Though there were no barriers to contain the people but a few whitewashed stones, there was no pushing or jostling, no encroachment on to the provisional road and no instances of bad manners or thoughtlessness. A sprinkling of African police were there, but their services were barely called upon. . . The visit has, if possible, strengthened the attachment of the African population of Bechuanaland to the Crown.'

In Zululand, which was part of the Union, by contrast, Baring reported, 'a large number of European Police were present – in Swaziland there were only some 20 at the Ndaba ground – the warriors in Zululand were not allowed to carry spears and Europeans attempted to organise the Zulu dance with the result that the Zulus themselves lost interest.'

In general, Baring wrote, 'the Union authorities have been the object of much criticism from educated Africans for their conduct of the visits to the native areas of the Union. They have been accused in the press of making arrangements which underlined "white supremacy".'[6]

There were a number of incidents and actions by members of the royal family which aroused particular comment. On his last day in Cape Town the King spoke for about half an hour with the Nationalist leader, Dr Malan. For this Malan was sharply criticised by members of his party, and some of the English-language newspapers seized on the incident with malicious delight.

An excellent impression was made by the Queen's action in handing President Kruger's family Bible to Smuts with the request that it should be returned to Kruger's descendants.[7] In Basutoland the two Princesses, after inspecting some Girl Guides, learnt that a busload of leper girls had not been included in the party to be inspected and insisted on walking round their bus and greeting them.[8]

Members of the official party confirmed from first-hand observation that the welcome given in town after town and at one wayside station after another was warm and spontaneous. 'As they trekked across South Africa,' Peter Townsend wrote, 'the Royal Family were greeted by all races.' He added: 'The most demonstrative response came from the Coloureds.' Peter Ashmore described the welcome as 'unqualified'. There was, he said, no visible evidence of protest.

The longer-term effects of the visit are difficult to assess. But the royal tour must at least be taken into account in any consideration of why, after the Nationalist party was returned to power, with men holding office who had been in sympathy with Hitler during World War II, the South African Government made no move for a long time to secede from the Commonwealth.

Throughout the tour the King continued to conduct much of the normal business of the monarchy. A Council of State, consisting of the Duke of Gloucester, the Princess Royal and Viscount Lascelles, had been appointed to act in Britain during the King's absence. But the Regency Act of 1937 did not, for example, apply to Canada, and none of the royal functions concerning Canada could therefore come within the Council of State's competence. As a safeguard against any omissions or misunderstandings, Lascelles wrote to Sir Eric Machtig at the Dominions Office on

2 January 1947: 'The King will continue to transact personally any business from the Dominions while he is absent from the United Kingdom.'[9]

Decisions were also required from the King on British domestic issues. On 24 March, as the winter was nearing its end, the Archbishop of Canterbury wrote to Attlee proposing a national day of prayer. 'The nation,' he wrote, evidently referring to the general state of the economy, 'is now facing an extremely critical period, as serious in its way as that which faced the nation at the beginning of the late war.'

While accepting the Archbishop's suggestion in principle, Attlee replied: 'I am not at all happy about the proposal in choosing a day as far ahead as Rogation Sunday. I feel that an earlier date might strike the public imagination more. The difficulty is, as you point out, the King's absence.' The Archbishop told Attlee that he needed time to prepare a suitable form of service, and the whole problem was referred by telegraph to the royal train in South Africa. After further discussion of dates by telegram it was officially announced that 'it is the desire of His Majesty the King that Sunday 6 July should be observed as a National Day of Prayer and Dedication to Almighty God in view of the tasks and duties which the nation is called to meet.'

Lascelles was then asked where the King would be when the day of prayer was held. To this he replied: 'The King, for all I know, may be in London on several Sundays this summer; including Sunday, July 6th. If so, he will certainly go to church somewhere or other.' It was eventually decided that on 6 July the King would attend a service in St Paul's Cathedral.[10]

The King found the South African tour both exhilarating and tiring. During the return journey on board HMS *Vanguard* he had to spend a week in bed. He was aware of muscular pain and stiffening in the thighs. This condition was later diagnosed as Buerger's disease, an arterial affliction of the lower limbs, and a necessary part of any treatment of the disease was that the patient should give up smoking. The King continued to smoke cigarettes heavily.

Like other Viceroys of India before him, Mountbatten reported regularly and formally to the King. Unlike others he was also able to communicate by the kind of letter in which he and the King addressed each other by their Christian names, and from time to time they exchanged unofficial comments on individuals which revealed their own opinions and prejudices. When Mountbatten told the King that he was resisting suggestions that Cripps should accompany him on his journey to India, the King wrote: 'I should never relish the idea of having him either on my staff or staying in my house.'[11]

Fairly soon after his appointment as Viceroy Mountbatten accepted that two separate and independent nations, India and Pakistan, must emerge on the sub-continent. It was not immediately clear whether either or both would remain within the Commonwealth, but as an immediate measure it was generally agreed that Dominion status would be conferred on both countries, and Governors-General would therefore have to be appointed by the King.

On 2 June 1947 a meeting of senior officials was held at 10 Downing Street to consider a report from Mountbatten. In this he stated that 'the Congress leaders, while willing that India should accept allegiance to the Crown as long as it remained a Dominion, regarded it as essential that the words "Indiae Imperator" and "Emperor of India" should be excluded from the royal title.' The ministers concerned, the officials were told, considered this 'not an unreasonable request'. The proposed changes would require legislation and also the assent of Parliaments in the other Dominions.

On 10 June Attlee discussed with the King the question of his title, and two days later wrote that he intended to include a clause changing the title in the India Dominions Bill. The King agreed to this the next day.

The King saw Attlee again on 29 July, when it was accepted that he would sign himself 'George R' on all papers relating to India and Pakistan and 'George RI' on all other documents until the Dominions Parliaments had passed legislation approving the changes.[12]

As an indication of what he thought Pakistan's attitude to remaining within the Commonwealth might be Mountbatten reported a conversation he had had with Jinnah on 26 April. Jinnah had wanted to know whether India or parts of India would have the right to secede and, if they chose not to do so, would automatically remain within the Commonwealth. He had then added: 'It is quite clear to me that you cannot kick us out. There is no precedent for forcing parts of the Empire to leave against their will.'[13]

The obvious choice for the post of first Governor-General of India was Mountbatten, particularly as he would clearly be acceptable to Nehru. Attlee consulted the King, who telegraphed to Mountbatten: 'I had a long talk with Prime Minister and Ismay. . . I hope very much that you will see your way to undertake Governor-Generalship of India irrespective of what happens in Pakistan.'

When Attlee finally informed Mountbatten that he had been chosen Mountbatten wrote in reply: 'I am most grateful for all the thought that the King, yourself, the Cabinet and the Opposition have given to this question. In view of your personal appeal and the overwhelming advice of all parties I feel in these special circumstances that I cannot but agree to have my name submitted to His Majesty for appointment as Governor-General of the new Dominion of India during the transition period though I must confess I still have some misgivings.'[14]

Mountbatten went to some lengths to try to persuade Jinnah that it would be in Pakistan's interests to have the same Governor-General as India in the interim period. He did not succeed. As Attlee succinctly put it to Mountbatten in a letter on 4 July, 'I have today asked Jinnah to let me have in writing the name of the individual whom he would wish me to recommend for formal submission to the King. This is going to be Jinnah.' He was right in his assumption.

As arrangements for the transfer of power on the Indian sub-continent neared completion the voice of a former Viceroy of India also made itself heard. This was Lord Halifax, who on 12 June wrote to Attlee to congratulate him on 'the courageous part' he and his colleagues had played in their dealings with India. He then suggested that, subject to the Viceroy's concurrence, Attlee should 'get the King and Queen to go to Delhi in the autumn for the purpose of formally saying good-bye and wishing them luck'. He went on: 'I would not let them do anything else but the formal farewell ceremony.' Attlee replied that he would put the suggestion to Mountbatten, adding: 'I do not know at all whether it will be possible for the King and Queen.' In fact he consulted Pethick-Lawrence, who was sceptical.

After conceding that 'a visit by Their Majesties might well be most valuable', Pethick-Lawrence wrote that it would be too early at any time during the cold weather of 1947–48 to be sure of a suitable welcome, and that it was doubtful whether 'the administration will be able to cope with the additional burden thrown on them'. Attlee thereupon dropped the proposal, and he does not seem even to have referred it to the King.[15]

Although the Indian sub-continent was in 1947 the part of the Commonwealth in which the need for change seemed most insistent, the Government accepted that elsewhere, too, major changes were likely to come about, and in June 1947 a small committee of ministers was appointed to consider the future structure of the Commonwealth. It was significant that Attlee was himself the chairman of the committee.

One of the first problems the committee had to consider was the anomalous status of the High Commissioners of the Dominions in London. A paper prepared by the Dominions Office in May 1947 stated: 'The view has hitherto been that as subjects of the King they cannot be given the complete diplomatic status given to Ambassadors of foreign countries, since the King cannot accredit in one capacity a representative to himself in another capacity. As a consequence they have been given in this country a lower precedence.'[16] This absurdity, arising, as it did, from common allegiance to the Crown, clearly had to be rectified.

In October 1947 a conference was held in London with representatives present from the British colonies. The delegates were received by the King on 8 October. In the course of the discussions which followed it was formerly recorded, to the gratification of the British Government, that 'the delegates dismissed the idea that the present economic policy of the United Kingdom towards the colonies was a cloak for the exploitation of the colonies in the interests of the United Kingdom and recognised its importance to their own development.'[17]

Among the contentious measures in the Government's home policy in 1947 were a National Service Bill and an Emergency Powers Bill. When they came under the scrutiny of Parliament Attlee explained with some care his thoughts about them to the King. On 3 April he wrote to Lascelles:

'The King may be interested to have my comments on the result of the debate in the House of Commons on the National Service Bill. The vote against the Government on the Bill was rather heavier than was expected. Labour members voting against were predominantly elderly members traditionally opposed to all forms of conscription and members from Wales. Having regard to the past traditions of the Labour Party on this matter I am not disposed to take the adverse vote too seriously, though there may be difficulties in the Committee stage.

'I think that a shortening of the period of service from 18 months to a year is desirable.'[18]

The Emergency Powers Bill, which was designed to prevent the kind of disruption which would bring industry to a standstill, was described by Churchill as 'a blank cheque for totalitarian government'. The King duly asked Attlee for an explanation of its needs and provisions. After receiving this he wrote to Attlee: 'I know very well that as long as you are at the head of any Government due regard will be given to the rights of Parliament itself. . . I know that your attitude towards this supremely important matter is the same as my own.' Attlee reassured the King that 'no question of evading Parliamentary control would arise.'[19]

By the autumn Attlee had come to the conclusion that new measures were needed to restore the economy and that these should, so far as possible, be under the control of a single minister. This he explained in a letter to the King on 26 September, which by Attlee's standards was of exceptional length.

'I am proposing,' Attlee wrote,

to relieve Mr Morrison, who is too heavily burdened at present, of his functions in relation to economic planning and to transfer them to a Minister without Portfolio who will devote his whole energies to this work.

His functions would be:

(1) General supervision and coordination of the whole production programme for home and export including coal and power, raw materials, building, shipbuilding and agriculture.

(2) With the Chancellor of the Exchequer be responsible for coordinating and supervising the import programme.

(3) Preside over a Committee of Ministers the nucleus of which would be those concerned with economic functions.

(4) Supervise the Economic Planning Group staff including the Economic Policy Unit.

(5) The economic section of the Cabinet Secretariat would work primarily to him.

(6) He would have control of the National Production Advisory Council for Industry and the regional organisation.

I desire to submit to Your Majesty that Sir Stafford Cripps should hold this office.

As there are already in the Commons three Ministers without Portfolio, which is the number allowed by Statute, I have asked for the resignation of Mr Greenwood who is getting on in years and is not now so effective as formerly. Mr Morrison would take over his present duties.

I desire to recommend as President of the Board of Trade Mr J. H. Wilson, the present Secretary for Overseas Trade. Although he is the youngest member of the Government he has shown great ability in trade matters and has done exceptionally well at international conferences.

I shall have the opportunity of giving a further account of these matters when I see Your Majesty on Monday next, before I make my formal submissions.[20]

In the following week Attlee submitted a number of other names to the King for ministerial appointments. They included those of Emanuel Shinwell, whom he had surprisingly yet shrewdly chosen for the War Office, and Hugh Gaitskell, who became Minister of Fuel and Power.

The principal objection to loading Cripps with such an immense burden came from Morrison, who on 2 October wrote to Attlee that 'the super minister idea has been overdone.' He added: 'I anticipate and hope that your own attendance at No.10 Economic Policy Committee will be regular, but I should wish to be clear that in your absence I should automatically preside. That is essential to my position as Deputy PM.'[21]

Among the visitors whom the royal family received in 1947 was Evita Perón, the wife of the Argentinian dictator and a formidable political figure in her own right. The invitation to Señora Perón to visit Britain came from the Government, not from the King or Queen. This she found inappropriate, and she voiced her dissatisfaction to Sir Noel Charles, the British Ambassador to Italy, a country she was visiting in the course of a European tour.

On 6 July 1947 Charles reported to the Foreign Office: 'I spoke to Señora Perón this evening and she insisted that she could not come to the United Kingdom unless her visit was regarded as official and she were received by the Queen.' After pointing out that 'it was most awkward for the Queen to change her programme' the Ambassador had told Señora

Perón that the King and Queen would be in London about 25 July. 'Señora Perón,' he reported, 'thereupon said that she would like to put off her visit so as to arrive on July 25th – she could fit in her visit to Paris and probably Lisbon before that. . . She expressed her desire to visit Great Britain, with which country Argentina had particular feelings of friendship.'

Sir Noel Charles continued: 'I asked both the Italian Prime Minister and Minister for Foreign Affairs later in the evening whether the Italian invitation to Señora Perón had been official. They were rather amused and admitted they had been bounced into doing more than had originally been intended. The invitation originally was semi-official but, as Count Sforza said, "*l'appétit vient en mangeant*," (appetite comes with eating) and the lady had contrived to obtain more and more by the simplicity of her approach.'[22]

The approach was no less successful in Britain, and Señora Perón duly had tea with the Queen.

On 22 October 1947 the King unveiled – rather belatedly, it might be thought – the memorial statue to King George V. Sir Henry Channon, who, having felt some regret at the departure of Edward VIII, was not one of George VI's uncritical admirers, wrote in his diary: 'The King read a speech more effectively than I have ever heard him: the matter, a serious tribute to his father's virtues, was a masterpiece.'[23]

Earlier in the year the King paid a visit to Cambridge for the celebrations on 3 June of the fourth centenary of the foundation of his old college, Trinity. The Master of Trinity was then the eminent historian G. M. Trevelyan, and after hearing the King's speech he said: 'The speech to which we have just listened was the King's own. His secretary had asked me to supply a few notes in aid, and I accordingly sent some suggestions of what are called "suitable remarks". But I perceive with delight that His Majesty put them straight into the waste-paper basket and preferred to give something from his own heart. After all he is a Trinity man.'

If Trevelyan's deduction was correct, the King had just given an impressive display of erudition. He had begun by saying that the appointment of the Master of Trinity, 'alone among the heads of Cambridge colleges, has remained to this day in the hands of the Crown.' This he might have known from first-hand experience. Nor was it surprising to hear him mention the names of Bacon and Newton, Byron and Tennyson, as former members of the college. But the full list he cited was a formidable one, and he added to the entertainment by referring to Dr Whewell, the Master who in 1847 had suggested that 'to preserve the reverence of undergraduates for their professors a century should be allowed to elapse before any new discovery in science should be admitted to the curriculum.'[24]

In fact, of course, it seems reasonable to deduce that Lascelles, or an Assistant Private Secretary, had performed yet another service calling for no public acknowledgment.

On 10 July 1947 a statement issued from Buckingham Palace read: 'It is with the greatest pleasure that The King and Queen announce the betrothal of their dearly beloved daughter The Princess Elizabeth to Lieutenant Philip Mountbatten, RN, son of the late Prince Andrew of Greece and Princess Andrew, to which union The King has gladly given his consent.'

The announcement of the engagement, which came as no surprise to the general public, had been delayed because the King wanted his daughter to visit South Africa, pass her twenty-first birthday and begin to accept some of the responsibilities of public life before she was formally betrothed. He also thought it desirable that Prince Philip should first acquire British nationality.

The King formally gave his sanction to the engagement at a meeting of the Privy Council. This was held on 31 July. Those whom the King required to be summoned were the Prime Minister, the Home Secretary, the Secretary of State for Commonwealth Relations (as the former Dominions Secretary was now known) the Lord Chancellor, the Archbishop of Canterbury, Winston Churchill and representatives of Australia, Canada, New Zealand and South Africa. Lascelles wrote to the Clerk of the Privy Council, Sir Eric Leadbitter: 'Do you see any objection in my asking the King if I also can be present at this historic Council?' Sir Eric did not, and the King agreed.[25]

The Government was unwilling to make any special financial provision for Princess Elizabeth or for Prince Philip after their wedding because of the general state of the nation's finances. The King accepted the immediate need for economy but did not want any departure from the established precedent that the heir, or heiress, to the throne was provided for by Parliament after marriage. After some discussion of the subject Hugh Dalton, as Chancellor of the Exchequer, came to see the King on 27 October. He spoke first to Lascelles and later wrote in a report to Attlee:

> Lascelles warned me beforehand that H.M. attached great importance to retaining the traditional procedure of a message to the House of Commons requesting that provision should be made, and to the setting up of a Select Committee to consider this request. On the other hand, H.M. would be prepared to send a further message ... which would be read by me, as Chairman of the Select Committee, at their first meeting, and would be willing that the provision, for the time being, should be only a token or peppercorn payment such as £10. Lascelles added that H.M. was fully aware of the embarrassment, both for the Royal Family and for the Government, and for

loyal opinion throughout the country, which would result from any public or acrimonious debate on the financial affairs of the Royal Family.

Dalton expressed his agreement with the King's proposals. His report continued:

When I went in to see the King he seemed to be in a very happy mood, and at once proposed to me the plan which Lascelles had explained ... H.M. said that he could not go on indefinitely making the additional provision from his own resources, but we both agreed that it was not possible, or desirable, to name any period at present during which this agreement should continue. I said I hoped we might be through the worst of our troubles in two years, but that, in view of all the uncertain factors, no one could be sure. I feel that this affair, so delicate from so many different points of view, has moved forward with an unexpected smoothness.[26]

In the end it was agreed that £25,000 a year should be paid to Princess Elizabeth from the day of her marriage in addition to any sum payable to her under the Civil List Act 1937, and £10,000 a year to Prince Philip from the same date. The Select Committee on the Civil List then recommended that 'towards the extra allowance for Princess Elizabeth H.M. the King should be asked to contribute a lump sum of £100,000.'

In the formal message which the King sent to the House of Commons no reference to the £100,000 was made, the King stating that he was 'willing to place at the disposal of the faithful Commons a sum derived from the savings on the Civil List made during the war years.'

On 15 September the Cabinet discussed a suggestion that the day of the wedding, which had been fixed for 20 November, should be a public holiday and came to the conclusion that this would be 'undesirable in the present circumstances'. A school holiday was thought to be appropriate. After the Cabinet meeting an official was deputed to propose to Lascelles that it might be announced that the decision to have no public holiday was Princess Elizabeth's wish. The King would not accept this. It would, he was reported as saying, 'throw upon her the responsibility for a decision which, if expressed in this form, might arouse criticism.'[27]

Another cause of some political concern was a report that silk for the Princess's wedding dress had come from abroad. At the time such an action, if proved correct, would have been deemed unpatriotic. Lascelles went to considerable trouble to ascertain the facts and on 10 October wrote personally to Attlee:

The wedding-dress contains silk which originally emanated from Chinese silkworms but was woven in Scotland and Kent;
The wedding train contains silk produced by Kentish silkworms woven in London;

The going-away dress contains about 4 or 5 yards of Lyons silk, which was not specially imported but was part of the stock held by the dress-maker (Mr Hartnell) under permit.

I am satisfied that those of my colleagues who are concerned with such matters are fully alive to that aspect of them which you mentioned to me last night. Only a few days ago, for example, the Keeper of the Privy Purse was obliged to point out to the Board of Trade that, in answer to an application for guidance as to where he might get the ornaments necessary for the wedding-dress, they had recommended to him a firm called Pompadour Products, run by an Austrian lady who only very recently became a British subject – a recommendation which threatened us with an appreciable amount of embarrassing publicity.[28]

The wedding, like that of the bride's parents, took place in Westminster Abbey. Shortly before, the King had created Prince Philip Duke of Edinburgh with the additional titles of Earl of Merioneth and Baron Greenwich.

After the wedding the King wrote to his daughter: 'You were so calm and composed during the service and said your words with such conviction, that I knew everything was all right.' He was particularly gratified that she had told her mother she considered the long wait before she had become engaged had been for the best. He had feared, he wrote, that she had thought he was being 'hard hearted'.[29]

CHAPTER TWENTY-THREE

Silver Wedding and Problems of Health
1948

On 3 June 1948 it was formally announced that two self-governing Dominions of the Commonwealth, India and Pakistan, had come into being, with the right, if they chose, to secede from the Commonwealth. The policy of Attlee's Government was to make every reasonable effort to ensure that they remained within it.

The gaining of independence had been preceded by civil wars, causing loss of life on a huge scale, and in India the murder of Mahatma Gandhi had increased the likelihood of widespread violence.

The judgments of the Viceroy, Lord Mountbatten, and of one of the ministers in Attlee's Government on likely future developments were ably summarised in a letter dated 2 February 1948. It was addressed to the Commonwealth Relations Office in London and came from the Office of the Deputy High Commissioner in Madras. The writer was John Hunt, a future Cabinet Secretary. The Government minister was Patrick Gordon Walker, Under Secretary of State at the Commonwealth Relations Office. 'Lord Mountbatten,' Hunt wrote,

raised with Mr Gordon Walker the question of India staying within the Commonwealth. He said that Gandhi's death had lessened the chances somewhat, as the latter's view would probably have been decisive. Patel wished to stay in, at any rate for the next few years, but Nehru's mind was changing.

Mountbatten said that he thought a lot would turn on the names and phrases used. The actual word 'dominion' would not do. India would be content not to call herself a republic if we did not insist on calling her a dominion. Mr Gordon Walker said that he had been very struck by the way in which both India and Pakistan referred to themselves as dominions; there was also the new Army instruction laying down the double loyal toast as 'The King – India.' Lord Mountbatten thought this was because they wished to behave well while still in the Commonwealth and not because they were ready to remain there. He suggested that a new word was needed that they could put into their constitution such as 'partnership' or 'partnerate'.

Mountbatten also told Mr Gordon Walker the curious story that a representative of India had been to consult Mr De Valera in Dublin. Mr De Valera had said that the link with the Crown was important. He might himself have difficulty in keeping it, but he advised India to do so. At the beginning of his struggle he had fought for 'association' and had been alone in the cabinet. He had then thought of 'external association' which was just acceptable.[1]

Southern Ireland did not retain the connection with the Crown, the Republic of Ireland Act, which formally severed the link, being passed through the Dail at the end of November 1948.

In India, by contrast, the debate on whether or not to remain within the Commonwealth was a prolonged one. Early in 1948 Attlee decided to set out his own views on the subject in a personal letter to Nehru. He sent a draft of it to Cripps, who considered it suitable. Much of the letter, which was despatched on 11 March 1948, was concerned with the functions and traditions of the Crown.

'In my own view,' Attlee wrote,

it is better to have the King or the Governor-General as someone above the political battle rather than a protagonist. There is also much to be said for having a personage who is a symbol of the State more readily understood by all sorts and conditions of men than an abstraction. For instance, in the British Commonwealth and Empire are many simple people who can understand a king better than they can comprehend a formula.

In India, I think, there is no native tradition of republicanism. It is really an importation from the West. There is a good deal to be said for having as the ultimate head of the State someone who does not belong to any section of the community and therefore has no special affinity to any one of them. This has shown itself in practice. When, for instance, the King and Queen visited Canada they got an equally cordial reception from French and English-speaking Canadians and in South Africa it was the same in regard to British and Dutch, Europeans, Indians and Africans.

After stating that he knew how much importance Nehru attached to maintaining the unity of India, Attlee wrote:

It will, I think, be of very material assistance in promoting this unity if India and Pakistan are both within the Commonwealth, and it will also help relations with Ceylon and Malaya, for in my view it is right and natural that India should increasingly take a leading part among the nations of Asia.

I should very much like to have your views on these high matters, for I know that you have in mind not only the affairs of India but also of the world. I think you would agree that what we need today is more unity in the world and that unnecessary fragmentation is to be deprecated. In my view the British Commonwealth is a unique experiment, in that we have there close association with complete freedom on the part of its constituent parts and a remarkable degree of flexibility owing to the absence of any constitution.[2]

Nehru's reply was friendly but altogether non-committal. In it he paid a warm tribute to both Lord and Lady Mountbatten. 'I have often wondered,' he wrote, 'what the history of India would have been if they had come a year earlier.'

In commenting on the draft of Attlee's personal letter Cripps had described Nehru as 'a very tired man and anxious to get away and come here as soon as he can.' An invitation had been sent to Nehru to attend Princess Elizabeth's wedding, but he had decided that he was too busy to leave India.[3]

Early in 1948 John Colville, who a year earlier had been appointed Private Secretary to Princess Elizabeth, put forward the suggestion that she and Prince Philip should visit Paris. In doing so he had been influenced by the evident interest shown throughout western Europe in their wedding.[4]

Princess Elizabeth discussed Colville's suggestion with the King, who said he had no objection provided the visit was undertaken with a specific object. Agreement having been reached within the royal family, the proposal was put forward for formal consideration by the Foreign Office.

Bevin had learnt from a number of sources that there was a likelihood of intensified communist activity, possibly leading to *coups d'état*, in a number of western European countries in March 1948, and he told Colville he did not want Princess Elizabeth's visit to take place before May. The proposal was then put to the British Ambassador in Paris, Sir Oliver Harvey, who discussed it with the French Foreign Minister, Georges Bidault. On 3 March Harvey reported to Bevin:

'M. Bidault received me today when I told him that you had been considering the desirability of a visit to Paris by Their Royal Highnesses, The Princess Elizabeth and the Duke of Edinburgh. Her Royal Highness had not yet visited the continent and it was unnecessary to emphasize the appropriateness of her first visit being to France. The visit would be highly significant in Anglo-French relations.' The nature of Bevin's preliminary instructions was revealed as Harvey continued: 'Your idea was that the visit should be informal and arranged so as to enable Her Royal Highness to see as much as possible of Paris and the environs. Their Royal Highnesses would stay at the Embassy and you were anxious that no undue public expense should be incurred.'

It was provisionally agreed that the visit should take place in mid-May and that Princess Elizabeth should be asked to open an exhibition of English life in Paris, which was to be staged under the joint auspices of the British Council and the French Ministry of Foreign Affairs.

That Princess Elizabeth should have reached the age of twenty-two before setting foot on the continent of Europe was an indication of the sheltered life which a combination of the King's wishes and the circumstances of war had caused her and Princess Margaret to lead. People who were close to the King have emphasised how determined he was that, until they were obliged to take their full part in public affairs, his daughters should enjoy a normal family life, with none of the rigours of his own early upbringing. They have also said that he prepared them for their future roles very much more by example than by precept.[5]

Smuts described the young Princess Elizabeth as 'serious and wise beyond her years'.[6] The future was to show that she had a dedication to the duty of the monarch which was as deep as that of her father. That this was so can be ascribed to her inherited nature, and to the way in which members of a closely-knit family can, almost without effort, influence each other's attitudes.

Princess Elizabeth's academic education had also been much more effective than her father's, and in Paris she surprised people by her accent and ease of delivery when making speeches in French. The crowds also observed that she had a flawless complexion and eyes which no photograph had ever up to then successfully conveyed.

Bevin's request that the Princess should be allowed to see something of the environs of Paris was met, and visits were paid to Fontainebleau, Versailles, Barbizon and Vaux.

In a report to Bevin after the event Sir Oliver Harvey wrote: 'By this visit Their Royal Highnesses have performed fine service in the cause of Franco-British friendship. What began as a warm welcome to the representatives of a friendly and admired country turned in a few hours to a universal expression of personal affection and admiration. The latent enthusiasm of the French people for the pomp and pageantry of monarchy was clearly revealed. It was an unusual experience to see the townsfolk of Paris cheer an English Princess from the Place de la Bastille.'[7]

Harvey was also impressed by the reaction of French newspapers. 'Even the Communist Press,' he wrote, 'which normally dismisses Royal occasions in contemptuous silence, published good photographs and sympathetic accounts of the visit and paid the Princess the indirect compliment of complaining that police arrangements for her security were such as to make it impossible for the people of Paris to approach her as closely as they wished.'

The people of Paris, Harvey concluded, 'flocked in their thousands wherever there was any hope of seeing the Royal visitors, waited for hours patiently and good-humouredly, shouted their momentary applause and came away smiling.'[8]

The extravagant language used and the popular reaction it described recalled events which had occurred ten years earlier, when the Princess's parents had visited Paris. If there seems to be a suggestion of loyal exaggeration in the reporting, it should be borne in mind that professional diplomats, such as Phipps and Harvey, who reach the eminence of being appointed British Ambassador in Paris, have had long training in objective reporting. They are not mindless sycophants.

The King was understandably pleased that his eldest daughter, in the most important public engagement which she had yet undertaken, had made such a favourable impression. Her husband, in spite of being unwell during much of the visit, had also been seen to advantage.

Lord Mountbatten's political enemies, whose numbers had been increased by many who thought the handing over of power on the Indian sub-continent had been too precipitate, had begun to voice fears that, with his nephew married to the King's daughter, he himself might become a kind of manager for the heiress to the throne.[9] In reality it had soon become apparent that the Duke of Edinburgh, much though he respected his uncle, had a mind of his own and intended to exercise his own judgment.

As the end of Mountbatten's term of office as Governor-General approached, the King again gave thought to the problem of finding the best employment for a man with such a record and such gifts. Mountbatten himself was determined to return to naval duties. There was a suggestion that he should be sent to the West Indies, but the King favoured an appointment in the Mediterranean theatre, where, as he put it, the fleet was 'a going concern'. In the end Mountbatten was posted to Malta.

Princess Elizabeth's visit to Paris, meanwhile, had brought to the surface a problem in Commonwealth relations which called for delicate handling. The Canadian Ambassador in Paris, General Vanier, while behaving with exemplary decorum, had pointed out that he was senior to Harvey in the Diplomatic Corps in France, and that it would have been reasonable for the Princess to turn to him for official advice during her visit. The question was not merely one of niceties of protocol, but was indicative of difficulties which might lie ahead as the different Dominions pursued increasingly independent policies in external affairs.

Lascelles asked the Foreign Office for guidance and was given the opinion that members of the royal family, when abroad on official or semi-official visits, should turn to the United Kingdom representative, who would decide whether to consult his Commonwealth colleagues. Lascelles questioned whether this would always be found satisfactory in Commonwealth countries.

He also asked, in a letter dated 29 June 1948, whether in future the Palace should seek the advice of the Ministers of External Affairs in Commonwealth countries before a visit such as the one Princess Elizabeth had made to Paris was undertaken. This led to further consultations between the Foreign Office and the Commonwealth Relations Office.

The judgment was confirmed that, when abroad, a member of the royal family should turn first to the United Kingdom representative. Lascelles accepted this, no doubt as the most convenient solution in practice.

He also recommended that in future, when royal visits were planned, it should be the responsibility of the Private Secretary of the royal visitor to convey the necessary information through High Commissioners. It was, he pointed out, 'obviously wrong (and likely to make trouble)' for Ministers for External Affairs to learn from newspapers that royal visits were to take place.[10]

By 1948 Attlee's Government was in mid-term. Its policies at home aroused both widespread admiration and loud condemnation. In July 1948 there came into operation what Attlee called 'the most comprehensive system of social security ever introduced in any country'. This was a consequence of the National Insurance, Industrial Injuries, National Assistance and National Health Acts. 'The scheme as a whole,' Attlee said in a broadcast on 4 July, 'is designed to cover you and your family throughout your life.'[11]

In contrast with this popular success Attlee received, five days before his broadcast, a report headed 'Nationalisation Developments to Date'. This called attention to 'the disappointment and frustration of both workers and Socialist Members of Parliament at the methods and results so far achieved.'[12]

It was on issues such as these that the Government was to be judged by the electorate, yet a high proportion of the energies of Attlee himself and a number of his senior colleagues had to be expended elsewhere, on problems arising from the transformation of the British Empire. Indeed, with the possible exception of that of Lord North at the time of the rebellion of the American colonists, there was almost certainly no other British government which gave so much of its time to the affairs of British territories overseas. Many of the problems called for consultation with the King.

In February 1948 it was confirmed that the King's correct title was now 'George VI (Albert Frederick Arthur George of Windsor) by the Grace of God, of Great Britain, Ireland and the British Dominions beyond the Seas, King, Defender of the Faith'. This anomalous description, following, as it did, the rupture by the Republic of Ireland of its connection with the Crown, was deemed necessary because governments in the Dominions had not yet had time to introduce legislation defining the status of Northern Ireland.

In June the King finally confirmed his new standing in India by signing a proclamation that 'in all instruments wherein Our Style and Title are used, in the Latin tongue the words "Indiae Imperator" and, in the English tongue, the words "Emperor of India" shall be omitted'.[13]

A new Commonwealth tour of major importance by the King and

Queen was also proposed. This was to be to Australia and New Zealand. The proposal was accepted by the King, and the tour was planned to take place in 1949. The choice of these countries for a royal visit was an obvious one, as the King and Queen had already visited Canada and South Africa. But it was incidentally hoped that the visit would serve to improve political relations with Australia, since these continued to be strained.

One reason for this was that, like Conservative Ministers before them, Ministers in Attlee's Government, including Attlee himself, found it almost impossible to establish tolerable relations with the Australian Minister for External Affairs, Dr Hubert Evatt. Describing a meeting between Attlee and Evatt in Paris, Patrick Gordon Walker wrote on 15 December 1948: 'Evatt seems to have been extremely rude and aggressive. . . I look forward with real concern to the prospect of weeks more of his presidency at Lake Success. The strain on Commonwealth relations will be grave.'[14]

Events in Palestine also affected the official advice given to the King. In July 1948 Sir Bernard Waley Cohen, President of the United Synagogue and a future Lord Mayor of London, asked for enquiries to be made to discover whether the King would receive the new Chief Rabbi on his appointment. Attlee consulted the Home Office and decided to advise the King not to receive him. His Private Secretary, Laurence Helsby, wrote to Lascelles on 16 July: 'It would create an awkward precedent; moreover the reception by His Majesty of the head of the Jewish religion in this country would certainly be regarded as a sign of favour by Arab communities, and it is undesirable that this should occur at the present time.'[15] It was advice reminiscent of that given to the King after the death of Cardinal Hinsley.

In April 1948 there were a number of ceremonial events that did require the presence of the King. One was the unveiling of the Roosevelt memorial statue.

There had been much discussion on how the life and work of the President could best be commemorated in London. Churchill, after leaving office, had interested himself closely in the question. On 4 December 1946 he had written a memorandum, in which he had stated: 'I am sure the statue ought to be seated. It was in the seated position that Roosevelt fought his way through the party politics of the United States for more than a decade, and it was thus that he played his great part in world history.' This opinion was not accepted.

Lord Jowitt, as Lord Chancellor, was assigned the task of finding a suitable place in Westminster Abbey for a memorial tablet. 'The walls of the Abbey,' he wrote to Attlee, 'are hopelessly congested with memorials, most of which have no artistic merit and many of which commemorate persons of no national importance.' The Dean of Westminster offered an empty space in the chapter house, but Jowitt thought it would be more appropriate to make room by removing the tablet commemorating a certain Dr Bell, 'who was responsible for some educational improvements in Madras'.[16] In the end a compromise was reached.

To pay for the main statue in Grosvenor Square the Anglo-American benevolent body known as the Pilgrims launched an appeal, and on 7 November 1947 its chairman, Lord Derby, wrote to Attlee: 'I have already written to His Majesty the King informing him of the date and expressing the hope that he would attend the unveiling. The King approved my suggestion that Mrs Roosevelt should unveil the monument.' Mrs Roosevelt was accordingly invited. She spent a week-end at Windsor with the King and Queen and then stayed in Claridge's Hotel as the guest of the British Government. A detachment of the United States Marines was also sent to London to mark the occasion.

Mrs Roosevelt believed for some time that she would be performing the unveiling ceremony and reasonably enough since the King had agreed that she should do so. But Attlee decided otherwise, and in the end the unveiling was done jointly by himself and Churchill. After the ceremony he had the modesty to write to Mrs Roosevelt: 'I wish I could have done more justice to the President in my speech, but I shall never be an orator.'[17]

A more colourful occasion was the six hundredth anniversary of the founding of the Order of the Garter, which was celebrated on St George's Day, 23 April, with a service in St George's Chapel in Windsor. The concept of the orders of chivalry appealed strongly to the King, and with Attlee's renunciation of the Prime Minister's right to recommend appointments to the Order of the Garter he took an even closer interest in them. He appointed a number of distinguished war leaders, including Alanbrooke, Alexander, Montgomery, Mountbatten and Portal, to the Order. Then, shortly before their marriage, he added Princess Elizabeth and, a week later, Prince Philip ('so that she will be senior,' as he wrote to Queen Mary) to the limited number that the statutes of the Order permitted.

For the six hundredth anniversary the elaborate pageantry of the Order was revived, and Princess Elizabeth and five knights, including the Duke of Edinburgh, had the insignia of the Order bestowed on them in the throne room in Windsor Castle.

But the most prolonged and popular celebrations in 1948 were those connected with the silver wedding of the King and Queen on 26 April. A small committee of officials had been formed back in December 1947 to make recommendations on how the silver wedding should be celebrated. The committee proposed a service in St Paul's Cathedral, some ceremonial drives, addresses from both Houses of Parliament and a school holiday. For some reason the committee members thought that the production of souvenirs, other than a souvenir programme, should be discouraged.

The Home Secretary, James Chuter Ede, was not at all attracted by these proposals. He believed there would be a new economic crisis in April 1948. The hand-over of power in Palestine was due to take place then, and he thought this would accentuate the problems of providing security, particularly around St Paul's Cathedral in the City of London, which was less easy to police than the area around Westminster Abbey. He even suggested that the King and Queen might celebrate their silver wedding, not on the actual anniversary, but on a Sunday, as he considered it undesirable to bring large crowds to London on a weekday so soon after Princess Elizabeth's wedding.

Chuter Ede conveyed his opinions to Lascelles, who passed them on to the King. On 2 February Lascelles wrote to Chuter Ede: 'Their Majesties are still most anxious that the service should be held in St Paul's rather than the Abbey; though they appreciate the security considerations which you described to me, they wish to ask, before they make a final decision, whether it is still thought that the arguments against using St Paul's on this occasion will definitely outweigh those on the other side.'[18]

It was the Queen, Lascelles told Laurence Helsby, who felt most strongly that, as King George V and Queen Mary had celebrated their silver wedding with a service in St Paul's, the tradition ought to be upheld. In a written report Helsby summarised other points which Lascelles had made.

'So far as the arguments for celebration of the anniversary on the Sunday rested on "austerity",' Helsby wrote, 'it had to be borne in mind that within a few days of April 26 there would be (a) the Cup Final, which the King was to attend in company with 140,000 other spectators, and (b) the unveiling of the Roosevelt memorial, in connection with which there was to be a dinner in the evening (to be attended by the Prime Minister) for, it is understood, some 800 people. It would be very difficult to make the public understand, against this background, that there was good reason for stopping Their Majesties from going to church on the anniversary of their marriage.'

Attlee saw the King and Queen on 10 February and agreed that the service should be held in St Paul's and on the day of their choice.

In brilliant sunshine on 26 April the King and Queen drove to the cathedral in a state landau through large and cheering crowds. In the afternoon they drove through some twenty miles of London streets in an open car. Happily no overt threat was made to their security.

In moving in the House of Commons 'a humble address to Their Majesties to congratulate them on the twenty-fifth anniversary of their wedding', Attlee took the opportunity to express his own appreciation of the manner in which the King and Queen had performed the duties of the monarchy. As usual he aspired to precision rather than oratory.

'I have a congenial task in moving this resolution,' he said, 'nor should it be difficult, for no eloquence or courtier's skill are needed to point the significance of the occasion. . . The King and Queen and their family are so entrenched in our affections that this anniversary cannot be other than an occasion for general satisfaction. They stand high in the regard which they have earned.' He went on to recall something of the part which the King and Queen had played during World War II.

'The King and Queen,' he said, 'shared the fortunes of their people under enemy attack. . . There are many examples, but perhaps I might refer to the royal visit to Coventry immediately after the bombing which the city had suffered. Bombing raged far and wide over the country, but there was a special malevolence in the attack on that town. The sympathy shown by the royal family in their visit, typical as it was of many like occasions, will not be forgotten and did much to help the spirit of our people to surmount all the trials to which they were subjected.'

These were events of which others had spoken and written, but Attlee then passed on to his own first-hand experiences of the functioning of the monarchy. 'I should like,' he said, 'to add one thing which I feel may not always be appreciated, and that is that the duties of a constitutional monarch are unending. They are continuous and there is no relief. Formal though many of the Sovereign's duties may be, the responsibility still remains. This is a burden which statesmen do not carry, for we come in and out of office and at times we can delegate our responsibilities. In speaking therefore of Their Majesties' devotion to duty, we must realize that behind this formal phrase there lies a real dedication of life.'

As a silver wedding present Mr and Mrs Attlee gave the King and Queen a silver beaker made by Bernardus van Asten of Leeuwarden in the Netherlands in the early eighteenth century,[19] while members of the Cabinet each subscribed £1-19-3 towards the purchase of a Georgian sauceboat.[20]

By the autumn a deterioration in the state of the King's health was becoming increasingly apparent. His left foot was continually numb, and he was in constant pain. He consulted his medical advisers, and they decided to call in Professor James Learmonth, an eminent Edinburgh specialist. He diagnosed an early condition of arteriosclerosis. The King's doctors committed themselves to the public statement that the King's general health 'gave no reason for concern'.[21] Nevertheless they advised rest. This was not easily to be had.

As his father had once done, the King defied medical advice and attended the Remembrance Day service at the Cenotaph on 7 November. A week earlier he had reviewed a massive Territorial Army parade in Hyde Park. The King's commitment to duty may not have been the cause of his physical decline, but it certainly accelerated his illness and made recuperation difficult.

He was at this time exceptionally well served by his personal staff. Lascelles was a man of learning, and outstanding as a Private Secretary. His grasp of the intricacies of Commonwealth affairs exceeded that of all but a very few of the ablest civil servants. His judgment was admirable and he could use words with ease and to powerful effect.[22] As Assistant Private Secretaries there were Michael Adeane, grandson of King George VI's Secretary and mentor, Lord Stamfordham, who was himself to become Private Secretary to Queen Elizabeth II, and Edward Ford, a man of charm and balanced judgment whom Lascelles had recommended to the King. Between them they were fully capable of relieving the King of much of the paper work which would otherwise descend on him. The King, for his part, had the ability to delegate. Nevertheless there were tasks which he insisted on performing because he accepted them as the peculiar responsibility of the monarch.

Many of these had to do with the armed forces. He studied carefully, for instance, the findings of courts-martial and would not infrequently ask for more information. Sometimes this led to the reversal of a decision. Many of his questions to ministers were concerned with service affairs. He took the greatest care too when preparing for investitures. At all times he was determined not to hold up the business of government by failing to deal with papers.[23] Such conscientiousness added to the strain inevitably imposed on a man whose physique was not strong. It is possible too that another of the King's characteristics, the occasional outbursts of violent temper to which he was subject, was indicative of a tendency to mild epilepsy.

The King himself, however, was not convinced that his physical condition gave grounds for concern. On the last day of 1948 he wrote to Mountbatten: 'Time will soon make me recover bodily but the mental strain will take longer to calm down.'[24] Nevertheless he accepted reluctantly that a major decision must be taken on medical advice. This was that the visit to Australia and New Zealand, which was due to take place in 1949, should be postponed.

Towards the end of 1948 an event occurred which gave the King the deepest pleasure. This was the birth on 14 November of his first grandchild, who a month later was christened Charles Philip Arthur George.

CHAPTER TWENTY-FOUR

The New Commonwealth
1949

In the first two months of 1949 the King was in a semi-invalid state, being obliged to rest in bed in the afternoons. Even so, his condition did not improve much, and early in March it was agreed that Professor Learmonth should perform the operation known as a lumbar sympathectomy. This, it was hoped, would improve the circulation of the blood to the King's foot. The operation was performed on 12 March in Buckingham Palace and was successful. Afterwards there was a steady improvement in the King's condition. He was able to resume normal duties within weeks and even to carry out physically demanding social engagements. Sir Henry Channon noted that at a ball at Windsor on 18 June 'the King had his foot up on a footstool to rest, though he seemed quite well and often danced.' He added that 'the Queen danced every dance vigorously.'

During the King's illness Attlee conscientiously kept him informed on affairs of state. On 13 January 1949 he sent the King a summary of a debate in the House of Commons on Palestine, informing him that Bevin, 'if he had chosen could have made a strong case against the Israeli Government for their aggression and against the United States Government for their constant changes of policy.' Bevin had preferred, Attlee added, 'to suffer misrepresentation rather than jeopardise the prospects of a settlement.'[1]

A month later a letter began:

'Mr Attlee with his humble duty to the King.

'Mr Attlee hopes that there has been sustained improvement in Your Majesty's health.

'The last two weeks in Parliament have been quiet, the only notable debate being on the report on the Lynskey Tribunal.'

The Lynskey Tribunal had been set up under the terms of the Tribunals of Enquiry (Evidence) Act of 1931 to investigate an affair which was an almost inevitable consequence of a prolonged period of rationing and controls in time of peace.

During the late 1940s a number of persuasive individuals, who were in effect conmen, convinced their victims that they were able to influence ministers and senior officials who had the tasks of allocating scarce materials or granting permits. As a result, by the end of 1948 there were persistent rumours of corruption in high places. It seemed that not enough evidence could be obtained to justify a prosecution, and Attlee was reluctant to set up instead the investigative machinery of a tribunal, the proceedings of which would be fully reported and before which unsubstantiated allegations against individuals could be made with little or no restraint. Such tribunals had, he said, all of what Baldwin had called 'the unthinking cruelty of modern publicity'. The rumours did however suggest that ministers in his own Government had been guilty of misconduct, and in consequence he had no alternative other than to set up the tribunal.

In a society weary of austerity and controls, the hearings under Mr Justice Lynskey developed into a popular entertainment. The principal contact man, Sidney Stanley, was a showman with a highly developed sense of theatre, and the slender newspapers of the time devoted a high proportion of their limited space day after day to reporting the proceedings in which he was involved.

The principal sufferer was the Parliamentary Secretary to the Board of Trade, John Belcher, who had received some entertainment and a few gifts in kind. Although these were trifling his political career was ruined.

The contact men, it was revealed, achieved next to nothing, and the conduct of ministers and officials generally was impeccable. On 10 February Harold Wilson, the President of the Board of Trade, sent Attlee a long personal letter, in which he explained that, apart from Belcher's 'intemperate habits' and 'his being too much addicted to entertainment by the business world', neither Wilson himself nor his predecessor at the Board of Trade, Sir Stafford Cripps, had had any grounds for suspecting him.[2]

All this was true. Nevertheless the tribunal, not least because its proceedings repeatedly descended into buffoonery, did substantial damage to the Labour party's electoral prospects, as much, arguably, as the decision taken in the autumn to devalue the pound.

In informing the King of the consequences of the tribunal Attlee stated that he was 'considering issuing a directive in regard to the responsibilities of junior ministers' and 'setting on foot inquiries as to the activities of so-called contact men.' Lascelles, thanking Attlee for his reports, wrote on 3 March that the King had 'found much to interest him.'[3]

Attlee kept the King even more fully informed of his plans for the new structure of the Commonwealth. These plans would, he hoped, be largely put into effect in 1949, although there was evidence of problems and differences of opinion in Ireland, Canada, Pakistan and India.

On 12 January the Commonwealth Relations Office put forward what probably seemed at the time a fairly routine proposal. This was that, subject to the King's approval, the various Commonwealth Governments should be asked to agree that in the King's title the words 'Northern Ireland' be substituted for 'Ireland'. This, it was felt, was a necessary consequence of the passing by the Dail of the Republic of Ireland Act.

The Governments of Australia and New Zealand agreed. So did the Government of the newly independent Ceylon. In South Africa the Nationalist leader, Dr Malan, who was now in power, personally raised a pertinent question. This was whether the Irish Government had been consulted, and if so what its answer had been.

The question was referred to the United Kingdom representative in the Irish Republic, Sir Gilbert Laithwaite, who replied: 'Any approach to the Eire Government would not only serve no useful purpose. It would provoke violent rejoinder on the whole question of partition.' He therefore suggested that the South African Government should be told there was no dispute on the point in question between the British and Irish Governments. This seems to have satisfied Dr Malan, who raised no further objections.[4]

The Canadian Government, now headed by Louis St Laurent and with Lester Pearson as Minister of External Affairs, had decided views on the subject of the King's title. These were conveyed to the United Kingdom High Commissioner in Canada, Sir Alexander Clutterbuck, in an interview which he had with Pearson on 17 January. Pearson, he reported, 'was not yet in a position to give the Government's views since he had not yet spoken to the Prime Minister, but his own view, which he held very strongly, was that it would be politically impossible for Canada to accept the proposal.' The report went on:

His reasons were
(1) Change in itself was open to question as giving undue prominence to Northern Ireland inconsistent with its position as part of the United Kingdom.

(2) In any case Government could scarcely be expected to legislate here for such a change while leaving alone the outdated phrase 'British Dominions beyond the seas'.

As I knew, there was keen anxiety to get rid of this phrase which was altogether inappropriate to the nationhood of Canada and other Commonwealth countries. That they should continue to be lumped in with the Colonies in this way was highly derogatory to them, and this would be all the more marked if Northern Ireland were to be mentioned specially in the King's title with no corresponding mention of Canada or the other members of the Commonwealth. He felt sure that any Government attempting to legislate on these lines here would run into serious trouble, all the more so as the case of those who want a radical revision of the title was virtually unanswerable.

Pearson, Clutterbuck went on, considered there were two possible courses open. These were:

(a) to agree to take up now not merely the Northern Ireland question but also the wider changes which would be necessary to meet the difficulties of all concerned, or

(b) to defer dealing with the change . . . until there was a suitable opportunity for members of the Commonwealth to discuss and agree upon a revision of the title as a whole.

All the questions arising, Pearson thought, were 'more suitable for discussion in the first instance rather than for correspondence'.[5]

What had seemed to be the comparatively simple issue of whether the one word 'Northern' should be added to the King's title was clearly bringing to the surface doubts among Canadian political leaders about the structure and, indeed, the purpose of the Commonwealth. On 19 January 1949 St Laurent sent a telegram to Attlee. Referring to the proposed change in the King's title he stated: 'This proposal, in my opinion, raises a fundamental issue which affects the entire basis of the Commonwealth structure.' He added: 'I shall, therefore, be grateful if you will kindly elucidate to me the nature and scope of the Commonwealth association to enable me to understand the position with particular reference to the special advantages which a Dominion enjoys if it continues to remain under the Crown of England and which it would cease to enjoy if it seceded from the Commonwealth.'

Some three weeks later the Canadian Government put forward a suggestion that 'His Majesty's title need not necessarily be the same in relation to each unit of the Commonwealth'. In Canada, it suggested, the King's title might be 'George VI by the Grace of God of Canada and of the other nations of the British Commonwealth King.'

On 11 March a telegram was sent from London to all United Kingdom High Commissioners in the Dominions informing them that because of lack of unanimity the proposed change in the King's title would not be included in legislation about to come before Parliament. Attlee had had to obtain the King's agreement before the telegrams could be sent.

The departure of the Republic of Ireland from the Commonwealth took place in an atmosphere of general goodwill and even with suggestions of regret at the final severing of the link with the Crown.

On 12 April 1949 Philip Noel-Baker, the Secretary of State for Commonwealth Relations, informed Attlee of a meeting he had had with John Dulanty, the Irish High Commissioner. Dulanty had, he reported, asked him 'with some diffidence, but with genuine hope, whether it would be possible for a message to be sent by the King to the President of the Republic.'

Noel-Baker stated that he had originally been against sending any such message. His reasons were:

(1) The Eire Government have gone out of their way to choose Easter Monday for the entry into force of their Republic, this being the anniversary of the rising in 1916;

(2) among the ceremonies they propose is the hoisting of their flag at the Dublin Post Office, which was the main centre of the rising;

(3) a message from the King to the President might be taken as emphasizing the foreign status of the new Republic in relation to the United Kingdom, and indeed the Commonwealth, and as such might make it more difficult for us to defend internationally our declared policy of treating Eire as 'non-foreign';

(4) it seems likely that a message from the King would be unwelcome to the Northern Ireland Government.[6]

The United Kingdom High Commissioner, Sir Gilbert Laithwaite, was however in favour of sending a message, and on reflection Noel-Baker agreed with him. Attlee put the suggestion to the King, and on 14 April Lascelles telephoned Helsby to say that the King was 'attracted by the proposal and favourably disposed towards it'. He added that the King wanted to make some small amendments to the draft. The reason for one of these was that he had a prejudice against beginning any message with an adjective.

Two months later the Lord Chancellor, Lord Jowitt, heard from Sir Shane Leslie, a distinguished man of letters and relation of Winston Churchill, that the Irish President, Seamus O'Kelly, would be passing through London on his way to visit the Pope in Rome and wanted to do 'the friendly and respectful thing and call on His Majesty'. The President wanted to know whether the King would receive him. The answer came from Lascelles.

'The King,' he wrote, 'gladly approves in principle the idea that the President of the Irish Republic should, on his way to Rome next winter, pay an official call on him.' Lascelles added: 'The King is strongly of the opinion that it would be quite out of order for him to return such a call by another Head of State passing through London in the course of a journey elsewhere. I may be wrong, but I cannot recall any instance of this having been done in my lifetime.'[7]

What Noel-Baker called the policy of treating the new Irish Republic as 'non-foreign' served, it could be argued, to give the Irish virtually all the benefits of membership of the Commonwealth with none of the obligations, such as they were. In particular Irish citizens would have unrestricted access to Britain, either to find work or for other reasons. Whether these facilities were offered from magnanimity, an underlying sense of unity in spite of differences, or because Britain still wanted to attract able-bodied workers is debatable. Certainly the anomalous nature of the new relationship did not escape notice in other Commonwealth countries, in particular Pakistan.

On 19 January the United Kingdom High Commissioner in Pakistan, Sir Laurence Grafftey-Smith, passed on a message from the Pakistan Government which called attention to the British Government's proposal 'to introduce a Bill to cover the various controversial measures which would ensure that Eire should not be regarded as a foreign country despite her becoming a Republic.' This, the Pakistan Government stated, 'affects the entire basis of the Commonwealth structure.'

A number of questions, it was pointed out, would be asked in Pakistan, such as 'what particular advantage Pakistan will derive from retaining the link with the British Crown which she would lose if that link were broken', and 'whether it will be open to the Commonwealth to admit foreign countries as new members irrespective of their existing constitution'. The message also stated that 'as the Constituent Assembly has still to decide the question of Pakistan's future relations with the Commonwealth any explanations given will possess special and important significance.'[8]

More important than the problems raised by the other Commonwealth nations, complex though some of them were, was, in Attlee's judgment, the attitude of India. This, he felt, was likely to determine the whole future structure and strength of the Commonwealth, and on 13 February he set out his views on this subject at length in a submission to the King. It began:

During the past week the Commonwealth Relations Committee have been giving prolonged study to the problem of India's relationship to the Commonwealth. Your Majesty will have seen the report of the Official Committee and the minutes of the meeting, which exhibit very fully the difficulties and dangers which attend the adoption of any possible line of action. The Committee has, as yet, come to no decision on what to recommend to the Cabinet. The intrinsic difficulties of the problem are increased by the limitations of time imposed on all concerned. It seems clear that a decision by all the Governments of the Commonwealth must be arrived at before the new constitution for India is adopted. It does not appear to be practicable to get the Indian Government to postpone their decision. The probability of elections in three of the Commonwealth countries in the autumn makes it necessary for a decision to be reached early.

It is, in Mr Attlee's view, vitally important to take every possible step to prevent any matter affecting the Crown becoming a subject of political controversy. It would seem, therefore, essential to have a Conference of Commonwealth Prime Ministers not later than May in order to reach a collective decision. It is unlikely that there has been in any of the Commonwealth countries the detailed consideration of the subject which has been given here. Mr Attlee therefore has it in mind to send a Minister or official to every one of the Governments concerned to explain fully the pros and cons in order that the Government may be fully apprized of all the arguments before the Conference is held. He may also wish to consult the Leaders of the Opposition in some of these countries. In this connection Mr Attlee has it in mind to inform the Opposition Leaders here of this intention before very long. It is unfortunate that Mr Eden should be away, as Mr Churchill's emotions on India tend to prevent him giving calm consideration to the larger problem of the future of the Commonwealth when the future of India is in question.

Attlee went on to explain the importance which he attached both to the links which the Crown could provide within the Commonwealth and the foreign policy which India was likely to pursue in the future.

Mr Attlee has always found it difficult to discover any satisfactory nexus for the Commonwealth other than allegiance to the Crown, and it is therefore difficult to see how a Republic can be included. He is, at the same time, impressed by the fact that India is anxious to remain within the Commonwealth, and that the other Dominions, especially Australia and New Zealand, have stressed strongly the desirability of retaining her. If India, against her will, is obliged to leave the Commonwealth, it would encourage Russia in her efforts to disrupt South-East Asia, while India, as the most important national state in that area, would tend to become the leader of an anti-European Asiatic movement. On the other hand, if she remains within the Commonwealth, there is a great possibility of building up in South-East Asia something analogous to Western Union.

Attlee summarised his thinking by concluding:

The arguments are therefore well balanced. It is an open question whether the inclusion of a Republic in the Commonwealth would lead to the spread of republicanism, or whether the insistence of allegiance to the Crown as an essential nexus might not lead to other Commonwealth states going out. In Mr Attlee's view it is clear that this question can only be settled at a Commonwealth Conference, and it is impossible to forecast what conclusion will be reached by the Conference members.[9]

The emissaries of whom Attlee wrote were in fact despatched to the various Commonwealth countries, and a conference of Commonwealth Prime Ministers was convened. Before it took place further efforts were made to find a solution to some of the problems raised by the various Dominions. In this the King himself took a leading part. Michael Adeane prepared a lengthy memorandum on the subject of the King's title based on notes which the King himself had made. Even when this had been done the King listed, in a note to Lascelles, seven more questions to which answers were needed.[10]

The conference which was to decide the future form of the Commonwealth met in London on 21 April. The only country whose Prime Minister did not attend was Canada. Lester Pearson, an Oxford Rhodes scholar with a good understanding of British politics, came in place of St Laurent. The other countries, in addition to Great Britain, whose Prime Ministers were present, were Australia, Ceylon, India, New Zealand, Pakistan and South Africa.

At the end of a week the work of the conference was completed, and on the afternoon of 26 April the ministers had an audience of the King. The next day, at Attlee's suggestion, the King received them in the white drawing room in Buckingham Palace. He began by congratulating them on the speed with which they had completed their task. Then, in what may be assumed to be a reference to the deliberations of the United Nations, he added: 'I wish that certain other countries, who are not privileged to belong to our British Commonwealth, could show an equal degree of common sense and good temper when they meet us round the conference table.'

As Attlee had foreseen, the principal task of the conference had been to find a formula, satisfactory to all, which would enable India to remain within the Commonwealth. This preoccupation was reflected in the formal declaration, to which the representatives of the eight nations subscribed and which Attlee read out to the King. Its wording was:

The Governments of the United Kingdom, Canada, Australia, New Zealand, South Africa, India, Pakistan and Ceylon, whose countries are united as Members of the British Commonwealth of Nations and owe a common allegiance to the Crown, which is also the symbol of their free association, have considered the impending constitutional changes in India.

The Government of India have informed the other Governments of the Commonwealth of the intention of the Indian people that under the new constitution which is about to be adopted India shall become a sovereign independent Republic. The Government of India have, however, declared and affirmed India's desire to continue her full membership of the Commonwealth of Nations and her acceptance of The King as the symbol of the free association of its independent member nations and as such the Head of the Commonwealth.

The Governments of the other countries of the Commonwealth, the basis of whose membership of the Commonwealth is not hereby changed, accept and recognise India's continuing membership in accordance with the terms of the declaration.

Accordingly the United Kingdom, Canada, Australia, New Zealand, South Africa, India, Pakistan and Ceylon hereby declare that they remain united as free and equal members of the Commonwealth of Nations, freely co-operating in the pursuit of peace, liberty and progress.

The adoption of the term 'Head of the Commonwealth', conferring, as it did, a new title on an ancient monarchy, was probably decisive in bringing about general agreement.

Attlee had the intention of including the new title in the British coinage, and in May, when dining in Oriel College, Oxford, he said that he was looking for a suitable Latin equivalent to 'Head of the Commonwealth'. The problem was discussed with some enthusiasm in the Senior Common Room, and it was decided to seek the advice of the eminent classical scholar and orientalist, Professor David Margoliouth. He came up with the suggestion 'Civitatis Gentium Supremum Caput'. Its abbreviation, CIV GEN SUPR CAP, would, he pointed out, take up little more space on the reverse of a coin than the letters FID DEF IND IMP, with which the public was familiar.

When the subject was brought to the attention of Attlee's Private Office a number of senior civil servants took up the challenge, and the consensus was that 'Consortionis Populorum Princeps' would be a better rendering than the Professor's. Enthusiasm waned when it was realised that all the Commonwealth Governments might have to be consulted. On 5 July Attlee noted on a memorandum on the subject: 'Not unduly pressing.'[11]

That the arrangement whereby India became a republic yet retained its links with the Crown was a popular one in India was illustrated by events later in the year. On 17 December the United Kingdom High Commissioner in New Delhi, Lieut-General Sir Archibald Nye, recommended that the King send a message to the President of the Indian Republic, Rajendra Prasad, on the inauguration of the new constitution. He cited the precedent of the Irish Republic and added: 'A great deal of attention is paid in this country to the sending of congratulatory messages on important occasions.'

The King duly sent a message of good wishes, in which he expressed the hope that the people of India would enjoy 'the full blessings of peace and prosperity in the years to come'. Nehru then suggested that at the swearing-in ceremony of the new President the outgoing Governor-General, Sir Chakravarty Rajagopolachari, as the King's representative, should read a message from the King to the people of India.

The King felt that two separate messages from him to the people of India would be excessive. He therefore compromised by sending a message to Rajagopolachari himself, making it clear that he was at liberty to read it out if he chose. The message described the swearing-in of the first President as 'a new chapter in the long and illustrious history' of the people of India.[12]

Winston Churchill once said that he did not become the King's First

Minister in order to preside over the dissolution of the British Empire. Attlee did, and it was one of his more memorable achievements. Indeed, when asked on one occasion what he thought he might be remembered by, he replied with characteristic terseness and diffidence: 'India perhaps.'

After World War II the ending of the British Empire in its old form was inevitable. Neither Attlee nor any other British statesman could have prevented this from happening. Nor could the King, as a constitutional monarch, have halted the course of events. Attlee's achievement was, for better or for worse, to have been the principal architect of the new structure of the Commonwealth and to have determined very largely the manner in which the transformation was made. In this work he was in continual consultation with the King. For his part the King showed flexibility and an understanding of the need for change and for tact and delicacy in its application. These were qualities in which his ancestor, King George III, in circumstances in some ways comparable, had been sadly deficient.

The process of change was to continue after 1949, with a steady acceleration in the rate of decolonisation. The main structure had however been brought into being by then, and it was of such a kind that the former colonies could easily be accommodated within it. Whether this structure was ideal, and whether the people of Britain in particular derived substantial benefits from it, is clearly debatable. But the likeliest alternative to what was brought about in the second part of George VI's reign would have been an ultimate void preceded by even more bloodshed.

The appraisal made by the British Government as a whole in the late 1940s of the future role and potential of the Commonwealth was admirably realistic. On 9 May 1949 a comprehensive paper was produced within the Foreign Office. Two of its conclusions were: '(a) The Commonwealth alone cannot form a third World Power equivalent to the United States or the Soviet Union. (b) Commonwealth solidarity is more likely to be promoted by the consolidation of the West than by the formation of a third World Power independent of America.'

Less perceptive were the observations on the economy of Europe. From these one conclusion drawn was: 'Whereas in the case of the Commonwealth the principal difficulties in the way of consolidation as a third World Power are political, in the case of Western Europe the difficulties lie mainly in the economic and military weakness of the members, though the political will to union must always be doubtful.'[13]

On 13 and 14 January 1949 the British Foreign Secretary, Ernest Bevin, had a number of discussions with the French Foreign Minister, Robert Schuman. At the end of a dinner which Bevin gave on the 13th he told Schuman that it had been the King's intention to invite the President of the

French Republic, Vincent Auriol, to London, but that the plan had had to be postponed because of the state of the King's health. The official record of the Foreign Ministers' meetings stated:

'Mr Bevin had discussed the whole question with the King, and he knew that His Majesty was most anxious to issue this invitation as soon as possible. M. Schuman very much appreciated the King's intention, and was clearly much touched to hear of it unofficially in this way. He said he would mention the matter to the President.'[14]

When they dined together again the next evening Bevin and Schuman talked with some frankness about the future of Europe. Bevin said he was 'not opposed to the union of Europe in principle' and that he had himself advocated this when addressing the Trades Union Congress in 1927. He had even persuaded the Congress to accept his proposal. But, the official record stated, 'he hoped that the French, with their more logical ideas, would not insist on building the whole fabric at the outset.' In strict confidence he then told Schuman that he thought Strasbourg should be the centre for what he called 'a European conference'.

On the same day Bevin wrote to the King to tell him that he had spoken to Schuman about a visit by the President and that the idea had been well received.

In the course of the year the King had the pleasant task of knighting Robert Hyde, with whom he had been associated for so long in the Industrial Welfare Society. He enjoyed, too, a gift he received from General Eisenhower. This was a book of the general's memoirs. On 1 March Lascelles wrote to Eisenhower that the King had read the book 'from cover to cover' – a compliment in itself, for the King did not read widely for pleasure – and that he had found it 'a wonderfully true picture of the great events that it records.'[15]

A reminder of the King's visit to South Africa two years earlier came in November. This was a petition signed by the Paramount Chief of Basutoland, Mantsebo Seeiso, and thirty-one other Basuto chieftains. It had been forwarded from Long Island, New York, by Rev. Michael Scott, an Anglican clergyman, who was attempting to interest the United Nations in the fate of the inhabitants of Basutoland. This method of transmission was used because the chieftains feared that the petition, if sent through the orthodox channels, might not reach the King.

One paragraph in the petition read:

Your Majesty.
Although we believe that those who were enemies of Basuto at the time our father Moshesh asked for protection are now under your government, and therefore are members of the same family to which we belong, we are afraid of them when we see them among your servants who are administering the

Government of our country, and we are compelled to pray that it may graciously please Your Majesty to send us children from the home of the Saviour of our Nation, Queen Victoria the Good, and all those already stationed in our country be transferred to the other territories. Your Majesty, we are afraid of them, and the object of their Government at the present time is to sever their connection with the British Crown and establish their independence as a Republic, which thing we Basotho detest to the bottom of our hearts.

The petitioners received a discouraging reply from the Government. This called attention to a statement which had been made in Parliament expressing 'every confidence in the officers serving in the Territory, from whatever country they may have been recruited.'[16]

By the end of the year the King was thought to have recovered his health sufficiently for him to undertake in the near future a number of engagements which had had to be postponed. These included two important state visits to Britain and his own tour of Australia and New Zealand. It was also certain that there would be a general election in Britain in 1950 with the likelihood of a close result and more than a possibility of a change of government.

The King was only fifty-four at the end of 1949, and it was reasonable to suppose that, physically, he would be able to meet the extra demands which would be made of him in the following year.

CHAPTER TWENTY-FIVE

General Election and Korean War
1950

The General Election which was held in the United Kingdom on 23 February 1950 was described by Winston Churchill as the 'most sedate' he could remember. If indeed it was sedate, this was not a consequence of apathy, for the poll was the heaviest in the nation's history.

The Labour party was returned to power, but as it obtained only 315 seats out of a total of 635, the business of managing Parliament was clearly going to be difficult and the strain on ministers likely to be intense.

The King formally opened the new Parliament on 6 March. Soon after it had met speculation began to grow about the possibility of a constitutional crisis in which the King might be called upon to act. With such a slender majority, it was suggested, Attlee might well ask the King to dissolve Parliament in the hope of obtaining a better result by a new election. The question which would then arise was whether the King would be obliged to meet his Prime Minister's wishes. Opinion among constitutional experts was divided.

Lord Simon, an eminent legal authority, who was to be Lord Chancellor in a future Conservative administration, stated emphatically that the King might properly refuse to dissolve Parliament. This opinion was contested in letters published in *The Times*.

One of these was written by a young Labour politican, Roy Jenkins, who pointed out that the prerogative of the Crown to refuse a dissolution had not been exercised since the Reform Bill of 1832. He added that if the King refused Attlee's request and asked Churchill to form a government, Churchill would also be forced before long to ask for a dissolution. The Crown, Jenkins wrote, would then be placed in 'the intolerable and dangerous position of granting to a minority Prime Minister what it had already refused to a majority Prime Minister.'

The correspondence was effectively ended by Lascelles, whose letter *The Times* published over the pseudonym 'Senex'. The decision whether or not to grant a request for a dissolution, was, Lascelles wrote, 'entirely personal to the Sovereign, though he is, of course, free to seek informal advice from anybody whom he thinks fit to consult.' Lascelles went on: 'No wise Sovereign – that is, one who has at heart the true interest of the country, the constitution, and the Monarchy – would deny a dissolution to his Prime Minister unless he was satisfied that: (1) the existing Parliament was still vital, viable, and capable of doing its job; (2) a General Election would be detrimental to the national economy; (3) he could rely on finding another Prime Minister who could carry on his Government, for a reasonable period, with a working majority in the House of Commons.'

Attlee did not in fact ask for a dissolution until late in the following year. Had he done so at any time in 1950, Lascelles's letter, in which he assumed for a time something of the role of Bagehot, makes it clear that the King would have met his request.

The visit to Britain by the French President, Vincent Auriol, which Bevin had proposed a year earlier, began less than a fortnight after the General Election. It was not therefore known until shortly before the President's arrival which British ministers would be in office to greet him. In fact Attlee did not make many significant changes in his administration, and Bevin remained in charge of the Foreign Office.

Bevin's ideas on what should be included in the programme for the President's visit seem to have puzzled the King somewhat. One suggestion which Bevin made was that an 'address on industry' should be included. This was considered by a committee which had been set up by the King to make arrangements for the visit, and after a meeting in the Lord Chamberlain's Office, the committee's secretary, John Russell, wrote:

'The King had accepted the inclusion of the item in the first instance as it had been suggested by the Secretary of State and as the King saw from the papers submitted to him that Mr Bevin evidently attached considerable importance to it. The King had, however, on being told over the weekend that the item was to be dropped, expressed considerable relief.'[1]

The King also made his wishes felt after studying the arrangements for entertaining the President at the Royal Naval College in Greenwich. 'The King,' Lascelles wrote to a member of the Foreign Office staff, 'feels strongly that at the end of the luncheon the Secretary of State should merely propose the two toasts without any speech, however short.'[2]

In the briefings which it prepared for the King the Foreign Office made it clear that the French President would welcome proposals for closer cooperation in various fields between Britain and France. The President was no de Gaulle, harbouring private grievances and bitterly resentful of the fact that the liberation of France had owed more to British than to

French arms. Instead the man the King would be meeting had had first-hand experience of life in occupied France and of what British help to the resistance had meant.

During the occupation, one of the briefings stated, Auriol had been warned by the BBC through a coded message that he should escape to London. He had made his way to Lyons, where the head of a resistance group had taken him to an airfield. From there he had been flown to London together with General de Lattre de Tassigny.

Auriol was described as 'a man of simple tastes and considerable charm', whose sentiments were Anglophile. He was also said to be a trout fisherman and fond of shooting. Mme Auriol, who had had a distinguished record in the resistance, was described as intelligent and cultivated and 'a very typical representative of the solid upper bourgeoisie that is the backbone of France'.

The President was to be accompanied by his Foreign Minister, Robert Schuman, whom the British Foreign Office described as 'scholarly, shy, gentle and retiring, deeply religious and universally liked and respected in France'.[3]

Encouraging though the sentiments of the visitors were thought to be, the King was nevertheless warned of pitfalls by a list headed 'Dangerous Subjects'. Among the observations were:

General de Gaulle
President Auriol is on bad terms with the general, but would not wish to admit this in England.

General de Lattre de Tassigny and General Montgomery
The absence of personal affection between these two leading players on the military stage is no secret in France.

Atomic Science
The French Government resent our refusal to exchange atomic information with them and attribute it to our distrust of Professor Joliot Curie, the Communist head of their Atomic Energy Commission.

Middle East
The average Frenchman still harbours the blackest suspicions of the alleged activities of the 'British Intelligence Service' in the Middle East. Syria and the Lebanon are still dangerous subjects.

Devaluation
The French regarded our failure to consult them before devaluing the £ last autumn as evidence that we considered them as having less importance to us than the Dominions or the United States. This action was also one of the things that made the French feel Great Britain was turning her back on Europe and seeking a special relationship with the United States.[4]

The visit clearly offered an opportunity for denying this last charge.

What remained unclear was whether British foreign policy would allow the denial to be made with any conviction. After drafting a speech for the King to make at the State banquet in Buckingham Palace John Russell, a talented diplomat who later became British Ambassador to Spain, wrote in a note which he appended to his draft:

'I have tried to give the speech some warmth and at the same time to avoid the stilted jargon traditionally associated with turtle soup.' He added: 'I have tried to write something that will be useful in allaying French fears of our pulling out of Europe and leaving them and our other Continental allies to save themselves by their own devices.'[5]

The President was met by the Duke of Gloucester at Dover. At Victoria Station in London he was met by the King, the Queen and both Princesses as well as by Attlee, Bevin and other members of the Government. The usual pageantry and speech-making followed, and of the warmth of President Auriol's sentiments and words there could be no doubt. Perhaps the most significant sentence in the various speeches which he made was: 'In the past England and France have dealt each other hard enough knocks to be able today, in pride, equity and reciprocity, to offer on the altar of our common cause the essential sacrifice of their individual sovereignty.'[6] From the British side there was no overt response to the implied offer, either from the King or from anyone else.

In reporting to Bevin on 17 March Sir Oliver Harvey, the British Ambassador in Paris wrote: 'There can be no question of the success of the President's visit or of the outstanding contribution which it has made to the cause of Franco-British understanding.'[7]

In retrospect this may seem a limited judgment. President Auriol's visit could have served as a watershed in British foreign policy, just as the King's visit to the United States in 1939 may be thought to have done. In fact this did not happen, and some years were to pass before Britain, belatedly seeking admission to the European Economic Community, would receive from General de Gaulle the ultimate insult of the blackball.

Within the Commonwealth a new manner of addressing the King was devised. On 27 May 1950 the Indian President, Rajendra Prasad, sent him an official communication which began: 'Great and Good Friend'. The King's reply began with greetings from 'George the Sixth by Grace of God to the President of the Republic of India'. He then addressed the President as 'Our Good Friend'.

The Prime Minister of Pakistan, Liaqat Ali Khan, on returning from a visit to the United States, told Attlee in London how impressed he had been by Truman's 'simple and direct approach' and by the personalities of Dean Acheson and General Omar Bradley. He then said how glad he was that Pakistan's constitution was 'based on the British and not the United States model'.[8]

A new status was conferred on Southern Rhodesia in 1950 following a visit by the Southern Rhodesian Prime Minister, Sir Godfrey Huggins, who lunched with the King and Queen at Buckingham Palace on 20 March.

Shortly before Huggins's arrival the Governor-General of Southern Rhodesia, Sir John Kennedy, sent a long report in which he summarised conditions and attitudes in the country. He wrote:

First, then, we must put the overwhelming spirit of loyalty to the Throne and to Great Britain. This spirit . . . is universal among the White Anglo-Saxon population. . . Next in importance I think I would put their tremendous pride in what they have accomplished in adding this country to the Empire and in developing it so swiftly and successfully by the sweat of their brows.

After referring to the growing influx of Afrikaners Kennedy wrote:

People in Southern Rhodesia believe most firmly that native problems are not properly understood in London. They feel about Africa just as the early settlers in America might have felt if the Colonial Office of those days had insisted on North America developing into a Red Indian State, or as the first settlers in Australia, if the policy of the Home Government had been to set up an Aboriginal Government there. They would not argue that it was right to have eliminated the Red Indians and the aboriginals, but would urge that their own liberal policy to the native was a great advance on that, and a more correct policy than that of the British Government.

On 10 March Patrick Gordon Walker, the Secretary of State for Commonwealth Relations, sent Attlee a paper advocating the appointment of a High Commissioner in Southern Rhodesia. The effect of this would be to remove the Governor-General, who was both the King's representative and the representative of the United Kingdom Government for what was known as 'reserved legislation' – i.e. largely that concerned with the indigenous Africans. Gordon Walker was instructed to discuss his proposals with Huggins. He found Huggins agreeable, and on 5 April the new status of Southern Rhodesia was publicly announced.

The Australian Prime Minister, Robert Menzies, expressed his intention on 16 June of visiting London in the near future. He was to go to Washington later. The United Kingdom High Commissioner in Canberra, Walter Garnett, reported that the main purpose of Menzies's visits was to discuss financial problems and that he had been 'having difficulties in Cabinet over economic policy'. Three meetings were arranged for him with Sir Stafford Cripps, the Chancellor of the Exchequer, and two with Attlee alone. On 18 July he lunched with the King.

In the briefings which the King received it was stated that 'of all the Commonwealth politicians Mr Menzies is the most devoted to the

Commonwealth connection and the only one who has given much thought to it. . . Mr Menzies has always shown himself a warm and true friend of this country. As Prime Minister in 1939 he was responsible for Australia's immediate entry into the war.' The King was also told that Menzies advocated common and distinctive Commonwealth policies in both foreign affairs and defence.[9]

On 25 June 1950 North Korean communist forces invaded the territory of South Korea, whose frontier, the 38th parallel, had been established after World War II under the supervision of the United Nations. Two days later President Truman announced that he had ordered American air and sea forces to give the South Koreans cover and support.

His action was later endorsed by the United Nations Security Council. Attlee immediately announced that British naval forces in Japanese waters would be placed under American command, and on 5 July the House of Commons, without dissent, supported the British Government's actions. Before long a Commonwealth division was in action in Korea.

The Parliamentary recess began on 5 August, but because of the military reverses suffered in Korea, and fears that the war might spread, there were demands by the opposition parties for an early recall of Parliament. Attlee informed the King of these in a letter he wrote dated 18 August.

'I was unable,' he wrote, 'to find any substantial reason for an earlier recall as it did not seem to me that another debate without any definite action by the House would be useful.' At this Churchill, he added, 'showed considerable annoyance.'[10]

The King had also wanted to know more of what was happening, and on 16 August Lascelles wrote to the Prime Minister's Office for 'confirmation if possible that His Majesty's ships had clear orders that while engaged under United Nations command against invading forces in Korea they were not to be involved in hostilities with China over Formosa.'

Lascelles's question was referred to the Admiralty, which confirmed that such orders applied to United Kingdom, New Zealand and Canadian ships. The tasks of Australian ships were less clearly defined. They had been placed unreservedly at the disposal of the United States Supreme Commander, though a telegram from Menzies to Attlee had stated that they were 'acting on behalf of the Security Council in support of the Republic of Korea'. Lascelles replied on 21 August that the King was 'now satisfied that everything is in order.'[11]

Parliament was in fact recalled a month earlier than usual, and on 12 September the Government announced a number of plans for strengthening national defences. The period of national service was extended from eighteen months to two years, and the limited military alliance known as the Brussels Pact was incorporated in the much more formidable body called the North Atlantic Treaty Organisation.

Attlee also decided to visit Truman in Washington in search of military policies which would be acceptable to both Britain and the United States. Before he left the King wrote to him: 'I know that you have contemplated this visit for some time, and I feel that this is the right moment when, as head of my Government in the United Kingdom, you can explain to the President the true picture, as we see it, of the present world situation.'[12] This Attlee did, but his success was otherwise limited, largely because of conflicting attitudes towards China.

That the United States and Commonwealth forces in Korea could claim to be fighting on behalf of the United Nations was a consequence of a decision of the Soviet Union to withdraw for a time from meetings of the Security Council. As a result she had been unable to exercise a veto when it was decided to resist North Korean aggression.

This somewhat fortuitous use of its authority did not serve to raise the standing of the United Nations itself in the eyes of British Government officials. On 11 October 1950 Peter Hope, a member of the United Nations department of the Foreign Office, wrote a minute stating: 'Mr Ivan Smith, who is the representative of Mr Trygve Lie in England and at the same time head of the United Nations Information Centre in London, called on me yesterday to ask confidentially if it would be appropriate for him to call at Buckingham Palace on October 24th (United Nations Day) to convey the respects of the Secretary-General to the King. The Secretary-General was anxious this year for calls to be paid by his representatives on heads of state in view of the greatly increased importance of the United Nations.'

Another minute was appended to this over an illegible signature. This stated: 'I take it that Mr Ivan Smith is not expecting to be received in personal Audience by the Sovereign for the purpose he has in mind. This would be altogether too much, I feel. The most he could hope for would be a few minutes interview with one of His Majesty's Private Secretaries.'

Another member of the Foreign Office staff passed on Ivan Smith's request to Lascelles, writing of Smith himself: 'He serves as a useful damper on some of the more outrageous schemes of the United Nations Association. . . For this reason we should like to support the suggestion. . . I should therefore be most grateful if you would take His Majesty's pleasure whether he would wish you to receive Mr Smith.'

Lascelles replied on 19 October: 'The King has gladly approved the suggestion that I should see Mr Smith on the morning of October 24th. . . He should also sign the King's Book.'[13]

It was generally agreed that the visit by the King and Queen to Australia and New Zealand, which had had to be postponed, should take place soon. But it was not thought expedient that they should go in 1951, largely because of the plans which had been made for holding a Festival of Britain. On 17 November 1949 Lascelles had written to Laurence Helsby at the Prime Minister's Office: 'It is almost unthinkable that The King and Queen should be away from this country for the whole – or at any rate much the greater part – of this Festival from which so much is expected.'[14]

It was however agreed that the King and Queen would visit Australia and New Zealand in 1952 in spite of the physical demands which such a tour would make on the King. It was also agreed that Princess Elizabeth and the Duke of Edinburgh would visit Canada in 1951.

An important step was taken too in preparing Princess Elizabeth for her presumed future role. This was explained by the Secretary to the Cabinet, Sir Norman Brook, when writing to Attlee on 14 June.

Princess Elizabeth's Private Secretary has suggested that during the coming months when she will be fulfilling no public engagements the Princess might take the opportunity of extending her experience of public affairs by reading a selection of the current Cabinet papers. Sir Alan Lascelles thought that this suggestion was worthy of consideration and consulted me about it.

There are precedents for allowing the heir to the throne to see Cabinet papers. The present King, when Duke of York, and the Duke of Gloucester, before Princess Elizabeth came of age, both received Cabinet memoranda (not minutes), in pursuance of specific Cabinet decisions taken in 1936 and 1937.

Brook went on to explain that the differences between memoranda and minutes were largely theoretical.

It is the 'proceedings' of the Cabinet which are, by constitutional doctrine, regarded as specially secret and it is the theory that these are reflected in the minutes rather than the memoranda. This theoretical distinction had, however, more force in the '30s than it has today; for Cabinet minutes were then written in a rather more graphic style which disclosed differences of opinion and attributed views to individual ministers.

From the practical point of view it is unsatisfactory, and may be positively misleading, for anyone to see the memoranda and not the minutes – for this means that they would know what proposals were being put to the Cabinet but would not know which of them were modified or rejected.

Brook therefore suggested that Princess Elizabeth should receive both minutes and memoranda, but added: 'I would suggest that confidential Annexes should not be sent to her.' He continued:

Sir Alan Lascelles suggests that, if you are disposed to approve such an arrangement, you might discuss it with the King at your next audience. If you will let me know whether you agree in principle, I will inform Sir Alan Lascelles so that he may warn His Majesty that you will be raising this question at your next audience.

Brook expressed the opinion that the specific authority of the Cabinet would not be needed for doing what was suggested, 'especially as it is not at present contemplated that this should be a lasting arrangement, but only a temporary arrangement forming part of a general plan for giving Her Royal Highness a wider experience of public affairs.'

Under this document Attlee wrote by hand: 'I will mention it to the King. I think it should be permanent.'[15]

On 24 January 1950 the Netherlands Ambassador had informed the Foreign Office that Queen Juliana of the Netherlands would be paying a state visit to France in May or June and would like 'thereafter' to pay a state visit to Britain, preferably in June. The Ambassador also spoke to Lascelles, who told him that the King generally preferred March or October for state visits.

From the Foreign Office Sir Ivo Mallet wrote to Sir Philip Nichols, the British Ambassador at the Hague: 'Lascelles feels that two state visits in one year would be a very heavy burden on the King, both physically and financially. The month of June is not convenient, since Their Majesties are already fully booked for the summer and, in any event, like to keep their summer engagements for their own people.' He suggested consideration should be given to a state visit in March 1951.[16]

Prince Bernhard of the Netherlands was in the habit of visiting London unofficially from time to time and, when lunching with the King in July, in an informal conversation he too raised the question of a state visit. He and the King then agreed that the visit could take place in November.

Reporting on this to the Foreign Office, Lascelles, still mindful of the King's health, hastily wrote from Buckingham Palace on 26 July: 'The programme for such a visit would be on a more modest scale than that for the French President's visit, and should comprise a State banquet here: a small dinner the following night at the Dutch Embassy, to be followed perhaps by a party given by HMG (not at Greenwich). A gala performance at Covent Garden could, it was thought, be dispensed with.'

A Foreign Office minute of the same date as Lascelles's letter nevertheless stated that the King and Prince Bernhard had agreed that a gala performance at Covent Garden was necessary. This was not for artistic reasons, but in order that the Dutch visit should be accorded parity with the earlier visit by the French.

Queen Juliana suggested that the cruiser in which she would be coming to Britain should sail up the Thames rather than berth at Dover. On this the Foreign Office informed the British Embassy in the Hague: 'The King has said that he wishes the traditional ceremonial of arrival at Dover and the journey thence by train to Victoria to be observed. There are in any case formidable technical difficulties in the way of bringing a cruiser up the Thames beyond Sheerness.' The King's wishes were met, and Queen Juliana and Prince Bernhard were greeted at Dover by the Duke of Gloucester and the Lord Warden of the Cinque Ports, an office which was now filled by Winston Churchill.

The notes prepared for the King reminded him that Queen Wilhelmina of the Netherlands had abdicated in September 1948 at the end of the fiftieth year of her reign. Queen Juliana, who succeeded her, had studied as a normal undergraduate at Leyden University, taking a degree in literature and philosophy. She had spent most of the war with her small children in Canada, with occasional visits to the United States. She had attended the coronation of King George VI in 1937.

'Prince Bernhard,' the notes went on, 'remained in London during most of the war as Commander-in-Chief of the Dutch forces. In addition he flew with and gained his wings in the RAF and played a considerable part in the organisation of the Dutch resistance forces. . . By all those who fought in the Resistance Movement Prince Bernhard is looked upon as a man to whom no appeal for help is ever directed in vain.'

Queen Juliana was accompanied by Dr Marie Tellegen, who was described as 'what we should call Queen Juliana's Private Secretary', The briefing claimed: 'She is the first woman to hold the post – called Director of the Cabinet of the Queen. . . Highly intelligent and well informed and enjoys a good deal of personal influence.'[17]

The 'dangerous subjects', of which the King was warned, numbered only three. The first of these was 'Colonies', on which the briefing stated: 'The Dutch feel that we, as another Colonial power in the Far East, supported them far too little during the troubles in Indonesia.' The other possibly contentious issues were naval and military, for which solutions could probably be found without great difficulty. During the French President's visit, by contrast, the number of so-called 'dangerous subjects' listed for the King had been twelve.

Like President Auriol, Queen Juliana emphasised in a public speech the need for greater unity in western Europe. But once again the response in the King's speech, prepared by the Foreign Office, was lukewarm. The most indicative words were: 'Whatever forms the closer association of the western world may take, it is already accepted among the free nations that we share the same precious heritage and that our interests lie in unity and cooperation, rather than in rivalry and division.'[18]

In the early months of 1950 it seemed likely that, in the furtherance of British policies, the King might soon be called upon to accept yet another state visit.

In January Bevin had a series of talks in Cairo. These followed receipt of information that King Farouk wanted to negotiate a secret treaty which would commit Britain to military intervention in support of Egypt in the event of a Soviet attack. The report of a discussion which Bevin had with Farouk on 28 January stated: 'King Farouk then mentioned the cloud under which he felt he had been since 1942, when he had been accused of being a Fascist working for the Italians and the Nazis. He said that while he was not seeking an invitation to visit London, he was conscious of the fact that he had not been invited there.'

Bevin told him that there had been no state visit to Britain since that by President Lebrun in 1939. He added that he too wanted to forget about the past. On his return to London he informed members of the Foreign Office staff that a state visit by King Farouk was a possibility.

King Farouk persisted. He bestowed on Princess Elizabeth the Order of El Kamal to mark the birth of Prince Charles. He also sent a telegram from Cairo on 7 March announcing his wish to confer an honour on the Duke of Gloucester. This, he suggested, might require the King's consent, and his telegram ended: 'Please inform the King.'

The King agreed to the proposal, and it was also decided that the Duke of Gloucester would visit Cairo and personally hand King Farouk a commission appointing him an honorary general in the British Army. This was duly done, but a report from the British Embassy in Cairo stated: 'King Farouk found that his father had anticipated him in conferring on His Royal Highness the order of Mohammed Ali and that he regretted therefore that all he could offer him was a signed photograph.'[19]

In spite of all this activity, the political and military negotiations did not advance far enough for a state visit by King Farouk to be thought appropriate.

By the summer of 1950 work had been completed on the new debating chamber of the House of Commons, which had had to be built to replace the old one destroyed by enemy action during the war. The King agreed to open it. As he would shortly afterwards be opening the new session of Parliament with all the familiar ceremonial dress and proceedings, he thought it would be appropriate for him simply to drive to the new House of Commons in a motor-car and to open it wearing morning dress. This did not please the ebullient Minister of Works, Richard Stokes, who expressed his opinion to Lascelles in conversation and later wrote:

> I know that the King alone can decide what he shall do when he comes to Westminster Hall on the 28th October, and I am not criticising his decision to come in a 'plain van'.
>
> What I am anxious is to assure that there is on record in your office my own opinion that a very great deal of disappointment will be felt throughout the

Empire and much of the romance taken out of the whole celebration at a time when there is all too little romance of the right kind in the world. This is a special occasion as you know, and I do not suppose ever before Speakers of the Commonwealth Houses of Commons have been together ceremonially. So far as the general public is concerned, it will be no occasion at all.

Stokes's letter drew a sharp rebuke from Attlee. 'The King's decision,' Attlee informed him, 'was reached after discussion with me and I fully agreed with it. It can only lead to confusion if another minister writes to place on record a view which is at variance with the advice which I have given.'[20]

The burden which ceremonial duties were placing on the King in the spring, summer and autumn of 1950 was already formidable. Attlee, it may be assumed, did not want to add to it further.

CHAPTER TWENTY-SIX
The Final Year
1951

On 4 January 1951 the King wrote to Mountbatten: 'We have our hands and minds full of Dominion PMs today for lunch and separate interviews with each one timed so that they don't interfere with their talks. It's like a jigsaw puzzle fitting them all in.'[1] Shortly afterwards, when writing to Mountbatten, he told him how impressed he had been by Nehru.[2]

At the end of their meetings the Prime Ministers issued yet another communique calling attention to the unique nature of the Commonwealth and expressing confidence in its power to act cohesively and effectively. 'Our historic Commonwealth,' the communique stated, 'which comprises one-fourth of the world's population and extends over all the continents and oceans of the world, is singularly well constituted to enable it to study and in some measure to comprehend the vexed questions which beset the world.'

Passing from the general to the particular, the communique went on: 'In the last few days we have directed our efforts to the securing of a cessation of hostilities in Korea, so that around the conference table the Great Powers concerned may compose their differences.'[3] It was a hope which was not immediately to be fulfilled.

1951, the last full year of George VI's reign, may be thought to have comprised the high point of the hopes that the Commonwealth, acting in unison, could serve to heal quarrels in other parts of the world and become a force for the better management of human affairs everywhere.

In the early months of 1951, additionally, the King was much occupied with the plans for the Festival of Britain. This was an imaginative project intended to commemorate the Great Exhibition of a century earlier and to give, as its predecessor had done, an impetus to trade and the arts. It was also a deliberately planned attempt to bring relief to the nation from the rigours of a period to which the term 'austerity' was already widely applied. As such it was remarkably successful.

Unlike the Great Exhibition the Festival of Britain extended over much of the country and gave rise to a variety of pageants and spectacles, art exhibitions, housing schemes and trade shows. The main display was on a previously derelict site on the south bank of the Thames near Waterloo Station. The most important building erected as an integral part of the Festival was a new concert hall.

Herbert Morrison was the minister principally responsible for the Festival arrangements, and in his autobiography he described how the King 'took a personal interest in all the plans for the South Bank site'. He and the King discussed the Festival Hall project in some detail, and, according to Morrison, the King said that 'the ideas indicated such a lovely building that it merited being titled "Royal".'[4] The title was duly conferred.

At the inaugural concert in the Royal Festival Hall Sir Malcolm Sargent conducted Arne's *Rule Britannia*, which he had himself arranged. It was performed by singers from seven London choirs and players from five London orchestras. State trumpeters in full uniform accompanied the singers in the final chorus. After the performance the King told Sargent that he was not very musical, but that he had never been moved by any music so much as he had been by the rendering of *Rule Britannia*. He added that if he came to another of Sargent's concerts he would be tempted to command him to perform it again. Sargent commented that this might be difficult if the concert had just included music such as Bach's B Minor Mass or the St Matthew Passion. The King replied drily that it would not be difficult, as in that event he would not have been present.[5]

The King formally opened the South Bank Exhibition on 4 May. After that he was reported to have moved 'briskly' from pavilion to pavilion. It was to be one of the last demanding public engagements which he performed with apparent ease. Three weeks later he became ill, influenza being diagnosed.

In June Princess Elizabeth deputised for her father at a number of events. One of these was the Trooping the Colour ceremony. Another was an unofficial visit from King Haakon of Norway. In June too Margaret Truman, the President's daughter, came to Buckingham Palace, where she discussed plans for a visit by Princess Elizabeth and the Duke of Edinburgh to the United States.

Among the engagements which had been planned for June was a visit by the King and Queen to Northern Ireland. This had been publicly announced on 8 February, when it was stated that the last joint visit by the King and Queen to Northern Ireland had been in June 1942, when they had spent a day with the first United States troops to arrive in the United Kingdom. The Queen and Princess Elizabeth had paid a visit in July 1945.

The reaction in ministerial circles in Dublin was violent. Sir Gilbert Laithwaite, the British Ambassador, was summoned by the Foreign

Minister, Sean MacBride, who said he was 'profoundly disturbed' by the news of the impending royal visit and that he expected 'a storm of criticism'. MacBride considered the reference to United States troops as particularly 'provocative'.

Laithwaite's account of his talk with MacBride evoked a corresponding response in London. A telegram, whose text was shown in advance to Attlee, was sent by the Commonwealth Relations Office to Laithwaite stating:

> This is a piece of impertinence which is deeply resented here and will not be tolerated. You are therefore instructed to see Mr MacBride forthwith and to speak to him in the following terms.
> *Begins*: His Majesty's Government in the United Kingdom of Great Britain and Northern Ireland are not (repeat not) prepared to discuss with the Government of the Irish Republic a visit by His Majesty the King to a part of his dominions. *Ends*.
> When you have done so, beyond listening to anything he may have to say, you should leave.

Lascelles wrote to Sir Percivale Liesching at the Commonwealth Relations Office to inform him that he had put the relevant papers before the King, 'who,' he added, 'I am sure will approve the tenor of the telegram sent to Laithwaite.'

Laithwaite carried out his instructions and reported that MacBride had 'muttered something about the talk having been informal'. He also dined with De Valera, who was then the Toiseach, and had friendly talks with a number of other ministers. From these he concluded that 'everything goes to suggest that Mr MacBride's intervention was not only improper and very ill-advised, but entirely personal.'[6]

In Northern Ireland Alderman H. Diamond of the Irish Labour party was ordered by the Speaker to leave Stormont for referring to the forthcoming visit by 'foreign royalty'. An unsuccessful attempt was made to blow up Belfast police station, where thirteen men were held following a round-up of IRA suspects. The IRA then issued a warning that the King and Queen would come to Belfast 'at the peril of their lives'.

None of this served as a deterrent, and on 4 May details of the royal itinerary were made public. Then on 30 May it was announced that the King had 'not shaken off' the effects of his influenza and that his temperature remained 'unsettled'. He would not therefore be coming to Northern Ireland, but the Queen and Princess Margaret would carry out the programme which had been arranged. This they did without interruptions or violence.

Through the rest of the summer the King continued in a semi-invalid state. He spent some time in Royal Lodge, Windsor, and some at Sandringham. Early in August he moved to Balmoral. He was still able to do much public business and to concern himself with the welfare of his family.

Prince Philip, faced with the formidable task of addressing the British Association for the Advancement of Science, showed the draft of his speech to the King and asked his advice. Passages in the draft were clearly controversial, and in advising him to omit some of them, the King gave his son-in-law the useful advice: 'Stick your neck out, but don't actually pass the axe.'

Basil Boothroyd, who wrote a short biography of the Duke of Edinburgh, learnt from Michael Parker, who served first as Equerry and then as Private Secretary, that the Duke had to learn his duties largely by experience and that in practice it was the King who was his principal adviser.[7]

On 1 September the King, after a consultation with his doctors, agreed to go to London for a series of tests. The chief of these was to be a bronchoscopy, for cancer of the lung was suspected. The tests showed that the diagnosis was correct. There was a malignant growth, and an operation for the removal of the whole of the left lung was recommended. The King accepted the verdict, although, in accordance with the practice of the time, the dread word 'cancer' does not seem to have been mentioned in his presence. On 21 September he wrote to Mountbatten: 'The doctors want me to have an operation to clear up the lung trouble.'[8]

The operation was performed by the eminent surgeon Clement Price Thomas on 23 September and was wholly successful though there were fears that coronary thrombosis might occur either while the operation was taking place or shortly afterwards.[9]

Among the messages of good wishes which flooded into Buckingham Palace was one from the President of the United States, which read: 'I am watching eagerly for advices from your bedside and want you to know that I am hoping for the best and share with your beloved subjects everywhere their anxiety for your welfare. May I in extending heartfelt wishes for your speedy restoration to health assure you also of my prayers that the God of Our Fathers, under whose ruling hand all creatures live, may bless and sustain you in this hour of trial.'[10]

Only three days before undergoing his operation the King had written to President Truman to inform him that he was presenting two eighteenth-century British candelabra and a looking-glass of the same period to the White House, which was then undergoing restoration, and that the gifts would be brought to him by Princess Elizabeth.

Another message came in the form of a letter to Lascelles written by General Eisenhower from the Supreme Headquarters of the Allied Powers in Europe. This read: 'When opportunity presents itself, Mrs Eisenhower and I would appreciate it if you would tell Her Majesty The Queen that we are just two of the millions whose daily prayers include our earnest supplication for the early return to health of His Majesty The King. Both of them are important to the free world and, on the more personal side, they occupy a very abiding place in our affections.'[11]

At the height of the King's illness his ministers were discussing whether it would be prudent for Princess Elizabeth to cross the Atlantic and carry out her planned engagements in Canada and the United States. Attlee felt it right to consult Churchill as Leader of the Opposition, and on 23 September Churchill wrote to him:

'It would be, in my opinion, wrong for the Princess Elizabeth to fly the Atlantic. This seems to me more important than any of the inconveniences which may be caused by changing plans and programmes in Canada.' He added: 'Thank God the operation this morning has so far been successful, but a period of grave anxiety evidently lies before us.'

Attlee then telephoned St Laurent, the Canadian Prime Minister, and shortly afterwards a message was sent stating that 'the people of Canada would not wish the Princess to leave the King's side in present circumstances.'

Once it was known that the operation on the King had been successful the planning of the visit by the Princess and the Duke of Edinburgh continued. Attlee took the advice of the Chairman of the British Overseas Airways Corporation and was told that a Boeing Stratocruiser was probably the safest aircraft. After a Cabinet meeting on 27 September a minute written in Attlee's hand stated: 'Tell Lascelles I agree to Princess Elizabeth flying, if the King's condition allows of her going to Canada.'[12]

The Princess and her husband left Britain on 7 October. They visited every province in Canada and then went on to the United States, where they met President Truman in the White House. The President later described their visit in a letter to the King. In contrast with the form of address used by the patrician Roosevelt, 'My dear King George', Truman used the conventional 'Your Majesty'. But the warmth of his letter was evident. He wrote:

> We've just had a visit from a lovely young lady and her personable husband – their Royal Highnesses, Princess Elizabeth and the Duke of Edinburgh.
>
> They went to the hearts of all the citizens of the United States. We tried to make their visit a happy one.
>
> As one father to another, we can be very proud of our daughters. You have the better of me – because you have two!
>
> I hope you have an early and complete recovery. Please express my appreciation to Her Majesty the Queen for her kindness to my Margaret.
>
> Sincerely,
>
> Harry S. Truman.[13]

In the course of the year Princess Elizabeth and Prince Philip were both formally introduced into the Privy Council. The file recording the details of this, which is held in the Public Record Office in Chancery Lane, was thereupon marked 'Closed for 75 years'. Its contents will not therefore be revealed until the year 2026 – an exercise of discretion which must arouse speculation about what the file may contain.[14]

Attlee's health gave some cause for concern also in 1951. Three years earlier he had been treated for a duodenal ulcer, and on 16 March he was admitted to St Mary's Hospital in Paddington. The official announcement stated that 'because of the strain of a heavy parliamentary session the Prime Minister's doctor thinks it wise that he should now have a further examination.'

While Attlee was in hospital a crisis occurred within the Labour party. On 20 March he was sent a letter by Hugh Gaitskell, who was now Chancellor of the Exchequer, on the subject of the health service. There was a belief among ministers, Gaitskell reported, that a limit must be placed on the cost of the health service, and that this could be done only by imposing certain charges. Attlee wrote back that he was 'in general agreement', but added: 'I would stress the point of presentation.'

Aneurin Bevan, the Minister of Health, considered the issue to be not one of presentation but one of fundamental principle, and he therefore tendered his resignation. On this the King wrote to Attlee by hand from Sandringham:

'I have received your submission about Mr Bevan's resignation from the Government. I fear Mr Bevan's attitude towards the imposition of charges in the National Health Service has left you no other course of action.

'I do hope this added worry will not affect your health in any way, and that you are feeling better for your treatment in hospital.'[15]

The Government survived the internal conflict, but the Conservative party's tactic of Parliamentary harassment became increasingly effective. Divisions were continually called for: ministers and the sick had to be rushed to the House of Commons to vote; the business of government was impeded; and strain grew steadily greater. By the late summer Attlee had concluded that a new General Election must be held soon. A major consideration in his choice of polling day was the programme of the King's engagements.

In August both the King and Attlee still assumed that the King would be making a six-month tour of Australia and New Zealand in 1952. For this reason Attlee felt it would be desirable to hold the election months before the King's departure. The King took a similar view.

'It would be very difficult indeed for me,' he wrote to Attlee on 3 September, 'to go away for five or six months unless it was reasonably certain that political stability would prevail during my absence.' On the other hand, he added, it would be 'disastrous' if visits to self-governing

Dominions had to be 'postponed, or even interrupted, on account of political difficulties at home.'

'It would be a great relief to me,' the King added, 'if you could now – or even in the next few weeks – give me some assurance that would set my mind at rest on this score.'

Attlee gave the King the assurance he asked for. He would, he wrote on 5 September, ask for Parliament to be dissolved in the first week in October. 'Among the factors to which I have given particular attention,' he wrote, 'was the need for avoiding any political crisis while Your Majesty was out of the country.'[16]

The House of Commons met after the summer recess on 4 October. Attlee began the proceedings with a statement about the King's illness. He was joined by Churchill and Clement Davies, the Liberal leader, in paying tribute and expressing sympathy. The next day the King signed a proclamation dissolving Parliament, and the business of electioneering began.

The outcome of the election was a victory for the Conservative party, which, with its allies in Northern Ireland, gained an overall majority of seventeen seats. The Labour party received more votes than did the Conservative party, but the result, in terms of seats, was not quite as anomalous as this might suggest, for four Ulster Unionists, who were at that time whole-hearted supporters of the Conservatives, were returned unopposed and no votes were therefore cast for them. The Liberal party reached its lowest point in Parliamentary history by winning only six seats.

For the King the immediate consequence was a renewal of his association with Winston Churchill, and on 26 October he formally invited him to form a new government. But the partnership was now very different from that which they had formed more than eleven years earlier. The King was a dying man, and he did not even discuss Churchill's new appointments in any detail. Nor did he receive the outgoing members of Attlee's Cabinet, as would have been customary.[17] Churchill, for his part, was no longer the incomparable war leader, but a man of seventy-six, who, sadly, was unable or unwilling to accept that he was too old for the task which he was now assuming.

The King's projected tour of Australia and New Zealand, which had been such a major factor in precipitating the holding of the General Election, did not take place. On 18 November a bulletin was signed by five doctors which stated:

The King is suffering from an obstruction to the circulation through the arteries of the legs, which has only recently become acute; the defective blood supply to the right foot causes anxiety. Complete rest has been advised, and treatment to improve the circulation in the legs has been initiated, and must be maintained for an immediate and prolonged period.

Though His Majesty's general health, including the condition of his heart, gives no reason for concern, there is no doubt that the strain of the last twelve years has appreciably affected his resistance to physical fatigue.

We have come to the conclusion that it would be hazardous for His Majesty to embark upon a long journey, which might delay his recovery and which might well involve serious risk to a limb.

With deep regret, therefore, we have advised that The King's visit to Australia and New Zealand should not be undertaken next year.[18]

The recommendation not to undertake the tour was accepted, and all the King's public engagements for some months ahead were cancelled. He did however insist on making his usual Christmas broadcast, although he was so weak that it had to be recorded a sentence or two at a time.[19]

CHAPTER TWENTY-SEVEN

Retrospect

The King expected to convalesce in the early spring of 1952 in South Africa, where Dr Malan, the Prime Minister and Nationalist leader, whom he had come to know during his South African tour in 1947, had put a house at his disposal. On 27 January Lascelles wrote to Eisenhower: 'His Majesty seems to be going on very well and we all hope that his cruise will set him up again completely.'[1]

By then the King had returned from Sandringham to London, where he concerned himself with the final preparations for a Commonwealth tour which Princess Elizabeth and the Duke of Edinburgh were about to make. On 31 January he saw them off as they left Heathrow Airport for East Africa. There was a bitterly cold wind, but the King stood watching their departure bareheaded.

On 4 February the King wrote a letter in his own hand to Lord Halifax, whom he had made Chancellor of the Order of the Garter. 'Many of the Knights of the Garter,' he wrote, 'have often asked me whether it would be possible for us and them to wear the Garter on trousers in evening clothes. After much careful thought and trying out various ideas, I have devised a pair of overalls strapped at the bottom as is usual, but fuller around the seat and the front, and they are quite comfortable to sit down in.'

The King enclosed three photographs showing himself wearing the Garter with evening trousers. These, he explained, were taken by the Duke of Edinburgh. He went on: 'I want you to see the idea first as Chancellor before I send out a formal statement telling them where they can get this garment made. I feel it will look very chic.'

This may have been the last letter the King ever wrote. Halifax replied the next day, describing the King's idea as 'very ingenious', but his letter was never sent. Before it could be posted Halifax had learnt of the King's death.[2]

On that day, 5 February, the King went out shooting at Sandringham.

In the evening he seemed relaxed, and he retired to bed about 10.30. He died during the night, possibly in his sleep.

Princess Elizabeth, who was not in immediate telephone contact and to whom the news of her father's death came through a report in the *East African Standard*, and the Duke of Edinburgh immediately flew back to England.

The King's body was moved to Sandringham Church, where workers on the estate mounted guard over it. The lying-in-state in Westminster Hall followed, lasting for three days, and although for much of the time there was rain, sleet or snow outside, the queues extended up to four miles. The number who passed through Westminster Hall exceeded 300,000.

Four royal dukes followed the gun-carriage drawn by naval ratings, which bore the King's body to Paddington Station towards its final resting place in St George's Chapel, Windsor. They were the Duke of Windsor, who had returned from the United States for the funeral, the Duke of Gloucester, the Duke of Edinburgh and the young Duke of Kent.

For ten days the BBC broadcast only on a single radio channel, from which all frivolous matters were excluded, receiving towards the end of this period a rebuke from the Roman Catholic Church for treating the subject of death with excessive gloom.

On 7 February Winston Churchill broadcast a talk to the nation on the life and character of the late King. He spoke of the King's 'simple dignity', his 'sense of duty alike as a ruler and a servant', and his 'gay charm and happy smile'. He also described him as 'so self-restrained in his judgment of men and affairs, so uplifted above the clash of party politics, yet so attentive to them, so wise and shrewd in judging between what matters and what does not.'

He recalled how 'calmly, without ambition, or want of self-confidence, he assumed the heavy burden of the Crown and succeeded his brother, whom he loved and to whom he had rendered perfect loyalty.' The King's 'conduct on the throne', Churchill went on, 'may well be a model and a guide to constitutional sovereigns throughout the world today, and also in future generations.'

These were measured words, not an exercise in oratory, and they told the truth without exaggeration.

Another Commonwealth Prime Minister, Robert Menzies, paid his tribute in the Australian House of Representatives. He described the late King as 'possessed of great force of character, a most royal sense of duty, a keen perception of the movements and issues of the day.' He went on to describe how 'all those who saw England under daily and nightly attack in the great battle of 1940 and 1941 were stirred by the spectacle of an embattled nation, normally not unacquainted with internal divisions and hostilities, in which there was unity, cheerfulness, courage, a common resolution.'

Menzies concluded: 'It was that superb fusing of the common will which defeated the enemy, and did so much to save the world. King George and his Queen Elizabeth were among the great architects of that brotherhood.'

Supporting a motion in the House of Commons on 11 February, Attlee, now Leader of the Opposition, spoke of his own association with the late King. 'I feel,' he said, 'a deep sense of personal loss in the death of one to whom I was bound not only by loyalty and respect, but by affection. I received from him at all times the greatest kindness and consideration. The longer I served him, the greater was my respect and admiration.'

Michael Foot was later to write: 'Only once did I ever see Attlee emotionally affected in public. . . He was cool even when he spoke of Ernest Bevin whom he clearly loved. But when he spoke of George VI's death, tears were in his eyes and voice.'[3]

Among the letters of condolence which the new Queen received was one from General Eisenhower, who wrote on 7 February: 'He represented, for us, a model of character and deportment for those in high places. Our respect for him as an inspirational force was equalled by our affection for him as a gentle human being.'

Replying by hand, the new Queen wrote: 'Your beautiful words were a great comfort to me, and I am so happy to know that you appreciated and realized the King's fine and gentle and courageous character. It is difficult to grasp the fact that he has left us; he was so much better, and so full of ideas and plans for the future. One cannot imagine life without him, but I suppose one must carry on as he would wish.'[4]

On 29 April 1952 a meeting was held which Churchill had called with the approval of the Queen. Its purpose was 'to consider the best procedure for the initiation of a memorial to commemorate the life and reign of the late King.' Those present were the Dukes of Gloucester and Edinburgh, leading members of the Government, Attlee, Clement Davies and the Lord Mayor of London. The Duke of Edinburgh reported that it was the Queen's wish that there should be a statue in London and a philanthropic scheme covering the country generally. The philanthropic scheme, he said, 'might well bear some relationship to the work of industrial welfare, boys' camps etc., in which the late King George was especially interested.'[5]

After further deliberations it was announced on 20 September that the Lord Mayor of London, Sir Leslie Boyce, had set up the King George VI Memorial Fund, and appeals were made for contributions. The purpose of the philanthropic scheme was described as being to promote 'the physical, mental and spiritual needs of young and old people'. In spite of this somewhat uninspiring definition £1,665,000 was contributed to the fund within eighteen months of the launching of the appeal.

Among the sensible benefits provided was the creation of clubs, with recreational facilities, for old people in towns where such amenities were badly needed. The places selected for this purpose were Bootle, Dundee, Port Talbot, Stoke-on-Trent and south-east London. The Women's Voluntary Services, a body created in 1938 as a branch of the Civil Defence organization, were made trustees for the implementation of this project.

The statue provided through the fund is in Carlton Gardens and shows the King in the dress uniform of an Admiral of the Fleet, wearing the Garter mantle and Garter star and looking over the Mall towards Buckingham Palace. The sculptor was William McMillan.

The Queen unveiled the statue on Trafalgar Day (21 October) 1955. Before doing so she said of her father: 'The friendliness and simplicity which so endeared him to his people during the trials of war were the fruit of a lifelong interest in his fellow men and of a human sympathy which was one of my father's most lovable qualities... Throughout all the strains of his public life he remained a man of warm and friendly sympathies – a man who by the simple qualities of loyalty, resolution and service won for himself such a place in the affection of us all that when he died millions mourned for him as for a true and trusted friend.'

The words in *Twelfth Night*, 'some men are born great, some achieve greatness, and some have greatness thrust upon them', are all peculiarly applicable to the life of George VI.

He was born a member of the ruling house of the greatest empire in the world, and, although personally modest and indeed humble, he never lost a sense of the dignity and splendour of his inheritance. The crown was thrust upon him without his choosing, as it had been on the Emperor Claudius. The story of his reign is a record of how he achieved greatness as a constitutional monarch, of how, in Churchill's words, he became 'a model and a guide to constitutional sovereigns throughout the world'.

To have raised the status of the monarchy, and the popular esteem felt for it, from the trough which followed the abdication of Edward VIII to the height reached in 1952 was an achievement which is beyond dispute.

In time of war, when waves of popular feeling tend to be stronger and more widely shared than they are in peace, George VI showed a perfect understanding of how to blend the mystique of royalty with common humanity. The results were not easily measurable, but to their reality there is abundant witness.

The manner of transformation from Empire to Commonwealth owed more than has yet been generally acknowledged to his flexibility, understanding, and his talent for winning the liking and respect of political leaders from different continents.

It has sometimes been suggested that the King presided over a social revolution at the end of World War II. This is an over-statement, but he did play a significant part in maintaining continuity, and thus assuring general assent, while major changes in the social structure were effected between 1940 and 1950.

By other crowned heads, not only in Europe, he was accepted as a leader. This was partly because of the peculiar standing of the British monarchy, but even more because of his personal qualities which, through proximity, these monarchs had better opportunities than most of discovering and appreciating.

The King did not have a profound intellect. His opinions tended to be conventional and were rarely original. His attitude to the arts was mildly philistine, although in this field too his conscientiousness asserted itself in the care he showed for the royal picture collections in Windsor and elsewhere.

Against these relative weaknesses must be set a quality which is not easily taught, but which the King, in the opinion of many who knew him well, possessed in unusually full measure. This was the quality of judgment, the capacity, in Churchill's words, to distinguish between 'what matters and what does not'. Sir Edward Ford, who for a number of years was the King's Assistant Private Secretary, said of him: 'He had a very good instinct for what was the right thing to do in any circumstances.'

His religious faith was deep, unquestioning and uncomplicated. He was an exemplary husband and father. He was also an admirable employer, showing a consideration for the comfort and welfare of those who worked directly for him far exceeding what had been instilled into him as a duty by the rigours of his upbringing.

No less important than these qualities in the performance of his task was his understanding of the peculiar nature of kingship. This was revealed in relative trivia as well as in the conduct of great affairs of state.

Numerous incidents have been recalled illustrating his concern with details of dress, decorations and ceremony. In many another man these might have indicated nothing more than excessive fussiness. The King understood instinctively the position which ceremonial and pageantry occupy in the exercise of monarchy, and therefore to him correctness of dress was, very properly, as important as it is to a regimental sergeant-major or to a stage director.

After describing the qualifications needed to make a human being 'fit material for a constitutional king' Bagehot wrote: 'Such kings are among God's greatest gifts, but they are also among His rarest.'

George VI proved by his life's work that he was fit material for a constitutional king. That he did so was a moral triumph, attributable predominantly to innate decency, loyalty, and an awareness of his obligations to others.

The nations over which George VI ruled may be thought to owe him a debt for the success, not only of his own reign, but also for that of the reign which followed. The way of life, the standards, and the beliefs which shaped his own conduct were accepted and have been adopted, to a remarkable degree, by the Queen who followed him. In consequence there has perhaps been no century in which the people of England and of Scotland were, on the whole, more fortunate in their monarchs than they have been in the twentieth century.

NOTES

(PRO = Public Record Office, Kew. PRO CL = Public Record Office, Chancery Lane.)

CHAPTER ONE

1. James Hinton, *Labour and Socialism*
2. Elizabeth Longford, *Queen Victoria*
3. Kenneth Rose, *King George V*
4. John W. Wheeler-Bennett, *King George VI*
5. Harold Nicolson, *King George V*
6. James Pope-Hennessy, *Queen Mary*
7. Rose, *King George V*
8. Pope-Hennessy, *Queen Mary*
9. Wheeler-Bennett, *King George VI*
10. Duke of Windsor, *A King's Story*
11. Denis Judd, *King George VI*
12. Rose, *King George V*
13. Windsor, *A King's Story*
14. Rose, *King George V*
15. Lord Birkenhead, *Walter Monckton*
16. Pope-Hennessy, *Queen Mary*
17. Lady Helen Hardinge, *Loyal to Three Kings*
18. Rose, *George V*
19. Windsor, *A King's Story*
20. Wheeler-Bennett, *King George VI*
21. Countess of Airlie, *Thatched with Gold*

CHAPTER TWO

1. Talk with the late Peter Hansell
2. Taylor Darbyshire, *The Duke of York*
3. Windsor, *A King's Story*
4. Darbyshire, *The Duke of York*
5. Windsor, *A King's Story*
6. Rose, *King George V*
7. Ibid.
8. Wheeler-Bennett, *King George VI*

9. Nicolson, *King George V*
10. Rose, *King George V*
11. Wheeler-Bennett, *King George VI*
12. Ibid.
13. Windsor, *A King's Story*
14. Ibid.
15. Wheeler-Bennett, *King George VI*
16. Judd, *King George VI*
17. Windsor, *A King's Story*
18. Wheeler-Bennett, *King George VI*
19. Navy List
20. Keith Middlemas, *The Life and Times of King George VI*
21. Wheeler-Bennett, *King George VI*
22. Ibid.
23. E. B. Haslam, *The History of RAF Cranwell*

CHAPTER THREE

1. Wheeler-Bennett, *King George VI*
2. PRO FO 371/3165
3. Ibid.
4. Ibid.
5. Ibid.
6. Wheeler-Bennett, *King George VI*
7. Judd, *King George VI*
8. Ministry of Defence, Air Historical Branch
9. Private information
10. Walter Bagehot, *The English Constitution*
11. Wheeler-Bennett, *King George VI*
12. Robert Hyde, *Industry was My Parish*
13. Introduction to Hyde's *Industry was My Parish*
14. Pope-Hennessy, *Queen Mary*
15. Rose, *King George V*
16. Elizabeth McLeod, *Sixty Years of Achievement*
17. Hyde, *Industry was My Parish*
18. Ibid.
19. Minutes of Council Meetings of Industrial Welfare Society
20. Ibid.
21. Wheeler-Bennett, *King George VI*

CHAPTER FOUR

1. Mountbatten papers
2. IWS minutes
3. Wheeler-Bennett, *King George VI*
4. IWS minutes
5. Hardinge, *Loyal to Three Kings*
6. Pope-Hennessy, *Queen Mary*
7. Hardinge, *Loyal to Three Kings*
8. Talk with Dan Maskell

9. Windsor, *A King's Story*
10. Aubrey Buxton, *The King in His Country*
11. Private information
12. Hannah Pakula, *The Last Romantic*
13. PRO FO 371/7679
14. Ibid.
15. Ibid.
16. Ibid.
17. PRO FO 372/1926
18. Ibid.
19. Mountbatten papers
20. Ibid.
21. Philip Ziegler, *Mountbatten*
22. Mountbatten papers

CHAPTER FIVE

1. Airlie, *Thatched with Gold*
2. Mountbatten papers
3. Private information
4. PRO CL PC 8972
5. Wheeler-Bennett, *King George VI*
6. Andrew Barrow, *Gossip. Fifty Years of High Society*
7. Wheeler-Bennett, *King George VI*
8. IWS minutes
9. Harold Macmillan, *The Past Masters*
10. Brian Masters, *Great Hostesses*
11. Elizabeth Longford, *The Queen Mother*
12. Rose, *King George V*
13. Wheeler-Bennett, *King George VI*
14. Ibid.
15. Mountbatten papers
16. PRO CO 533/292
17. Macmillan, *The Past Masters*
18. PRO CO 533/293
19. PRO CO 533/314
20. Ibid.
21. Wheeler-Bennett, *King George VI*
22. PRO CO 533/328
23. Wheeler-Bennett, *King George VI*

CHAPTER SIX

1. Nicolson, *King George V*
2. PRO CL PC 8 1070
3. Rev. W. H. M. Aitken and Lord Cholmondeley
4. Peter Lane, *The Queen Mother*
5. Wheeler-Bennett, *King George VI*
6. Nicolson, *King George V*

7.   *Royalty in New Zealand*
8.   PRO DO 35/24
9.   *Royalty in New Zealand*
10. Wheeler-Bennett, *King George VI*
11. PRO FO 372/2597
12. David Duff, *George and Elizabeth*
13. Darbyshire, *The Duke of York*
14. Duff, *George and Elizabeth*
15. Mountbatten papers

CHAPTER SEVEN

1.   Darbyshire, *The Duke of York*
2.   Diana Cooper, *Autobiography*
3.   Pakula, *The Last Romantic*
4.   Princess Bibesco, *Feuilles de Calendrier*
5.   Talk with Sir Edward Ford
6.   Private information
7.   Duff, *George and Elizabeth*
8.   Nicolson, *King George V*
9.   PRO FO 371/13460
10. Talk with the Duke of Portland
11. Bibesco, *Feuilles de Calendrier*
12. Wheeler-Bennett, *King George VI*
13. IWS minutes
14. Nicolson, *King George V*
15. Rose, *King George V*
16. PRO FO 371/18791
17. Michael Bloch (ed.), *Wallis & Edward Letters*

CHAPTER EIGHT

1.   Francis Watson, The Death of George V, *History Today*, December 1986
2.   Hardinge, *Loyal to Three Kings*
3.   Wheeler-Bennett, *King George VI*
4.   Frances Donaldson, *Edward VIII*
5.   Hardinge, *Loyal to Three Kings*
6.   Windsor, *A King's Story*
7.   India Office Library, EUR F 125/139
8.   PRO CL Coronation File
9.   Birkenhead, *Walter Monckton*
10. J. Bryan III and Charles J. V. Murphy, *The Windsor Story*
11. Duchess of Windsor, *The Heart has its Reasons*
12. Birkenhead, *Walter Monckton*
13. Bryan and Murphy, *The Windsor Story*
14. Dr Alan C. Don, *Diaries*
15. Ibid.
16. Windsor, *The Heart has its Reasons*
17. H. Montgomery Hyde, *Baldwin*

18. PRO FO 371/20734
19. Sir Robert Menzies, *Afternoon Light*
20. Hardinge, *Loyal to Three Kings*
21. Wheeler-Bennett, *King George VI*
22. Ziegler, *Mountbatten*
23. Don, *Diaries*
24. Bloch, *Wallis & Edward Letters*
25. Hyde, *Baldwin*

CHAPTER NINE

1. Chamberlain papers, NS7/5/31
2. Lord Reith, *Diaries*
3. Don, *Diaries*
4. Ibid.
5. Hyde, *Baldwin*
6. PRO FO 372/3234
7. PRO FO 371/3283
8. PRO FO 372/3234
9. PRO FO 372/3233
10. Ibid.
11. PRO CL PC8/1338
12. PRO FO 372/3233
13. PRO FO 371/20882
14. PRO FO 371/20884
15. Hyde, *Baldwin*
16. Winston S. Churchill, *The Gathering Storm*

CHAPTER TEN

1. Ziegler, *Mountbatten*
2. Bryan and Murphy, *The Windsor Story*
3. PRO FO 954/33
4. Ibid.
5. Ibid.
6. Ibid.
7. Ibid.
8. Ibid.
9. Ibid.
10. Ibid.
11. PRO FO 371/20681
12. Ibid.
13. PRO FO 954/29
14. India Office Library. MSS EUR F 125/139
15. Ibid.
16. Chamberlain papers
17. Pashanko Dimitroff, *Boris III of Bulgaria*

CHAPTER ELEVEN

1. PRO PREM 4
2. Sir Anthony Eden, *Full Circle*
3. Stephen Roskill, *Hankey Man of Secrets*
4. Chamberlain papers, NC 7/3/23
5. Ibid.
6. J. A. Cross, *Lord Swinton*
7. PRO FO 371/21606
8. Ibid.
9. Chamberlain papers
10. PRO FO 371/21607
11. PRO FO 371/21606
12. Ibid.
13. PRO FO 800/311
14. Chamberlain papers
15. Ibid., NC 7/3/270
16. Ibid., Dep 57 F 157
17. Pope-Hennessy, *Queen Mary*
18. Duff Cooper, *Old Men Forget*
19. Diana Cooper, *Autobiography*
20. PRO FO 800/322
21. PRO FO 371/22445
22. Ibid.
23. Ibid.
24. PRO FO 371/22334
25. Dimitroff, *King Boris III of Bulgaria*
26. PRO DO 121/45
27. Ibid.

CHAPTER TWELVE

1. Don, *Diaries*
2. Chamberlain papers, NC 7/3/31
3. Ibid., NC 7/3/35
4. Archives Nationales, Paris
5. PRO FO 800/318
6. PRO FO 800/321
7. Ibid.
8. PRO FO 371/22304
9. PRO FO 371/21548
10. Ibid.
11. W. L. Mackenzie King papers, C 3748
12. PRO DO 121/65
13. Ibid.
14. Ibid.
15. Mackenzie King papers, C 3743
16. PRO FO 371/21548
17. PRO FO 371/22799
18. Wheeler-Bennett, *King George VI*
19. William Buchan, *John Buchan*

20. PRO DO 121/65
21. Mackenzie King papers, C 3743
22. Ibid.
23. Rose, *King George V*
24. Mackenzie King papers, 234466
25. Wheeler-Bennett, *King George VI*
26. Ibid.
27. PRO FO 371/22801
28. John Colville, *Footprints in Time*
29. Mackenzie King papers, 227335

CHAPTER THIRTEEN

1. Chamberlain papers, NC 7/3/36
2. PRO FO 371/23626
3. PRO FO 800/321
4. Chamberlain papers
5. PRO FO 371/21607
6. Chamberlain papers, NC 7/3/37
7. Ronald W. Clark, *Tizard*
8. Churchill papers, CP 19/2
9. Ibid.
10. Dimitroff, *King Boris III of Bulgaria*
11. PRO FO 371/23783
12. Wheeler-Bennett, *King George VI*
13. PRO FO 800/309
14. Roskill, *Hankey Man of Secrets*
15. Mountbatten papers
16. Nigel Nicolson, *Alex*
17. Chamberlain papers
18. Martin Gilbert, *Finest Hour*
19. Halifax papers, A2 278 26A 1–6

CHAPTER FOURTEEN

1. Wheeler-Bennett, *King George VI*
2. R. J. Minney (ed.), *The Private Papers of Hore-Belisha*
3. Gilbert, *Finest Hour*
4. PRO FO 800/326
5. PRO FO 800/324
6. Dermot Morrah, *The Work of the Queen*
7. Wheeler-Bennett, *King George VI*
8. Gilbert, *Finest Hour*
9. Macmillan, *The Past Masters*
10. Hyde, *Baldwin*
11. Churchill papers, CP 20/1
12. PRO PREM 4/24/2
13. Gilbert, *Finest Hour*
14. PRO FO 371/24407
15. Wheeler-Bennett, *King George VI*
16. Mackenzie King papers

17. PRO PREM 3/461
18. Churchill papers, CP 20/9B
19. Ibid., CP 20/9A

CHAPTER FIFTEEN

1. Hugh Dalton, *Diaries*
2. Chamberlain papers
3. David Wood and Derek Dempster, *The Narrow Margin*
4. Charles de Gaulle, *The Call to Honour*
5. Winston S. Churchill, *Their Finest Hour*
6. Harold Nicolson, *Diaries and Letters 1939–1945*
7. PRO PREM 4/100/3
8. Chamberlain papers
9. Wheeler-Bennett, *King George VI*
10. PRO FO 371/24348
11. PRO FO 371/24303
12. Ibid.
13. Churchill, *Their Finest Hour*
14. Gilbert, *Finest Hour*
15. PRO FO 800/321
16. Ziegler, *Mountbatten*
17. Wheeler-Bennett, *King George VI*
18. PRO FO 954/29
19. David and Sybil Eccles, *By Safe Hand*
20. Gilbert, *Finest Hour*

CHAPTER SIXTEEN

1. Halifax papers
2. Gilbert, *Finest Hour*
3. PRO PREM 4/10/4
4. Ibid.
5. Gilbert, *Finest Hour*
6. Dalton, *Diaries*
7. Halifax papers, A4 410 4 8
8. Wheeler-Bennett, *King George VI*
9. PRO PREM 3/461/3
10. Halifax papers, A2 278 26 1–7A
11. PRO PREM 4/17/2
12. Halifax papers, A4 410 4 8
13. PRO FO 954/6
14. PRO FO 371/30265
15. Ibid.
16. Gilbert, *Finest Hour*
17. Wheeler-Bennett, *King George VI*
18. Averell Harriman and Elis Abel, *Special Envoy to Churchill and Stalin*
19. Lord Butler, *The Art of the Possible*
20. Relations with France (Canada House Archives)
21. PRO PREM 4/84/2A

22.   Colville, *Footprints in Time*
23.   PRO FO 954/4
24.   PRO PREM 4/84/2A
25.   Talk with the Dowager Viscountess Hambleden
26.   PRO FO 954/29
27.   Ibid.
28.   PRO FO 954/33
29.   PRO FO 371/29696

CHAPTER SEVENTEEN

1.   Churchill papers, C20/59
2.   Martin Gilbert, *Road to Victory*
3.   Wheeler-Bennett, *King George VI*
4.   Halifax papers, A4 410 4–8
5.   Halifax papers, A2 278 06 1 74
6.   PRO DO 43A/14
7.   Ibid.
8.   Gilbert, *Road to Victory*
9.   Gilbert, Ibid.
10.   Wheeler-Bennett, *King George VI*
11.   Halifax papers, A2 278 26 1–4
12.   Princess Alice, *Memoirs*
13.   Halifax papers, A2 278 26 1–4
14.   John Colville, *The Fringes of Power*
15.   PRO PREM 4/83/2
16.   Mountbatten papers
17.   Dalton, *Diaries*
18.   Churchill papers, CP 20/52
19.   Gilbert, *Road to Victory*
20.   Eisenhower papers
21.   PRO FO 954/29
22.   Ibid.
23.   Joseph P. Lash, *Eleanor and Franklin*
24.   Halifax papers
25.   PRO FO 954/29
26.   Noël Coward, *Diaries*
27.   Ziegler, *Mountbatten*
28.   Coward, *Diaries*
29.   Mountbatten papers
30.   PRO PREM 4/82A
31.   PRO FO 954/19
32.   Ibid.
33.   Halifax papers, A2 278 26 1–24
34.   Churchill papers, CP 20/52
35.   J. G. Lockhart, *Cosmo Gordon Lang*
36.   Halifax papers, A4 410 4–8
37.   Gilbert, *Road to Victory*
38.   Wheeler-Bennett, *King George VI*

39. Gilbert, *Road to Victory*
40. Winston S. Churchill, *The Hinge of Fate*
41. PRO FO 371/31695
42. Gilbert, *Road to Victory*
43. Churchill papers, CP 20/52
44. Gilbert, *Road to Victory*

CHAPTER EIGHTEEN

1. Dalton, *Diaries*
2. Churchill papers, CP 20/92
3. Gilbert, *Road to Victory*
4. Churchill papers, CP 20/92
5. Gilbert, *Road to Victory*
6. Churchill, *The Hinge of Fate*
7. Ibid.
8. PRO PREM 497/9
9. Harold Macmillan, *War Diaries. The Mediterranean 1943–1945*
10. Admiral of the Fleet Viscount Cunningham of Hyndhope, *A Sailor's Odyssey*
11. PRO PREM 497/9
12. Macmillan, *War Diaries*
13. Nigel Hamilton, *Monty, Master of the Battlefield*
14. PRO PREM 497/9
15. Gilbert, *Road to Victory*
16. E. C. W. Myers, *Greek Entanglement*
17. PRO PREM 3/346/1
18. PRO PREM 3/344/1
19. PRO PREM 4/50/11
20. PRO DO/121/52
21. Ibid.
22. Macmillan, *War Diaries*
23. Peter Townsend, *Time and Chance*
24. Talk with Sir Edward Ford
25. PRO FO 954/30
26. PRO PREM 4/58/1
27. Wheeler-Bennett, *King George VI*
28. Halifax papers, A4 410 4–8
29. Ibid.
30. Churchill papers, CP 20/129
31. Mountbatten papers
32. Churchill papers CP 20/120
33. Halifax papers, A4 410 4–8

CHAPTER NINETEEN

1. Mountbatten papers
2. Gilbert, *Road to Victory*
3. Ziegler, *Mountbatten*
4. Mountbatten papers

5. Ibid.
6. Ibid.
7. Ziegler, *Mountbatten*
8. Wheeler-Bennett, *King George VI*
9. Gilbert, *Road to victory*
10. PRO FO 371/42674
11. Mountbatten papers
12. Nigel Nicolson, *Monty. The Making of a General*
13. Gilbert, *Road to Victory*
14. Churchill, *The Hinge of Fate*
15. PRO PREM 4/10/4
16. De Gaulle, *The Call to Honour*
17. PRO PREM 4/10/4
18. Cunningham, *A Sailor's Odyssey*
19. PRO FO 954/14
20. Macmillan, *War Diaries*
21. Lord Egremont, *Wyndham and Children First*
22. PRO FO 954/34
23. PRO PREM 4/10/4
24. Eisenhower papers, 1777–1778
25. PRO PREM 4/10/4
26. Alun Chalfont, *Montgomery of Alamein*
27. Airlie, *Thatched with Gold*
28. T. E. B. Howarth (ed.) *Monty at Close Quarters*
29. Mountbatten papers
30. PRO PREM 4/10/4
31. Mountbatten papers
32. Talk with the Dowager Viscountess Hambleden
33. Mountbatten papers
34. Private information
35. Wheeler-Bennett, *King George V1*

CHAPTER TWENTY
1. PRO FO 371/47692
2. PRO FO 954/23
3. Sir John Wheeler-Bennett, *Friends, Enemies and Sovereigns*
4. Thomas Barman, *Diplomatic Correspondent*
5. Gilbert, *Road to Victory*
6. Halifax papers, A4 410 4 13
7. Churchill papers, CP 20/199
8. PRO PREM 4/41/2
9. PRO PREM 4/41/5
10. Wheeler-Bennett, *King George VI*
11. PRO PREM 4/41/5
12. Churchill papers, CP 20/193
13. PRO PREM 4/84/1
14. Wheeler-Bennett, *King George VI*

15. Attlee papers, Dep 18 Folio 50
16. Kenneth Harris, *Attlee*
17. Attlee papers, Dep 18 Folio 75
18. Wheeler-Bennett, *King George VI*
19. Douglas Jay, *Change and Freedom*
20. Wheeler-Bennett, *King George VI*
21. Townsend, *Time and Chance*
22. Alan Bullock, *Ernest Bevin*
23. PRO FO 954/2
24. Winston S. Churchill, *Closing the Ring*
25. PRO FO 954/30
26. Truman papers
27. PRO PREM 4/10/3
28. Roy Jenkins, *Truman*
29. Wheeler-Bennett, *King George VI*
30. Talk with Sir Edward Ford
31. Ziegler, *Mountbatten*
32. PRO PREM 8
33. Attlee papers

CHAPTER TWENTY-ONE

1. Halifax papers, A4 410 4–8
2. Bryan and Murphy, *The Windsor Story*
3. Halifax papers, A4 410 4 10
4. PRO PREM 8/711
5. Wheeler-Bennett, *King George VI*
6. Attlee papers, Dep 36 Folio 64–69
7. Wheeler-Bennett, *King George VI*
8. Trevor Burridge, *Clement Attlee*
9. Wheeler-Bennett, *King George VI*
10. Harris, *Attlee*
11. Burridge, *Clement Attlee*
12. PRO PREM 8/657
13. PRO PREM 8/248
14. Nicholas Mansergh and Penderell Moon (eds) *Transfer of Power* series, Vol 8
15. Wheeler-Bennett, *King George VI*
16. Burridge, *Clement Attlee*
17. Ziegler, *Mountbatten*
18. Philip Warner, *Mountbatten*
19. Wheeler-Bennett, *King George VI*
20. PRO FO 371/30265
21. PRO FO 371/59538
22. Conversation with Prince Tomislav
23. Eisenhower papers

CHAPTER TWENTY-TWO

1. PRO FO 900/443
2. PRO FO 371/4079
3. Talk with Vice-Admiral Sir Peter Ashmore
4. PRO FO 371/65575
5. Norman Hill, *The Royal Tour Trains*
6. PRO FO 371/65575
7. Dermot Morrah, *The Royal Family in Africa*
8. Brigadier Stanley Clark, *Palace Diary*
9. PRO DO 35/3143
10. PRO PREM 8/617
11. Ziegler, *Mountbatten*
12. PRO PREM 8/802
13. *Transfer of Power* series
14. Mountbatten papers
15. PRO PREM 8/575
16. PRO PRO FO 371/65588
17. PRO PREM 8/732
18. PRO PREM 8/598
19. Harris, *Attlee*
20. Attlee papers, Dep 61 Folios 27–29
21. Ibid., Folio 135
22. PRO PREM 8/407
23. Sir Henry Channon, *Diaries*
24. Information supplied by Dr Robert Robson
25. PRO CL PC8/1557
26. PRO PREM 8/652
27. PRO PREM 8/656
28. Attlee papers, Dep 51 Folio 221
29. Wheeler-Bennett, *King George VI*

CHAPTER TWENTY-THREE

1. PRO DO 35/2232
2. PRO PREM 8/820
3. PRO PREM 8/814
4. Colville, *The Fringes of Power*
5. Talks with Sir Edward Ford and the Dowager Viscountess Hambleden
6. Princess Marie-Louise, *My Memories of Six Reigns*
7. PRO FO 372/6683
8. Ibid.
9. Ziegler, *Mountbatten*
10. PRO FO 372/6684
11. Attlee papers, Dep 72 Folios 40, 63, 128
12. Ibid., Folio 23
13. PRO FO 371/6680
14. PRO FO 800/444
15. PRO PREM 8/829
16. PRO PREM 8/915
17. Attlee papers, Dep 69 Folio 170

18. PRO PREM 8/884
19. Attlee papers, Dep 18 Folio 318
20. PRO PREM 8/884
21. Wheeler-Bennett, *King George VI*
22. Talk with Sir Edward Ford
23. Private information
24. Mountbatten papers

CHAPTER TWENTY-FOUR

1. PRO PREM 8/1015
2. Attlee papers, Dep 75 Folios 261–263
3. PRO PREM 8/1015
4. PRO DO 35/2160
5. Ibid.
6. PRO PREM 8/1011
7. PRO PREM 8/1223
8. PRO DO 35/2160
9. PRO PREM 8/1015
10. Wheeler-Bennett, *King George VI*
11. Attlee papers
12. PRO DO 35/4221
13. PRO PREM 8/1223
14. PRO 800/465
15. Eisenhower papers
16. PRO DO 35/4111

CHAPTER TWENTY-FIVE

1. PRO FO 371/89192
2. PRO FO 371/89194
3. PRO FO 371/89192
4. PRO FO 371/89194
5. PRO FO 371/89191
6. PRO FO 371/89194
7. PRO PREM 8/1333
8. PRO PREM 8/1216
9. PRO DO 35/3870
10. Wheeler-Bennett, *King George VI*
11. PRO PREM 8/1243
12. Wheeler-Bennett, *King George VI*
13. PRO 371/88615
14. PRO PREM 8/1013
15. PRO PREM 8/1271
16. PRO FO 371/89410
17. Ibid.
18. PRO FO 371/89412
19. PRO FO 800/457
20. PRO PREM 8/1225

CHAPTER TWENTY-SIX

1. Mountbatten papers
2. Ziegler, *Mountbatten*
3. PRO PREM 8/1350
4. Herbert Morrison, *An Autobiography*
5. Charles Reid, *Malcolm Sargent*
6. PRO DO 35/3945
7. Basil Boothroyd, *Philip*
8. Mountbatten papers
9. Wheeler-Bennett, *King George VI*
10. Truman papers
11. Eisenhower papers
12. PRO PREM 8/1513
13. Truman papers
14. PRO CL PC8/1673
15. Attlee papers, Dep 119
16. Harris, *Attlee*
17. Wheeler-Bennett, *King George VI*
18. PRO PREM 8/828
19. Wheeler-Bennett, *King George VI*

CHAPTER TWENTY-SEVEN

1. Eisenhower papers
2. Halifax papers
3. Michael Foot, *Aneurin Bevan*
4. Eisenhower papers
5. PRO DO 35/3331

BIBLIOGRAPHY

I have not attempted to give a list of books which provide the general background needed for any deep understanding of the period covered by this book. The bibliography which follows is limited to works by responsible writers which throw light on King George VI himself and his life's work.

Addison, Paul: *The Road to 1945* (Cape 1975)
Airlie, Countess of: *Thatched with Gold* (Hutchinson 1962)
Alice, Princess, Duchess of Gloucester: *Memoirs* (Collins 1983)
Bagehot, Walter: *The English Constitution* (1867)
Barman, Thomas: *Diplomatic Correspondent* (Hamilton 1968)
Barrow, Andrew: *Gossip. Fifty Years of High Society* (Pan 1978)
Bibesco, Princess: *Feuilles de Calendrier* (Plon 1939)
Birkenhead, Lord: *Walter Monckton* (Weidenfeld & Nicolson 1969)
Bloch, Lionel (ed.): *Wallis & Edward Letters* (Weidenfeld & Nicolson 1986)
Boothroyd, Basil: *Philip. An Informal Biography* (Longman 1971)
Boyd Carpenter, John: *Way of Life* (Sidgwick & Jackson 1980)
Bradley, Omar N.: *A Soldier's Story* (Holt, New York, 1951)
Bryan III, J. and Murphy, Charles J. V.: *The Windsor Story* (Granada 1979)
Buchan, Walter: *John Buchan. A Memoir* (Buchan & Enright 1982)
Bullock, Alan: *Ernest Bevin. Foreign Secretary 1945–1951* (Heinemann 1983)
Burridge, Trevor: *Clement Attlee* (Cape 1985)
Butler, Lord: *The Art of the Possible* (Hodder & Stoughton 1982)
Carlton, David: *Anthony Eden* (Allen Lane 1981)
Cave Brown, Anthony: *Wild Bill Donovan. The Last Hero* (Times Books, New York, 1982)
Chalfont, Alun: *Montgomery of Alamein* (Weidenfeld & Nicolson 1976)
Channon, Sir Henry: *Diaries* (ed. Robert Rhodes James) (Weidenfeld & Nicolson 1967)
Charmley, John: *Duff Cooper* (Weidenfeld & Nicolson 1986)
Churchill, Winston S.: *The Second World War* (Cassell). *The Gathering Storm* (1948). *Their Finest Hour* (1949). *The Hinge of Fate* (1951). *Closing the Ring* (1952). *Triumph and Tragedy* (1954)
Clark, Ronald W.: *Tizard* (Methuen 1965)
Clark, Brigadier Stanley: *Palace Diary* (Harrap 1958)

Colville, John: *Footprints in Time* (Collins 1976)

Colville, John: *The Fringes of Power* (Hodder & Stoughton 1985)

Cooper, Diana: *Autobiography* (Russell 1979)

Cooper, Duff: *Old Men Forget* (Hart-Davis 1954)

Coward, Noel: *Diaries* (eds Graham Payn and Sheridan Morley) (Weidenfeld & Nicolson 1982)

Cross, J. A.: *Lord Swinton* (Clarendon 1982)

Cunningham of Hyndhope, Admiral of the Fleet Viscount: *A Sailor's Odyssey* (Hutchinson 1951)

Dalton, Hugh: *Second World War Diary* (ed. Ben Pimlott) (Cape 1986)

Darbyshire, Taylor: *The Duke of York* (Hutchinson 1929)

De Gaulle, Charles: *War Memoirs. The Call to Honour* (Cape 1984)

Dimitroff, Pashanko: *Boris III of Bulgaria* (Book Guild 1986)

Don, Dr Alan C.: *Diaries* (Lambeth Palace Library)

Donaldson, Frances: *Edward VIII. The Road to Abdication* (Weidenfeld & Nicolson 1974)

Duff, David: *Elizabeth of Glamis* (Muller 1973)

Duff, David: *George and Elizabeth* (Collins 1983)

Eccles, David and Sybil: *By Safe Hand. The Wartime Letters of David and Sybil Eccles* (Bodley Head 1983)

Eden, Sir Anthony: *Full Circle* (Cassell 1960)

Egremont, Lord: *Wyndham and Children First* (Egremont & Hutchinson 1965)

Fisher, Nigel: *Harold Macmillan* (Weidenfeld & Nicolson 1982)

Foot, Michael: *Aneurin Bevan. A Biography* (Davis & Poynter 1973)

Frankland, Noble: *Prince Henry, Duke of Gloucester* (Weidenfeld & Nicolson 1982)

Garrett, Richard: *Mrs Simpson* (Barker 1979)

Gilbert, Martin: *Winston S. Churchill* (Heinemann). *Finest Hour* (1983). *Road to Victory* (1986)

Grigg, John: *Nancy Astor* (Sidgwick & Jackson 1980)

Gwyer, J. M. A., and Butler, J. R. M.: *Official History of the Second World War.* Vol III (HMSO 1969)

Hamilton, Nigel: *Monty* (Hamilton). *The Making of a General 1887–1942* (1981). *Master of the Battlefield 1942–1944* (1983)

Hamilton, Willie: *My Queen and I* (Quartet 1975)

Hardinge, Helen: *Loyal to Three Kings* (Kimber 1972)

Harriman, Averell, and Abel, Ellis: *Special Envoy to Churchill and Stalin 1941–1946* (Hutchinson 1976)

Harewood, Lord: *The Tongs and the Bones* (Weidenfeld & Nicolson 1981)

Harris, Kenneth: *Attlee* (Weidenfeld & Nicolson 1982)

Haslam, E. B. *The History of RAF Cranwell* (HMSO 1982)

Hibbert, Christopher: *The Court of St James* (Harper 1964)

Hill, Norman: *The Royal Tour Trains* (South African Government)

Hinton, James: *Labour and Socialism* (Wheatsheaf 1983)

Holroyd, Michael: *Augustus John* (Heinemann 1975)

Howard, Philip: *The British Monarchy* (Hamilton 1977)

Howarth, T. E. B. (ed.): *Monty at Close Quarters* (Cooper 1985)

Hyde, H. Montgomery: *Baldwin: The Unexpected Prime Minister* (Hart-Davis MacGibbon 1973)

Hyde, Robert: *Industry Was My Parish* (Industrial Society 1968)

Ingham, Kenneth: *Jan Christiaan Smuts* (Weidenfeld & Nicolson 1986)

Interdepartmental Committee (Canada) on the Royal Visit: *Visit to Canada of His Majesty the King and Her Majesty the Queen, 1939*

James, Robert Rhodes: *Anthony Eden* (Weidenfeld & Nicolson 1986)

Jay, Douglas: *Change and Fortune* (Hutchinson 1980)

Jenkins, Roy: *Truman* (Collins 1986)

Judd, Denis: *King George VI 1895–1952* (Joseph 1982)

Lane, Peter: *The Queen Mother* (Hale 1979)

Lash, Joseph P.: *Eleanor and Franklin* (Deutsch 1972)

Lees-Milne, James: *Harold Nicolson. A Biography* (Chatto & Windus 1981)

Lewin, Ronald: *Slim* (Cooper 1967)

Lockhart, J. G.: *Cosmo Gordon Lang* (Hodder & Stoughton 1949)

Longford, Elizabeth: *Victoria R.I.* (Weidenfeld & Nicolson 1964)

Longford, Elizabeth: *The Royal House of Windsor* (Weidenfeld & Nicolson 1974)

Longford, Elizabeth: *The Queen Mother* (Weidenfeld & Nicolson 1981)

Longford, Frank: *The Grain of Wheat* (Collins 1974)

Macmillan, Harold: *War Diaries. The Mediterranean 1943–1945* (Macmillan 1984)

Macmillan, Harold: *The Past Masters* (Macmillan 1975)

McLeod, Elizabeth: *Sixty Years of Achievement. The Industrial Society 1918–1978* (Industrial Society 1978)

Mansergh, Nicholas (ed.): *Transfer of Power* series (HMSO)

Marie-Louise, Princess: *My Memories of Six Reigns* (Evans 1956)

Masters, Brian: *Great Hostesses* (Constable 1982)

Menzies, Sir Robert: *Afternoon Light* (Cassell 1967)

Middlemas, Keith, and Baines, John: *Baldwin* (Weidenfeld & Nicolson 1974)

Middlemas, Keith: *The Life and Times of George VI* (Weidenfeld & Nicolson 1974)

Minney, R. J. (ed.): *The Private Papers of Hore-Belisha* (Collins 1960)

Morrah, Dermot: *The Royal Family in Africa* (Hutchinson 1947)

Morrah, Dermot: *The Work of the Queen* (Kimber 1958)

Morrison, Herbert: *An Autobiography by Lord Morrison of Lambeth* (Odhams 1960)

Myers, E. C. W.: *Greek Entanglement* (Hart-Davis 1953)

Nicolson, Harold: *King George V. His Life and Reign* (Constable 1952)

Nicolson, Harold: *Diaries and Letters* (Collins). *1930–1939* (1966). *1939–1945* (1967)

Nicolson, Nigel: *Alex. The Life of Field-Marshal Alexander of Tunis* (Weidenfeld & Nicolson 1973)

Pakula, Hannah: *The Last Romantic. A Biography of Queen Marie of Roumania* (Weidenfeld & Nicolson 1984)

Pearson, John: *The Ultimate Family* (Joseph 1986)

Pope-Hennessy, James: *Queen Mary* (Allen & Unwin 1959)

Reid, Charles: *Malcolm Sargent. A Biography* (Hamilton 1968)

Reith, Lord: *Diaries* (ed. Charles Stuart) (Collins 1975)

Richards, Denis: *Portal of Hungerford* (Heinemann 1977)

Robertson, Bruce: A History of the Royal Flights, *Air Clues*, February 1970

Roosevelt, Eleanor: *This I Remember* (Hutchinson 1950)

Roosevelt, James: *My Parents* (Allen 1977)

Rose, Kenneth: *King George V* (Macmillan 1983)

Roskill, Stephen: *Hankey Man of Secrets* (Collins 1974)

Royal Visit to South Africa 1947 (South African Railways 1947)

Royal Wings Through Five Reigns (Air Ministry)

Royalty in New Zealand. Official Picture Souvenir of the Visit of TRH the Duke and Duchess of York 1927 (New Zealand Government Publicity Office 1927)

Sitwell, Osbert: *Rat Week* (Joseph 1986)

Townsend, Peter: *Time and Chance* (Collins 1978)

Warner, Philip: *Auchinleck. The Lonely Soldier* (Buchan & Enright 1981)

Warner, Philip: *Horrocks. The General Who Led from the Front* (Hamilton 1984)

Watson, Francis: The Death of George V, *History Today*, December 1986

Wheeler-Bennett, John W.: *King George VI. His Life and Reign* (Macmillan 1958)

Wheeler-Bennett, Sir John: *Friends, Enemies and Sovereigns* (Macmillan 1976)

Windsor, Duke of: *A King's Story* (Cassell 1951)

Windsor, Duchess of: *The Heart Has Its Reasons* (Joseph 1956)

Wood, David, and Dempster, Derek: *The Narrow Margin* (HMSO)

Ziegler, Philip: *Crown and People* (Collins 1978)

Ziegler, Philip: *Mountbatten* (Collins 1985)

PERMISSIONS

I was allowed to see the Halifax papers in the Borthwick Institute, York, through the good offices of the Earl of Halifax (who, incidentally, asked for a copy of the book to be sent to him) and the Mountbatten papers in Broadlands through Lord Brabourne. In both establishments letters from the King were marked 'not to be reproduced without the permission of the Keeper of the Queen's Archives.' This is Oliver Everett at Windsor Castle.

The passages in question are shown below:

Halifax papers

(Ch = Chapter, n = note)

Ch 13, n19, Ch 16, n13, Ch 17, n5, 11, 33, 36, Ch 18, n29, Ch 20, n6, Ch 27, n2.

Broadlands papers

Ch4, n19, 20, 21, Ch 5, n15, Ch 6, n17, Ch 16, n16, 29, Ch 18, n31, Ch 19, n4, 5, 6, 11, 29, 31, 33, Ch 23, n24, Ch 26, n1, n8.

The Chamberlain papers are kept at Birmingham University under the control of Dr Benedikt Benedikz, with whom I have long been on quite friendly terms. He indicated that his permission was needed for reproduction, but I do not foresee difficulties. The relevant passages are:

Ch 10, n17, Ch 11, n4, 5, 9, 14, 15, 16, Ch 12, n2, 3, Ch 13, n1, 4, 17, Ch 15, n2, 8.

For quotations from the Churchill papers I was told that permission must be got from Heinemann's. The relevant passages are:

Ch 13, n8, 9, Ch 17, n1, 34, 43, Ch 18, n2, 4, 30, Ch 20, n7

INDEX